Hall China
Tea and Coffee Pots
The First 100 Years

Gary and Paula Barnebey

4880 Lower Valley Road, Atglen, PA 19310 USA

Disclaimer and Acknowledgment of Copyrights and Trademarks

A number of the products, bottom marks, and designers mentioned or pictured in this book are registered copyrights and trademarks. None of the trademark or copyright holders have authorized this book nor approved the information used by the authors of this book. We have tried to recognize the copyrights and trademarks on first use.

Library of Congress Cataloging-in-Publication Data

Barnebey, Gary.
   Hall China tea and coffee pots : the first 100 years / by Gary and Paula Barnebey.
      p. cm.
   ISBN 0-7643-2196-X (hardcover)
1. Hall China Company. 2. Teapots—United States. 3. Coffeepots—United States. 4. Pottery, American—20th century. I. Barnebey, Paula. II. Title.

NK4210.H28A4 2005
738.3'09771'63—dc22

2004026853

Designed by Mark David Bowyer
Type set in Americana XBd BT/Souvenir Lt BT

ISBN: 0-7643-2196-X
Printed in China
1 2 3 4

Published by Schiffer Publishing Ltd.
4880 Lower Valley Road
Atglen, PA 19310
Phone: (610) 593-1777; Fax: (610) 593-2002
E-mail: Info@schifferbooks.com

For the largest selection of fine reference books on this and related subjects, please visit our web site at **www.schifferbooks.com**
We are always looking for people to write books on new and related subjects. If you have an idea for a book please contact us at the above address.

This book may be purchased from the publisher.
Include $3.95 for shipping.
Please try your bookstore first.
You may write for a free catalog.

In Europe, Schiffer books are distributed by
Bushwood Books
6 Marksbury Ave.
Kew Gardens
Surrey TW9 4JF England
Phone: 44 (0) 20 8392-8585; Fax: 44 (0) 20 8392-9876
E-mail: info@bushwoodbooks.co.uk
Free postage in the U.K., Europe; air mail at cost.

Dedication

This book is dedicated to our families who, when we talk Hall, just wanly smile and put up with our collector's insanity.

Contents

Acknowledgments 4
Introduction 5
   Book Organization 6
Brief History of Hall China 7
Bottom Marks 9
Common Collector's Questions 11
   Is it Hall? 11
   How old is it? 11
   What color is it? 12
   What is the difference between Silver Glo and Metal Clad? 12
   What is Pewter? 12
   What is Super-Ceram®? 12
   What does the paper label signify? 13
   Why buy pattern add-on pieces and reissues? 13
   What about price differences? 13
   Where do I find current collector information? 13
Teapot and Hot Water Pot Shapes 14
Coffee and Beverage Pot Shapes 67
Series
   Early Gold and Platinum Decorations 117
   Early Decals 124
   "Art Deco" Series 127
   "Novelty" Series 128
   Gold Decorated / Gold "Special" / Platinum Decorated 129
   "Victorian" Series 138
   Brilliant Series 139
   Gold Label 140
   Sixties Decorations 143
   Lipton Tea Company Shapes 144
   McCormick Tea Company Shapes 145
   Enterprise Aluminum Company Shapes and Decorations 147
   Forman Family, Inc. Shapes and Decorations 157
   Tricolator Company Shapes and Decorations 163
Decorations 175
Eva Zeisel Designs 201
Red-Cliff Ironstone 208
Ernest Sohn Creations 212
Colors 219
Bibliography 234
Appendix: Name Cross Reference 236
Index 237

Acknowledgments

First we would like to acknowledge The Hall China Company, without whom we would be collecting some other product. Hall China has built a reputation for producing the finest china products in the industry. This position has been achieved by maintaining an active Research and Development department which developed the "Single-Fire" process and such improvements as Super-Ceram® china bodies.

Over the years the R & D department has also developed a range of products such as outdoor speaker systems, glove molds, and tea cups, plus producing and testing over twenty-five thousand color glaze formulas. Along with research and development, Hall has been a leader in employing up-to-date manufacturing equipment and techniques. Their computer-controlled furnaces, semi-automated computer-controlled production lines, and high-pressure presses for large flatware are the pride of the industry.

In the area of production and design, it was necessary to keep up with the changing whims of the general public and institutional customers. Hall has maintained a capable in-house staff of designers and decorators and has also been associated with industry-honored designers such as Don Schreckengost, J. Palin Thorley, and Eva Zeisel. Hall maintains a custom-design department that claims to be able to create any logo on any Hall product or to design any custom shape the customer desires. (Well, almost any shape.)

The production capability would come to naught if it were not for the sales department. The Hall China Company has worked hard at sales since their super salesman, F. I. Simmers, rolled china lids across the customer's office floor to demonstrate Hall's quality. Hall also has fostered new arrangements with china distributors and institutions.

The Hall China Company's policy of allowing factory tours and access to company personnel has been a great help in providing accurate information to the public and collectors about Hall's products. We especially acknowledge the time and information provided by Mr. John C. Thompson, Chairman of the Board; Everson Hall, Historian; Michael Bowdler, Staff Designer; and Mrs. Margaret Thompson, Hall China's Official Hostess (great cookies).

Next, we would like to acknowledge the help of the East Liverpool Historical Society and the Museum of Ceramics at East Liverpool, Ohio. Phil Ricker at the museum has been most cooperative in facilitating access to the Society's collection. Researching old company newsletters, company catalogs, and trade journals made for hours of interesting research.

It would be a mistake not to acknowledge the works of other authors who have written about Hall China products. In rereading Harvey Duke's books and price guides, we always seem to find something we missed or about which our memories needed refreshing. Harvey Duke's, Jo Cunningham's, and Margaret and Kenn Whitmyer's books are industry standards and provide probably the best picture identification of the wide variety of Hall's product lines. Elizabeth Boyce's writings in *The Glaze* newspaper have provided details about Hall's products otherwise easily missed. The works of Jeffery Snyder, Richard Luckin, Michael Pratt, C. L. Miller, and Barbara J. Conroy have been a great help in adding to the published information on The Hall China Company collectibles. These authors were all aided by the willingness of collectors of Hall's products to share their knowledge about their collections and provide pictures for publication.

We extend an extra special acknowledgement to those collectors who opened up their homes and collections for our picture taking. There are some truly spectacular collections that exist. We have seen some and heard of others. Those providing pictures were Virginia Anderson, Winona Beckner, Shirley and John Boesch, Elizabeth Boyce, Phyllis and Donald Coppess, April and Terry Fredrickson, Everson Hall, NanSue and Bill Hamilton, Maggie and Tony Hughes, Barbara and Bill Johnston, Christine Layman, Gary Menke, Benjamin Moulton, Dorothy McCrane, Karen and Mike Parkinson, Judy and Harry Pomroy, William Ramey, Bill Rist, Sharon and Jim Roberts, Jane and Don Smith, Linda and Jim Terry, Margaret Thompson, and Joel Wilson and Virginia Lee – who are both of China Specialties, Inc.

We would also like to acknowledge those who provided research material and catalogs. We would like to thank Elizabeth Boyce, NanSue and Bill Hamilton, Matt Hargreaves, Vera C. Hinkelman, Chris Holtzleiter, Shirley Manning, Dorothy McCrane, Pat Moore, Benjamin Moulton, Naomi Murdock, Karen and Mike Parkinson, Kerilynn and Eric Perry, Bill Rist, Sharon and Jim Roberts, Judie and Dick Sanford, Jeffrey Schneidmiller, and John Walker.

A special thanks to those who previewed and assisted with the book. They are Virginia and David Anderson, Shirley and John Boesch, Elizabeth Boyce, Juli and Sammy Derezes, Stephanie Derezes, George Derezes, April and Terry Fredrickson, Everson Hall, Maggie and Tony Hughes, Barbara and Bill Johnston, Christine Layman, Sandra and Jim Nelson, Karen and Mike Parkinson, Judy Powell, Sharon and Jim Roberts, Linda and Jim Terry, John Thompson, and Dolores and Raymond Turner.

Finally, he said, we wish to acknowledge all current and future collectors of The Hall China Company products. It matters not if you collect teapots, coffee pots, creamers, custards, decanters, dinnerware, glove molds, kitchenware, lamps, or any other of Hall's fine products. Without you, this book would have no purpose.

Introduction

When we agreed to write this book, it seemed like a relatively easy task. After all, we limited the scope to just Hall China's teapots and coffee pots, with the primary emphasis on shapes. This fit with our personal goal of collecting an example of each shape and size of Hall's teapots and coffee pots. Also, to accomplish our own collecting goal, we have been collecting old and current catalogs and advertising material produced by Hall China and their distributors. But we were a little overly optimistic, as we found we still had some major obstacles to overcome. The tasks were (1) to identify all shapes and sizes of teapots and coffee pots that were made by The Hall China Company; (2) to obtain pictures of each; and (3) to provide size information for them so collectors would know which item they had found.

To accomplish the first task, we turned to our collection of catalogs; to the East Liverpool Historical Society and the Museum of Ceramics at East Liverpool, Ohio; to other collectors; published antique collector books; and The Hall China Company. Mr. Everson Hall, The Hall China Company Historian, and Mr. John Thompson, Chairman of the Board, were a great help in identifying Hall's products. By reviewing Hall's product identification records, we discovered there are far more teapots and coffee pots produced than are commonly known. The product identification book was started in about 1930 and does not provide complete descriptive or picture data on each item. Thus, for example, we know that Hall produced three teapots for the Manning Bowman Company, but only one of them is pictured in current antique collector information.

Hall China's product identification book is organized by a running number system with only an occasional cross-reference to teapot or coffee pot names known to collectors. In general Hall has not used names of items in manufacturing or sales except to support advertising, but uses a unique identification number for each size of the items produced. This numbering system was instituted about 1930 when the number of items produced began to grow. Items considered as viable sales candidates after 1930 were included in the product identification book and given numbers, while obsolete items were excluded. This means items produced by Hall prior to 1930, but discontinued in the 1920s or early 1930s, could only be found in old catalogs, Hall's advertising, or in the marketplace.

Identification of teapots and coffee pots is not complete. Correlation of the teapots and coffee pots produced based on the Hall product identification records to pictures in antique collector books and reference data seems to indicate up to five percent of Hall's teapots and coffee pots are yet to be found and identified.

One other minor problem occurred. When is a teapot a teapot, a hot water pot, a beverage pot, a coffee pot, or a creamer? The Hall China Company does not seem sure. Hall's catalogs can list the same item as any of these. For this reason, we have included hot water pots and beverage pots into the teapot and coffee pot shape sections. We grouped hot water pots with the teapots and beverage pots with the coffee pots.

The second task we faced was to obtain pictures of identified beverage pots, coffee pots, hot water pots, and teapots. We had some (fewer than we previously thought), but not all, in our collection. So we turned to other collectors for help. Thankfully they are most generous with their time and have been very helpful in allowing us to take pictures, or they provided pictures of some of their prize collections.

A new skill we needed to acquire was how to take pictures of the items. Taking pictures of china is not like taking family pictures. Many of the teapots have mirror-like surfaces, and the picture turns out to be a teapot with you and your camera in its middle! Front lighting washes out the gold decorations and side lighting over-exposes the teapot edges, so picture taking is more trial and error, lots of error.

In Seattle, we took sample pictures using slave flashes and white bounce boards. We showed the pictures to Schiffer Publishing on our visit and were told we were on the right track. Schiffer provided a short course on better picture taking techniques and picture backgrounds that was a great help.

Back across country we went, stopping at other collectors' homes to accumulate pictures. We did not develop any pictures until we returned to Seattle, so we were shooting blind. Unfortunately, many of the pictures looked like a blind man took them! So on to new trials for better pictures. We used photofloods, a variety of light sources, bounce boards, a photo cube, and spray starch for shiny pots. Forget the starch – but use an area with subdued light and a minimum of reflective surfaces. Coffee pots with decals seem the easiest to photograph, but we have yet to find a way to photograph Golden Glo and Copper Lustre Airflow teapots without including the camera and every wall and ceiling reflected in the picture.

The final task was to obtain size data for the items included in the book. Measurement data in Hall's catalogs is not consistent. For instance, teacup sizes vary from four ounces to six ounces depending on the catalog and coffee cup sizes vary between six ounces and eight ounces. In addition some pots are shown with size based on serving size rather than brimful size. Also, for some reason in the mid-1930s, Hall changed its five-cup and seven-cup teapots (marked on pot bottom) to six-cup and eight-cup without changing the mold sizes. Pot height measurements are usually without cover but sometimes the cover is included in catalog listings. For these reasons, we tried to be consistent by measuring pots in ounces as brimful or until liquid runs out the cover opening or spout. If Hall included a cup measurement with the pots, we included their cup sizes. Height measurements are without cover, except for pots like the Airflow, Football, Rhythm, etc., where we measured to the highest point on the pot. Height measurement with cover and width of pot from handle to tip of spout are included. Our measurements are to the nearest one-eighth inch.

Because china shrinks by 10-15 percent during the firing process, there will always be differences in the actual measurements of individual pots. Size variations are considered acceptable to Hall when the capacity is held to plus or minus ten percent (capacities listed are brimful measurements) or plus or minus one-eighth inch in physical size of the advertised size. The primary reason for including measurement data is to allow collectors to identify the pots they have collected. Sometimes a pot will only be one-eighth inch higher than another of the same shape but will contain four or six ounces more liquid, and be a two-cup rather than a 1.5-cup. It can be embarrassing to say you have a one-cup Philadelphia only to find it is a huge 1.5 cup.

One special size teapot was created for salesmen to use on sales calls. These are marked miniature one-fifth size salesman samples and have been found for the Boston, French, New York, and Philadelphia with standard gold decorations and have the H-2 bottom mark. These teapots are close to the 1.5-cup teapot size.

Book Organization

Now that we have decided to have sections for teapot/hot water pot and coffee pot/beverage pot shapes, the question was what order to present them. Collectors we talked to said to order them alphabetically. Great, but most of the teapots and some of the coffee pots have several names. Harvey Duke used Hall's names when known, other collector's names, and F. Scott Fitzgerald's character names, according to Jim Shepard, when no Hall or other name was known. The Whitmyer's used combinations of Hall's names, collector's names, and their own made-up names in their reference books. Other authors used names from these sources and added names of the collector or their friend, relative, or postman who found the pots not previously identified by other collectors. Remember, Hall primarily used numbers for identification after 1930, not names. Continuing research has revealed names used by distributors or retail sales companies for which the pot was made further complicating the naming of the pots.

We decided to present shapes alphabetically by using Hall China Company names or Hall's distributor or retail sales company's names if known. If that name is unknown, we used the name given by Kenn and Margaret Whitmyer and/or Harvey Duke. If the pot was still nameless, we gave it our name pending finding a Hall, distributor, or retail sales company name. When we used names provided by Kenn and Margaret Whitmyer, Harvey Duke, or ones we named, we used them with quotes. In a later section of this book, we provide a name cross-reference.

We took an exception to listing all the shapes in the shape sections of this book. Hall China produced a line of Red-Cliff® ironstone teapots and coffee pots. Harvey Duke provided some drawings of these pots in his book, *HALL II*. The ironstone pots have not been covered otherwise with much detail in collector reference books. Another line of teapots and coffee pots that has received little coverage has been the items produced for Ernest Sohn. Both these lines are uniquely different from Hall's other decorated teapots, coffee pots, and commercial china. Therefore, we separated these lines from Hall's other products, and provided a section for each. The teapot, hot water pot, beverage pot, and coffee pot shapes in these lines are not included in the alphabetical listings in the main shape sections of this book. We also provided a separate section for Eva Zeisel designed items and decorations.

It seemed that not including something about teapot and coffee pot decorations would be inappropriate, so we added them. We included pictures of early gold and platinum decorations which Hall used on teapots and coffee pots between 1920 and the early 1930s. The most popular of these early gold decorations became the start of the "Gold Decorated Line" of teapots. The initial "Gold Decorated Line" of teapots consisted of twelve teapots with a single standard gold decoration for each teapot. A table showing the "Gold Decorated Line" of teapots and colors was printed in the 1935 *Hall China Special Catalog No. 35*.

Next, we tried to provide pictures of the early decals used on Hall's teapots between about 1926 and 1935, before the dinnerware and kitchenware lines with decals were produced. In this period, decals were tried only on a limited number of five-cup and seven-cup teapots, but several decals were used on the Tea for Four Sets, Tea for Two Sets, and the Twin-Tee Sets. Early decals are on the French, New York, Philadelphia, and Newport, but strangely they have not been found on the Boston. Hall's customers seem to mainly have purchased floral decals on the two-pot sets used in hotels, restaurants, and tearooms.

Sections were then added for the "standard" series included in the other collector books – "Art Deco", Gold Decorated, Gold "Special", Platinum "Special", Gold Label, etc. While this covered the gold decorated teapots, it left out the teapots and coffee pots with decals, so we added them. (After all, it's only paper.)

Including patterns sounded easy, but it soon became complicated. Trying to include every commercial logo would be interesting and should be done, but we excluded them. Also we excluded hand-painted and silver overlay teapots and coffee pots. Generally these last two types of items were produced on Hall blanks and are not marked with a manufacturer's or decorator shop marking. This is not to say they would not make a great collection. Next we excluded patterned items especially produced for collector's organizations and clubs except the National Autumn Leaf Collectors Club and East Liverpool Alumni Association. Finally, we put patterns used by Enterprise Aluminum Company, Eva Zeisel, Forman Brothers, and Tricolator Company in separate sections.

Brief History of Hall China

In 1894, a company consisting of John W. Hall; Robert Hall, a successful lumber dealer; and Monroe Patterson, an iron founder, purchased the defunct Lincoln Pottery plant located on the southeast corner of East Fourth and Walnut Streets and operated it as The East Liverpool Pottery Company. Plain and decorated ironstone china was made until 1896, when they switched to the manufacture of semi-vitreous porcelain. Products included dinnerware, toilet ware, and commemorative pieces.

After seven years of successful operation, The East Liverpool Pottery Company combined with five other independent potteries to form the East Liverpool Potteries Company. The six potteries were the East End Pottery Company, East Liverpool Pottery Company, Globe Pottery Company, George C. Murphy Pottery Company, Wallace and Chetwynd Pottery Company, and United States Pottery Company of Wellsville, Ohio. Silas M. Ferguson of the United States Pottery Company became the general manager of the new conglomerate. The primary purpose of combining several smaller potteries into one larger pottery was to improve the chances of acquiring contracts considered too large for a single small pottery company.

The company in many ways acted like an association with each former pottery company maintaining its previous management structure and manufacturing facilities. In 1903, Robert Hall decided that the reasons for joining the East Liverpool Potteries Company were not being fulfilled, and he decided to leave. He left in July with the property and equipment that belonged to his former East Liverpool Pottery Company.

On August 14, 1903, thirty-eight days after Robert Hall left the East Liverpool Potteries Companies, he incorporated The Hall China Company at his old East Liverpool Pottery Company location. The company principals were John W. Hall, Charles Hall, and Robert Hall. Three bottle kilns were fired, and thirty-three potters began making bedpans and hotel items. HALL® and the H-1 bottom marks were established as Trademarks for the new company. These bottom marks are illustrated in the Bottom Marks section.

The company was off to a difficult start with a shortage of capital and stiff competition from more than a score of small potteries in the East Liverpool, Ohio, area. This was further complicated by John W. Hall's death in 1903 and Robert Hall's death in 1904. Robert T. Hall, son of Robert Hall, assumed management of the company. F. I. Simmers, his brother-in-law, and Malcolm Thompson soon joined Robert T. Hall in forming the management team of The Hall China Company. Mr. Simmers was in charge of sales and is credited for helping the young company stay solvent.

Robert Hall felt that in order to prosper, The Hall China Company would need to develop a competitive advantage. He decided if they could solve the age-old problem of pottery crazing, he would achieve his competitive advantage. He reasoned that if the ancient Chinese had developed a single-fire pottery that did not craze, the feat must be repeatable with modern technology. Most pottery is produced using a two-fire process. The shaped piece is air-dried and is called green-ware. The green-ware is fired to a temperature slightly higher than the glaze firing. The piece is now called bisque. Next the piece is glazed and fired for a second time. The result is a piece of pottery covered with a glaze coating which has a weak mechanical bond between the piece and the glaze coating. Moisture in the bisque and differences in the thermal properties of the bisque and glaze can cause small cracks to occur in the glaze coating, called crazing. In the single-fire process, the thermal properties of the glaze and clay body are matched and fired at the same time to increase the strength of the bond between the clay body and glaze, minimizing crazing. From 1905 until 1910, Mr. Hall and Mr. Meakin experimented tirelessly to produce a single-fire process and still keep the company profitable.

In 1908 Mr. Hall decided to reenter the domestic dinnerware market and purchased from the Mayer China Company of Beaver Fall, Pennsylvania, molds, blocks cases, and copper plates for a dinnerware set. Some coffee pots and teapots were made for this and subsequent dinnerware sets, and they will be found with the H-1 bottom mark.

The Company's income was just adequate to cover expenses during this time period. When vandals destroyed the pug mill, slip house machinery, and slip sifters on Memorial Day in 1910, the resulting $3,000 in damage was almost catastrophic for the company. Robert Hall responded by intensifying the research for the single-fire process with plant superintendent, Jackson Moore, who had replaced Mr. Meakin in 1910. The right combination of body materials, glaze composition, and firing temperatures was found in 1911, achieving a successful single-fired product.

Part of the secret for the development of the successful single-fire process was the development of a leadless glaze that allowed higher firing temperatures. Mr. Simmers, on examining the resulting test specimen, exclaimed, "Bob, if you continue to make ware like that, I'll sell so much of it you'll have to double the plant." The problem of converting experimental results to a production process ran afoul of a stubborn fireman who insisted that raising the kiln firing temperature would surely burn the pottery down. However, one day when he was sick, his substitute fireman, when asked to raise the kiln temperature, responded, "Sure, why not, it's your pottery." In the next few months production had grown from two-dozen bedpans per day to sixteen dozen.

In 1910 Hall started to add blue colored bodies to their specialty lines of hotel china. In 1911 Hall China decided to make hotel ware the leading feature of business. Their single-fire products were well suited for this market. Hall again entered this market by purchasing the models, engravings, and molds from a firm long established in this line of business. By 1913, Hall decided to leave the domestic dinnerware market because of competition from foreign china producers.

The First World War brought opportunities for American pottery companies, with the European potteries not being able to supply the American market. The American potteries were in an ideal position to add to their product lines of steam-table inserts, coffee urns liners, teapots, casseroles, and other vessels used in the preparation and serving of food. Hall took advantage of this expanding market and their single-fire, hard, nonabsorbent, and non-crazing products were rapidly accepted by the industry. At the end of the war, the industry had learned that even though more expensive than the overseas products, Hall's products saved money over the long run and had sanitation advantages as well. Hall's products proved to be stronger and odor free, requiring fewer replacements than competing products. Hall China has continued in this market to the present time.

In about 1917, Hall started experimenting with gold decoration and stampings on some of the institutional teapots. These decorated teapots were well received, and their popularity for use in hotels and restaurants grew. In 1919 Hall purchased the old Goodwin Pottery Company property at East Sixth and Broadway for the production of Gold Decorated teapots. The first teapots to sport gold decorations were from the institutional lines and were the Boston, French Light Weight, and New York. The addition of the newly designed Hollywood, Los Angeles, and Tea-for-Two Set shapes quickly followed.

Until 1920 most of Hall's advertising was directed toward keeping the Hall name present in the trade journals and reminding salesmen and distributors of the primary advantages of using Hall's products. In that year, however, Hall changed its strategy and started a three-pronged advertising approach. The first point was to teach distributors and salesmen how to sell Hall products to customers. This advertising was placed in the trade journals. The second point was to teach the ultimate consumers of the advantages of Hall's products so they would demand dealers to stock Hall items. This advertising was done through the popular household magazines of the day such as *Good Housekeeping*. The last point was to introduce the advantages of Hall's products to the households of business owners and society families by placing advertising in *Literary Digest*. This advertising strategy proved very successful.

In 1927, a third plant was opened for the production of a new line of soda fountain jars. In addition Hall started to distribute decorated cooking china through retail-trade channels. In 1928, they began featuring four new colors on their celebrated teapots. The four new colors were "Larkspur," naturally taking its name from the flower and the name suggesting a light blue; canary yellow; a shade of jade green; and a pretty shell pink. All of these were adorned with decal treatments. Medallions were featured on most of the teapots, although sprays were also used. In the cooking ware line, Hall introduced a new shape called the Newport in a rose color and cadet blue color. Other teapots introduced shortly thereafter were the Cleveland, Naomi, Columbia, Johnson, and Albany.

Also in 1928, Mr. Hall decided to build a new plant to consolidate all of the company's operations into a new single plant to be located on a twenty-one-acre site in the east end of East Liverpool. The new plant was a modern one story complex and contained a modern roller tunnel kiln. The plant was constructed in 1930 and operation began from this new plant late that year. Construction of this plant at this time was fortunate as the post depression recovery forced competing companies to offer premiums to customers to maintain their loyalty. Frequently premiums used by these companies were domestic china cooking ware and dinnerware sets. Companies like Jewel Foods Company, Cook Coffee Company, Enterprise Aluminum Company, McCormick Tea Company, Lipton Tea Company, and many others all bought Hall china products to use as premiums.

Business at Hall China was so brisk that four additions and two roller tunnel kilns were added between 1930 and 1938. During this period, Hall introduced the Baltimore, Moderne, Illinois, Ohio, Indiana, Kansas, and Streamline teapots. The period between 1938 and the start of World War II was also productive, with the introduction of the remainder of the decorated teapot shapes and many of the innovative coffee pot designs. Also introduced in this period were the refrigerator sets that were used by refrigerator manufactures as premiums in their products.

During WW II, Hall China's production supported the war effort, and new designs were delayed until the war's end. After the war, the Victorian teapot series was developed and reflected the desire of the nation to return to a less chaotic time. However, in the economic recovery following the war, design trends changed and a variety of gold decorations were added to the Victorian teapots to try to keep current with the public's tastes. The "Victorian" Series was followed by J. Paul Thorley's Brilliant Series and soon after that by the Eva Zeisel Hallcraft Dinnerware and Kitchenware lines. These were very successful designs. The last new decorated teapot series contained no new shapes but featured new decorations on old shapes and were known as the Sixties series. In the late 1950s, Hall produced teapots and coffeepots as well as companion pieces for the Red-Cliff China Company. These ironstone pieces are totally different from the previous Hall produced designs. The pieces are usually collected by collectors of English and American ironstone, rather that the traditional Hall collector.

In the 1970s Hall China produced another, different line of pottery for the Ernest Sohn Company that was very distinctive and not normally associated as Hall China produced products. Collectors are just beginning to appreciate these award-winning shapes. By the late 1970s, with the loss of tariffs, foreign potteries were making major inroads into the domestic dinnerware and kitchenware markets. Hall decided to concentrate on the commercial cooking and serving china fields and exited the domestic markets.

In 1982, in order to decrease the order and shipping time for Hall's commercial customers, Hall implemented an Express Service Catalog system. Hall supported this system by maintaining selected items in popular colors in stock at the factory for immediate delivery instead of the usual "produce on order" production system.

Between 1982 and 1991, the Hall China Company undertook a major upgrade to its facilities. It replaced the roller kiln with state of the art computer controlled gas fired tunnel kilns. The new kilns reduced the firing time from forty-eight hours to six hours and produced a more consistent quality product.

From 1991 to the present, Hall China Company has been producing the hollow ware pieces for the Longaberger® Basket Company. This project has led to further modernization of equipment such as high pressure presses for production of large flat platters, automated product handling equipment, and automated computer controlled production lines. In addition to the Longaberger contract, Hall has maintained its position as a quality commercial china producer and manufactures many custom items with unique shapes and logos in its custom design shop.

Bottom Marks

Potter's marks or bottom marks are used by a pottery company to identify their wares. Marks include ink stamped marks, impressed or stamped-in marks, incised marks, paper labels, logos, or other identifying marks molded into the product. Not all potters used marks but depended upon an item's unique design, shape, or decoration to serve as the potter's identification. Marks used by larger potteries are generally registered with the U.S. Patent Office and are protected by trademarks or copyrights. Patent office records are probably the best method for determining the date of first usage of a pottery mark. However, they are generally not helpful in determining the date when a product was discontinued. They only indicate that the trademark or copyright was not extended.

Most major potteries use many different bottom marks to indicate the pottery company, patterns, product lines, distributors, and customers. Bottom marks also may indicate product numbers and decorations to aid the pottery company in identifying the product and decoration for reordering. An item may be marked with several different marks – one being the mark of the shape, another for the manufacturer, and a third for a decoration.

Products and decorations have a limited life. New products are continually being introduced and older products discontinued as decorating ideas and public tastes change. Marks associated with these items are discontinued as these items are phased out. Potteries frequently marked discontinued dates for items long after the item had ceased to be produced, and the company expected no further reordering of this product.

Some of the reasons pottery companies do not maintain records of past products and marks are (1) except for tax purposes, federal, state, and local governments have not imposed requirements for extended record keeping; (2) records for previous products or on products not expected to be reordered are not required for current production; (3) because of the short production cycle and nature of the pottery products, spare parts do not have to be maintained; and (4) better use can be made of space, which would have to be dedicated for record storage.

Improvement in production methods and Hall China's philosophy of "produce-by-order only" have led to a reduction in the required factory floor space needed to produce the current products. This has allowed Hall space to store previous product molds that would have been destroyed. This has proved to be beneficial to collectors, collectors' clubs, and after-market decorators as these older molds have been found and revived to make add-on pieces for Hall's older product lines. These revived items are marked with current bottom marks.

Below are descriptions of some of The Hall China Company's marks used in the last one hundred years on teapots and coffee pots. The pictures indicate only the central feature of the mark and do not include extra items such as "Made in U.S.A.", shape number, or pattern data. Marks used in identifying the primary distributor or the company for which the item was produced are shown in those sections of this book, i.e. Enterprise Aluminum Company, Forman, Tricolator, etc. Not all marks are shown but some are described or shown with the shapes on which they were used. For a more complete definition of The Hall China Company's marks, see Lois

Lehrner's or Bill Gates' books on marks that are listed in the bibliography.

Our shorthand notation for this mark is HALL. The word "HALL" incised in the bottom of a molded product, printed or stamped on a product, or used in advertising related to a Hall product is The Hall China Company trademark. The first use of this trademark was listed as 1903, and it is a current trademark of The Hall China Company.

Our shorthand notation for this mark is H-1. This mark was registered in first use in 1903 and was discontinued about 1913 when Hall changed its product line. The mark was used on hotel ware and commercial cooking china. From 1908 to 1913 the mark was also used on white ware and dinnerware.

Our shorthand notation for this mark is H-2. This mark and slight variations thereof were used by Hall on products from roughly 1913 until the early 1930s.

Our shorthand notation for these marks is H-3. The mark on the left was first used in about 1930 and was registered in November 1930 and used until about 1970. This trademark has expired. The second of the two marks was registered in March 1934 and is currently active.

Our shorthand notation for this mark is H-4. This trademark was used in January 1969 and was registered in December 1970. It is currently active.

Our shorthand notation for this mark is HSQK. This trademark was used from about 1932 until 1970 on kitchenware items. Chinese red teapots and coffee pots made after 1970 will usually have the H-4 bottom mark.

Our shorthand notation for this mark is HD. This trademark was used on dinnerware items between 1936 and 1970.

Our shorthand notation for this mark is HK-Mary Dunbar. This bottom mark was used on products made for the Jewel Tea Company. It was first used on the Newport teapot in 1933.

Our shorthand notation for this mark is Super-Ceram. The first usage was in March 1961 and was registered in February 1962. It is a current trademark of The Hall China Company.

Our shorthand notation for this mark is NALCC. In 1986 Hall starting making pieces not previously produced with the Autumn Leaf decals for the National Autumn Leaf Collectors Club. Members could buy these pieces on a one-time basis only by a special club offering. Pieces were limited to one or two per member. One or two pieces are being produced yearly for this club.

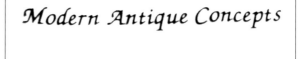

Our shorthand notation for these marks is China Specialties. Starting in 1990 Virginia Lee and Joel Wilson of China Specialties commissioned Hall China to make limited edition collectibles based on Hall dinnerware and kitchenware patterns. These items were on Hall China produced stock and were on shapes not originally made for the decals used. Recently China Specialties has had other potteries produce items on china stock not made by The Hall China Company. China Specialties has also applied new decal decorations to undecorated Hall China shapes — for example, a Little Red Riding Hood decal on a Hook Cover teapot. There are several variations of the bottom marks used by China Specialties.

Our shorthand notation for this mark is Thornberry. Between the 1970s and 1980s, an Ohio company added unique decals to undecorated Hall China teapot shapes. These were produced in limited numbers. The bottom marks are H-4 and/or Thornberry.

Our shorthand notation for this mark is ELHS Alumni. Starting in 1998, the Hall China Company produces between eighteen and twenty-four teapots to be auctioned by the East Liverpool Alumni Association, East Liverpool, Ohio. The teapots are from Hall China's historical line and have special decorations. The teapots are numbered serially.

Our shorthand notation for this mark is Modern Antique Concepts. In the late 1990s, decals the same as or very similar to the Thornberry decals were applied to undecorated Hall China shapes. These were produced in limited numbers and are marked with the H-4 and Modern Antique Concepts bottom marks.

Common Collector's Questions

Is it Hall?

Most Hall products have manufacture's marks on the bottom. The teapot and coffee pot marks will usually be HALL, H-1, H-2, H-3, H-4, HSQK, Drip-O-lator, Forman, Hallcraft, Red-Cliff, or Tricolator. If you are just going to collect gold decorated, gold label, or Chinese red teapots, that is probably all you need to know as most of these pots are marked. If you are going to collect Victorian or the Brilliant teapots, you must also know the shapes, as many of these pots escaped Hall's factory without being marked. If you are going to collect Forman or Tricolator, you are in luck, as they are well marked. However, you must also know the shapes as these companies used other pottery companies besides Hall to manufacture their wares. Luckily, the other products made by these other manufacturers are not of the same shapes as Hall produced items. The shapes produced by Hall for Forman and Tricolator are mostly known and well documented.

For Enterprise Aluminum Company coffee pot collectors, however, things are harder. Enterprise used primarily two Drip-O-lator bottom marks. These bottom marks belonged to The Enterprise Aluminum Company and were provided to all potteries making coffee pots and teapots for Enterprise. Only one of these bottom marks has been associated with coffee pots provided by Hall China. Fraunfelter Pottery, Porcelier Pottery, and at least one other pottery company also used this same bottom mark. Most of the Fraunfelter Pottery products are double bottom marked, both by the Enterprise bottom mark and a green diamond or two concentric green ovals with Fraunfelter printed between the ovals. Fraunfelter coffee pots look and feel like Hall coffee pots with shapes very similar to Hall produced coffee pots, so Hall produced shapes must be known by the collector. A complete match-up of Hall's mold book numbers and the pictures of Enterprise coffee pots has not been done, so some surprises will be in store as additional Hall's Drip-O-lator coffee pots are identified. Enterprise also distributed coffee pots and teapots from the dinnerware and kitchenware lines with Drip-O-lator or Tea-O-lator bottom marks.

If you are collecting railroad items, we hope you have deep pockets and are using the Richard Lunkin books on railroad china as a reference.

Collectors of commercial teapots and coffeepots need to know the bottom marks used by Hall and their distributors. Some of these are shown in Lois Lerner's book on marks and in The Hall China Company catalogs. Copies of many of the catalogs are available on CD-Rom from Hall Mania at HallChinaBook@cs.com. Different bottom marks were used depending upon the product line distributor or retail sales company.

Hall products made for the Red-Cliff Company are well marked, as are the Ernest Sohn products. However, Ernest Sohn and Red-Cliff products were made by other pottery companies in the same shapes as produced by Hall. The bottom marks are the same for Hall and non-Hall produced items. We know from Hall's records what was produced, but picture identification is still incomplete.

Luckily for all Hall collectors, no fake Hall products have been identified. Teapots produced for collectors clubs are sometimes not considered as desirable as the same item produced for the original purchaser. But they are not fakes produced by other companies and represented as being made by the Hall China Company with Hall's bottom marks.

If you are collecting H-1 or ELPC (East Liverpool Potteries Company) shapes, your task is hard, as no listing of teapot or coffee pot shapes is known for this period. Teapots and coffee pots produced during this period would be parts of dinnerware sets or tea sets. Also remember the ELPC bottom mark was used on H-1 style pottery long after Hall was associated with the East Liverpool Potteries Company.

One important thing to remember about Hall China is that the unglazed areas of the item appear bright white. If the unglazed areas are yellow or brown, it was not produced by Hall China. Also, some collectors think that all Hall China products have an unglazed area on the bottom where the item sits while being fired, but Hall produced many items using glazing stilts to support them during firing. The center of the bottom of Hall teapots and coffee pots may or may not be glazed.

How old is it?

The Hall China Company manufacturing process and glazes offer few clues to the age of an individual item. The most obvious clue to age, of course, is the bottom mark. The H-1 bottom mark was used from 1903 until about 1913; the H-2 from about 1913 to the early 1930s; and the H-3 bottom mark between the early 1930s and 1970. The H-4 bottom mark is the current mark for most of Hall's product lines. HSQK and dinnerware marks were used between 1936 and 1970. There was no specific date for the change in marks so some overlap occurred, and some items are found with dual marks. The use of HALL as a bottom mark doesn't help in dating an item as it has been used since 1903. HALL, H-3, and H-4 bottom marks are current Hall trademarks.

Colors can yield some indication of age since an item could not be ordered in a color before the availability of the color. If the item is platinum blue, it could not have been made in 1926. For example, a Kansas teapot will not be found in Golden Glo since the decoration was introduced after the teapot was dropped from production.

If a teapot has a strainer, it is probably older than the same teapot without a strainer. We have little date data on when Hall stopped making pots with strainers and started making free pour (without strainer) pots and the date would have varied for each style. Hall insists that the location of the cover vents is not an indication of age as no standard location for the vent was ever specified. The one manufacturing artifact that can help in determining an older item from the newer one is the amount of hand detailing of the spout and handle. Well-shaped fillets around the spouts and handles where they are attached to the body take time and skill and would indicate an older item. In order to stay competitive over time, the amount of hand finishing was reduced and spouts and handles were designed into the molds eliminating the need to attach them by hand. Therefore, an item with attached handle and spout will be older than one with molded spout and handle. Likewise, a pot with a well-finished spout (i.e. doesn't look like it had been drilled) is older than one without much hand detailing. When comparing items, one can say which item is probably older but not how much older.

When known, specific dates for the production of individual pots are listed in the shape sections of this book.

What color is it?

By 1957 the industrious Research and Development Department at The Hall China Company had formulated over 25,000 glazes, 2,000 engobes, 400 stains, 350 body compositions, and numerous over-glaze, under-glaze, and art glaze trials for Hall products. This was mostly required because Hall's hotter firing temperatures caused traditional color formulas not to work and the difference in materials at different times. Continued work on colors and body compositions is ongoing, driven by the customer requests for new colors and treatments and the need for better quality. A distinct advantage to the higher firing temperatures is that all of Hall's glazes are lead-free. Technically, a customer could order their product in any of the 25,000 plus colors at a slight additional cost.

Before 1910 Hall products were only available in white, green, and brown. Hall produced some popular item shapes in green and brown for inventory, but otherwise only produced items for current purchase orders. Inventoried items in green or brown were referred to by collectors as "stock green" and "stock brown". In 1911 Hall started advertising teapots in blue. This blue shade is now known as cobalt blue. It was not until about 1926 when the industrial designers were pushing the industry to produce colored china that expanded color choices began to be developed.

By 1935 Hall China was offering gold decorated teapots in thirteen "Gold Decorated" colors and twenty-six standard colors. To simplify ordering "Gold Decorated" teapots, Hall developed and published a table listing teapot styles across the top and colors down the side. At the intersection of any style and color was a Hall order number. To order, a customer only needed the style-color number and teapot size. As new teapot styles and colors were developed, they were added to this table. At more than twenty colors, however, this table had problems, since only twenty color numbers were allocated per teapot style. Duplicate numbers were added for seven more colors, but other new colors were considered as special order colors. For non-decorated teapots, Hall maintained a list of standard colors and optional colors. These color lists and options expanded as new colors were developed and customer requested new colors. Today approximately 150 standard colors and optional colors are available. In addition, by customer request, special color matching is available through Hall's custom shop.

Some teapot series or teapots made for a distributor or customer have unique colors or color shading. Examples are the "Art Deco" series and Lipton series of teapots. Coffee pots produced by Hall did not seem to be ordered in as wide a color range as the teapots. Solid colored coffee pots are usually found in maroon, delft blue, or ivory. The Tricolator Company did have coffee pots made in eight matte art glaze and solid colors with contrasting colored covers. Some coffee pot bottoms marked with H-3, Cube teapots and coffee pots, Tea for Four Sets, Tea for Two Sets, and Twin-Tee Sets have been produced in the same matte art glaze colors listed for Tricolator. Forman also used a mat black on some of its teapots and coffee pots. The only Enterprise Aluminum Company coffee pots found in solid colors are the "Basketweave" and "Trellis." Most of the Hall coffee pots are patterned, but a large number of them have red bottoms, ivory or white accents, and platinum trim. Many of these same coffee pot shapes can be found with black, blue, green, or yellow instead of the red.

The available colors over time are summarized in a later section of this book.

What is the difference between Silver Glo and Metal Clad?

Hall China made a number of metallic over-glazed teapots. Metallic over-glazes included Golden Glo, Silver Glo, and Copper Lustre. These glazes are made with metal in a liquid that, when fired, forms a glossy metal coating over the entire glazed area. The pot may be buffed to brighten the surface; but, as the metal coating is only slightly fused into the under-glaze, the metallic coating is easily damaged. The same technique is used for gold lining and gold stamping of decorated products. For a bright finish, Golden Glo and Copper Lustre glazes are used on light colored bodies. Silver Glo, however, is used on black bodies, giving the final product a smoky, mirror finish.

Metal Clad products initially have a mirror-like appearance, and the process adds a protective metal layer on the product. The main purpose of this metal layer was to give the pot resistance to chipping when used in commercial establishments. The manufacturing process included an over-glaze of silver to make the surface electrically conductive. Next, a nickel alloy was electroplated onto the silver over-glaze. Then a thin chrome layer was electroplated over the nickel alloy. Finally, the chrome surface was buffed to increase its mirror-like surface. The chrome gave the nickel cladding a protective surface and prevented oxidation. The metal cladding on these pots is thick enough to be felt at the edge of the cladding.

Metal Clad products suffered from three problems. The most significant problem was the high manufacturing cost. The second problem was that dishwashing wore away the chrome coating, allowing the nickel clad to oxidize, and the product to become dull. And finally, under extreme usage, the china body could become cracked without showing through the metal cladding. This made for unsanitary use, and the product needed to be discarded.

The cause of the termination of the Metal Clad line stemmed from customer unwillingness to pay a higher cost for increased durability, not from customer dissatisfaction with the product line.

What is Pewter?

Pewter is an over-glaze that, when fired, develops a mottled two-tone matte charcoal-like finish. The finish also may have a grainy appearance. This finish has been found mostly on small commercial beverage pots; however, a Tea Taster has also been found with the Pewter finish.

What is Super-Ceram®?

Super-Ceram is a body composition that is fired at a higher temperature than other Hall single-fire ceramics and results in a harder, more chip resistant product. The process is patented. Because of the higher firing temperature, special glazes had to be developed that would not burn out during the firing. Super-Ceram glazes are generally pastel and fewer color choices are available. Available colors are Dresden blue, Nile green, old wine, pink, flesh, shell, ivory, black, pearl gray, and white. Super-Ceram products are usually intended for the commercial trade; however, Ernest Sohn used some Super-Ceram bodies in his house-ware accessory lines.

What does the
paper label signify?

When a customer asks for a sample or Hall sends out promotional samples of their products to distributors and customers, Hall puts a paper label on the bottom of the item that identifies the product number, size, and color. These paper labels are intended to contain all the information for the customer to order the product. Products intended for a large promotion are made in batches, and the excess is usually sold through the Hall China factory store called the Hall Closet.

Prior to using paper labels, Hall would put the product number on the side, top, or bottom of a promotional piece in gold. This would give customers the shape information needed to order the item but not the size or color information.

Why buy pattern add-on
pieces and reissues?

Reissues are pieces made by a manufacturer that are copies of previously made products. Hall China Company has from time-to-time reissued products made from the same molds as previously sold pieces. Notably, in 1985, Hall reissued pieces in a series called The New Hall American Line. The Doughnut and Rhythm teapots were included in this series, and they are easily distinguished from the older teapots by their bottom mark of H-4. Doughnut teapots are still being sold at the Hall Closet, but mostly in newer colors and also marked with Hall's newer bottom mark. These items are worth collecting because they are genuine Hall China and produced in limited numbers and colors. These teapots will be as hard to find as their older cousins in a couple of years. Hall China has agreed not to reissue Autumn Leaf pieces that were previously made to protect collectors' investment in this pattern.

Pattern add-on pieces are those that have the same decoration as a discontinued pattern but are not the same shape as pieces originally produced in that pattern. Hall makes add-on pieces in the Autumn Leaf pattern for The National Autumn Leaf Collectors Club (NALCC) and the China Specialties Company. Hall also makes add-on pieces in other discontinued dinnerware and kitchenware patterns for China Specialties under the rule that previously produced pieces will not be duplicated. Approximately two different pieces of china with the Autumn Leaf decoration are produced for NALCC each year, and they are pre-sold to their members.

China Specialties has several pieces made each year in Autumn Leaf and other discontinued dinnerware and kitchenware patterns. These pieces are collectible if you like the way they add to your older collection. All of the China Specialties pieces are clearly marked and frequently have the production date included with the bottom mark. Because China Specialties orders on speculation, it buys only a limited number of any one item. The collector must be aware, however, that China Specialties does sell add-on pieces not made by the Hall China Company with the same decals used on Hall China's discontinued dinnerware and kitchenware. Unfortunately, these pieces are not always marked with their manufacturer. China Specialties makes this clear in their advertising, but in the secondary market the buyer must know which are made by Hall and which are not. These pieces may still be collectible as they add interesting pieces to an older collection or fill in for a lower priced item until an original older piece can be found.

What about price
differences?

The prices included with the picture captions in this book are estimated prices based on the authors' buying and selling of Hall China Company products over the last decade and collaboration with other collectors. Prices are for pieces in excellent condition. Prices are not for the purpose of setting prices in the collecting market but only as a guide to collectors of Hall China products.

Prices vary based on the supply of the products in different regions of the country, the knowledge of the seller or buyer, and the general economic climate. eBay has leveled the prices over the past several years by making a regional market into a national market. In addition, eBay and other Internet auction sites have increased the supply of Hall products for sale. Unlike a mall that has fixed prices, the Internet price is based on who is watching at that time and their desire for that object to be part of their collection. Auction prices may be unrealistic because of auction-fever or a large number of the same item being offered at the same time.

Where do I find current
collector information?

Several collectors clubs and Internet Bulletin Boards exist. For the collectors of the Autumn Leaf dinnerware pattern, there is the National Autumn Leaf Collectors Club, which publishes a bi-monthly newsletter. They hold a national convention and several regional conventions yearly. They can be reached on the Internet at http://nalcc.org.

Collectors of add-on Hall dinnerware and kitchenware pieces can subscribe to a newsletter published by the China Specialties Company, issued approximately bi-monthly. The newsletter covers more than advertisement for their current products. They can be reached at http://chinaspecialties.com.

The Hall China Company maintains a web site for products available through the factory store, the Hall Closet. Their web site is http://hallclassics.com.

The Longaberger Basket Company also maintains a web site. Hall makes the hollow ware for Longaberger. Their web site is http://longaberger.com.

The Eva Zeisel Times is published quarterly by the Eva Zeisel Collectors Club. Visit their web site at www.evazeisel.org for information about the club.

There is a Hall Bulletin board and a Yahoo Bulletin Board. There is also a social group called the "Haul Hall". Yearly there is a convention for collectors of Hall China in the spring. Information on the "Haul Hall" and the Hall Convention are posted on the bulletin boards. Their web sites are http://inter-services.com/HallChina and http://groups.yahoo.com/group/HallChina/. Resource information is on the web sites and links to additional information is provided.

Teapot and Hot Water Pot Shapes

The teapot and hot water pot shapes are listed in alphabetical order with measurements and capacities. The measurements were taken from actual pieces of china and cross-referenced with catalogs, brochures, advertisements, and the Hall China product number records. Pots are not included if we did not have a picture. We know that other pots exist based upon The Hall China Company records. For example, Hall's records show that an English Bone China teapot was over-glazed by Hall in the mid-1970s. The pot is not included since we could not find a picture. There are additional teapots and hot water pots that we know exist but are excluded for the same reason. Pre-production samples are not included. The Hall number listed with the size information for each pot represents the mold or catalog number used for product identification by Hall China. If Hall's number was not verified for the pot, then that information was left out.

The majority of the teapots and hot water pots are shown in solid colors to emphasize their shape. If a non-decorated teapot or hot water pot was not found, then the shape is shown with decoration. Decorations used on the teapots and hot water pots are listed in two categories, older and newer decorations, and exclude commercial advertising, most clubs, and other logos. Demarcation between older and newer decorations is approximately 1970. The newer decorations generally include China Specialties and National Autumn Leaf Collectors Club. Turn to the Series and Decorations sections of this book for examples of the decorations.

We tried to include the start of production date, and the date when Hall considered an item was no longer available for production, and the company or distributor for whom the pot was made. Special treatments are noted when a pot was made in Super-Ceram or Metal Clad.

Some of the pots have been renamed based upon documentation found in catalogs, advertisements, patents, brochures, or Hall China records. If unable to locate a teapot or hot water pot you are looking for, check the Name Cross-Reference section in the back of the book.

Known bottom marks of the teapots and hot water pots are listed with each shape. Frequently more than one bottom mark is found on a pot. Examples of the common bottom marks are shown in the Bottom Marks section of this book. Bottom marks unique to one or two pots are pictured or described with the shape.

The "#1 Teapot" is representative of dinnerware lines produced by the East Liverpool Potteries Company of which Hall China was a part between 1901 and 1903. The Hall China Company continued to produce this style of dinnerware until about 1913 with the H-1 bottom mark. Most decorations are gold lining or gold lining with floral decals. Some may be a combination of gold lining and gold stamping. These teapots and coffee pots were usually included in dinnerware or tea sets. Several shapes are known to have been produced, but they have not been cataloged.

The East Liverpool Potteries Company of Wellsville, Ohio, continued to make this style of dinnerware until the 1930s, and those pieces are marked ELPC (East Liverpool Potteries Company).

"#1 Teapot"

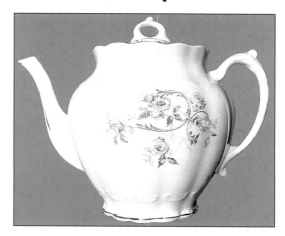

"#1 Teapot," ND (Price **N**ot **D**etermined).

"Adele"

Size:
6 cup, 40 ounces brimful, 5" high without cover, 6.125" high with cover, 9.5" wide, no strainer

The "Adele" is part of a distinct series called "Art Deco" by collectors. During the mid-1930s, the "Adele," "Damascus," and "Danielle" were distributed in blue, maroon, olive green, and yellow. The colors seem to be unique to this series of teapots. The color is considered an "all over color" as the inside of the teapot is the same color as the outside. The "Adele" is found with the H-2 or H-3 bottom mark or with no marking on the bottom of the teapot.

Maroon "Adele," $250-275.

Adjusto

Size:
6 cup, 24 ounces brimful in the large chamber with the strainer, 18 ounces brimful in the smaller free pour chamber, 7.75" high, 9" wide

White Adjusto, $90-110.

Adjusto is a two-chamber teapot made for the Forman Family, Inc. It is usually found in white but has also been found in Chinese red with a bottom mark of "Made Exclusively for Forman Family, Inc. by the Hall China Company." An Adjusto in white with fruit decals on both sides was available in 1985 in the Hall China Closet located at the Hall factory. There is a built-in strainer only on one side of the teapot, and the teapot handle has a tab on top showing which side has the strainer. The Adjusto differs from the similarly shaped Tea Taster teapot, with ridges on the bottom third of the teapot, and the cover knob goes in a different direction.

The bottom mark reads: "Adjusto Tea Pot – Adjust strength of tea to your taste. Exclusive product Forman 4 Family, Hall Porcelain." The tag that accompanied the teapot reads: "Adjusto Tea Pot – Adjust strength of tea to your taste. Step No. 1 - Brew tea in compartment with strainer … in the good old-fashioned way. Step No. 2 – Add hot water from other compartment … to adjust strength of tea to your taste. Exclusive Product Forman 4 Family, Brooklyn, New York 11211, Made of Hall Porcelain."

Airflow

Sizes:
6 cup, 38 ounces brimful, 6.75" high to top of handle, 9.5" wide, Hall No. 3111
8 cup, 46 ounces brimful, 7.25" high to top of handle, 10" wide, Hall No. 3112

Older decorations:
Blue Blossom, Blue Garden, Copper Lustre, French Flower, Gold Decorated, Gold "Special," Golden Glo, Mother of Pearl, Red Kitchenware, Silver Glo, solid colors

Indian Red Airflow, $150-185.

Newer decorations:
"Antique Rose," "Autumn Harvest," Autumn Leaf, "Ivy Trellis," "Lilac Mist," Red Poppy, Silhouette, solid colors, "Summer Song," "The Chase," "Winter Berry"

The eight-cup Airflow appeared in an April 1938 advertisement that said the graceful streamlined teapot shape was obtainable in DuPont colors of blue, green, red, or yellow. The Doughnut and Football appeared along with the Airflow. An advertisement in December 1941 states, "The Airflow is perfectly balanced and is as simple to lift as a purse. Easy to pour, and the lid won't fall off." The Patent for the Airflow was issued on June 21, 1938, to the designer, Leonard Bridley. The six-cup Airflow was introduced in 1939.

The Airflow can be found in many colors, both decorated and undecorated. The most common gold decoration is a single rose on each side with leaf sprigs around the top opening and gold lining on the cover and the handle. This teapot can be found with the same gold decoration but without the rose decals. The different bottom marks found on the Airflow are H-3, H-3 with the Gold Decorated or Gold "Special" number, H-4, and HSQK.

In 1985 Hall reintroduced the Airflow along with other teapots and coffee pots in their Hall American line. The Airflow could be ordered in the stock colors of black, blue, gray, red, tan, and white. Retailers could also special order their own colors from Hall's entire palette of over 100 colors. An antique dealer in San Francisco, Naomi's Antiques, ordered the Airflow in the special colors of solid cobalt, orange, and lavender. All of the reintroduced Airflow teapots are marked with the H-4 bottom mark. The older teapots have strainers inside the teapot whereas the newer ones do not.

In the 1970s Thornberry's of Ohio sold the Airflow in the "Ivy Trellis" decal. The bottom mark is Thornberry. China Specialties sold the Airflow in the Autumn Leaf, Red Poppy, and Silhouette decals in the early 1990s. They have the China Specialties bottom mark, but some are found without a bottom mark. In the late 1990s, Modern Antique Concepts sold the "Antique Rose," "Autumn Harvest," "Lilac Mist," "Summer Song," "The Chase," and "Winter Berry" decals on the Airflow. The bottom mark is Modern Antique Concepts.

Aladdin, Oval (with and without infuser)

Canary Oval Aladdin with Gold and Infuser, $80-95; Chinese Red Oval Aladdin with Colored Infuser, $280-310; Delphinium Solid Oval Aladdin, $100-125.

Size – with infuser:
6 cup, 38 ounces brimful, 4.5" high without cover, 7" high with cover and infuser, 11" wide, no strainer, Hall No. 1410.5; infuser 3.5" high

Size – without infuser:
6 cup, 38 ounces brimful, 4.5" high without cover, 6.625" high with cover, 11" wide, no strainer, Hall No. 1410

Top row, left to right: Solid Color Oval Infuser, Colored Oval Infuser with Gold; bottom row: Oval Cover to fit an Infuser, Oval Cover to fit Teapot without Infuser.

Older decorations with infuser:
Blue Bouquet, Blue Garden, Crocus, Gold Decorated, Gold "Special," Red Kitchenware, Red Poppy, solid colors, Wildfire

Older decorations without infuser:
Gold Decorated, Red Kitchenware, solid colors

The oval Aladdin was designed by J. Palin Thorley in 1939 and described as typical of the functional design of an entirely new style of Hall teapots. In the fall of 1939 the oval Aladdin without an in-fuser was advertised along with the Bird Cage and Melody and sold for $1.25 each. They came in Chinese red, delph blue, green, turquoise, and yellow. In the early 1940s Hall added an infuser to the oval Aladdin. This was Hall's fourth use of an infuser in a teapot, the first being in the twenties in several sizes of the Infuser/Percolator teapot, in the late twenties in a two-cup Boston for the railroads, and in the early thirties in the Ceylonator. The purpose of the Hall infuser was to hold the leaves while they are steeped to make a brew of desired, controlled strength. By using an infuser there is no tea bag necessary or leaves to strain.

In a 1942 *Hall China Special Catalog No. 24*, the oval Aladdin was advertised in Chinese red and in a variety of solid colors with a gold lining decoration. The Gold Decorated oval Aladdin is found with a matching solid or gold lined colored infuser, a white infuser with gold lining, or without an infuser. The covers on the oval Aladdin without an infuser do not fit inside the infuser of the oval Aladdin with infuser. The covers used with an infuser have a wider seat than those used in the teapots without infuser. One of the problems with the design of the oval Aladdin is that the cover is easily damaged by falling into the teapot. The most common bottom marks found on the oval Aladdin are H-3, H-3 with the Gold Decorated or Gold "Special" number, and HSQK.

The solid oval and round Aladdin teapots without infusers were sold to the Stephen Leeman Products Corporation of New York and were marked on the bottom with Epicurio or with "The Ming Tea Company, Epicurio No. 971, Made in U.S.A." Some teapots will be found with a sticker on the side that reads, "Filled with Ming Cha, The Tea Wine (A Flowery Orange Pekoe), Certified to be the finest tea grown." Some common colors found on the Epicurio Aladdin teapots are cadet, canary, cobalt, maroon, and turquoise.

Aladdin, Six-cup Round (with and without infuser)

Size – with infuser:
6 cup, 38 ounces brimful, 3.75" high without cover, 6.75" high with cover and infuser, 11" wide, no strainer, Hall No. 1411.5; infuser 3.75" high

Chartreuse Round Aladdin with Gold and Infuser, $80-110; Turquoise Solid Round Aladdin, $110-130.

Size – without infuser:
6 cup, 38 ounces brimful, 3.75" high without cover, 6.5" high with cover, 11" wide, no strainer, Hall No. 1411

Older decorations with infuser:
Blue Bouquet, Brown-Eyed Susan, Crocus, French Flower, Gold Label, Gold "Special," Golden Glo, Oyster White and Red Cooking Ware, "Pastel Morning Glory," Serenade, Silver Glo, solid colors, "Tulip," White Bake Ware, Wildfire

Older decorations without infuser:
Black Gold, "Floral Sprig," "Mini-Fleurette," Red Kitchenware, Royal Rose, Silver Glo, solid colors

Hall introduced the round opening Aladdin in 1948. Some of the teapots came with infusers, and some came without. In the early 1950s, the Aladdin without an infuser was advertised in Black Gold and Royal Rose patterns. From the mid-1950s to the 1960s, the round Aladdin was advertised with and without infusers and in solid colors, Gold Decorated, Gold Label, and Gold "Special." Infusers may have been added at a later date to those teapots that did not originally come with one. The Gold Decorated Aladdin has gold lining, and the Gold Label Aladdin has gold "Swag" or gold "Squiggle" stamping. The teapots are marked on the bottom with H-3; H-3 with the Gold Decorated, Gold Label, or Gold "Special" number; HSQK; Epicurio; or "The Ming Tea Company, Epicurio No. 971, Made in U.S.A."

Aladdin, Seven-cup Round
(with and without infuser)
Size:
7 cup, 45 ounces brimful, 4.375" high without cover, 6.75" high with cover, 7.5" high with cover and infuser, 11" wide, no strainer, Hall No. 3256; infuser 4" high

Ivory Undecorated Aladdin, $45-55.

Older decorations with infuser:
Autumn Leaf, Morning Glory
Older decoration without infuser:
"No Blue"

The seven-cup wide body Aladdin teapot was introduced in 1942. The Jewel Tea Company distributed the Aladdin with an infuser in the Autumn Leaf and Morning Glory patterns. By 1976 the teapot had been discontinued. The bottom marks are HSQK and HK-Mary Dunbar.

Many of the seven-cup undecorated Aladdin teapots have been hand-painted and are not bottom marked. In the 1950s an oval and round candle warmer was created by Hall and is usually found in the Autumn Leaf decoration.

Albany
Size:
6 cup, 32 ounces brimful, 5.5" high without cover, 7" high with cover, 9" wide, strainer, Hall No. 126
Older decorations:
Gold Decorated, Gold Label, Gold "Special," Red Kitchenware, solid colors

The Albany teapot was introduced in 1929. An advertisement in 1935 says the Albany is available in solid colors and in gold decorated under-glaze colors of black, blue (cobalt), brown, cadet, canary, emerald, green, green lustre, ivory, marine, maroon, rose, and yellow. At that time the Gold Decorated Albany sold for $1.15 and the solid ones for $1.08 wholesale. The standard gold decoration for the Albany is a gold emblem that was also used on the "Columbia" teapot. The Albany is part of the Gold Label series with the "Reflection" decoration and advertised in mahogany but came in other colors.

The Ceylonator teapot is very similar to the Albany, but the Ceylonator has a colored infuser and a special cover to fit the infuser. Bottom marks found on the Albany are H-3; H-3 with the Gold Decorated, Gold Label, or Gold "Special" number; HSQK; and HALL incised.

Lune Blue Albany, $100-120.

Alma
Size:
3 cup, 10 ounces brimful in the larger chamber, 8 ounces brimful in the smaller chamber, 4" high without cover at the highest point, 4.75" high with cover, 6" wide, Hall No. 3231

The Alma was made for the Twinspout Pottery Company, Inc. in the late 1930s. Patent No. 2135410 was issued on November 1, 1938, to Oscar Ottoson, inventor. One of the objectives of the patent was to provide a device so constructed that it will be divided into separate compartments, a larger one for tea and another smaller one for hot water. When serving tea, if the tea poured is too strong, hot water may then be poured from the teapot into the partially filled cup and dilute the tea in the cup. The larger compartment of the Alma holds two cups and the smaller holds one cup.

The teapot came in a variety of colors including black, Chinese red, emerald, ivory, marine, maroon, and turquoise. The design of the Alma is similar to the Irvine except the Alma is more triangular and the Irvine rounded. The bottom mark reads, "TWINSPOUT TEAMASTER Patent 2135410 MADE in U.S.A." "Twinspout" refers to the company that was distributing the teapots; "Teamaster" refers to the line of teapots. The four styles of Teamaster teapots made by Hall China for the Twinspout Pottery Company are the Alma, Irvine, Tea Taster, and Twinspout.

Marine Alma, $260-310.

Apple

Size:
8 cup, 44 ounces brimful, 4.5" high without cover, Hall No. 2515

The Apple teapot was introduced in November 1970 and made for the Carbone Company. The Apple shown in the picture is a prototype of the Apple produced, and it is missing the stem and leaves at the top of the locking cover. The teapot was produced only in white. During the 1970s, the Apple teapot was sold in the Hall Closet, a china outlet at The Hall China Company factory in East Liverpool, Ohio.

Apple, ND.

"Apple" ("Browning")

Size:
6 cup, 36 ounces brimful, 4.625" high without cover, 6.125" high with cover, 9" wide, strainer, Hall No. 1526

The "Apple" is part of the Brilliant Series. In early 1959 the "Apple" was introduced in solid colors of bright blue, gloss black, maroon, and white with 22-carat bright gold stipple decoration. In 1964 it was advertised in sky blue with the gold decoration and with colored brilliants selling for $4.95 each. The "Apple" was later produced in white with the Game Bird decal.

The bottom marks found are H-3 for the solid teapots, HSQK for the Game Bird decal, and H-3 with the Gold Decorated number on those with the gold stipple. Many of the bottom marks will include the Hall identification number.

Sky Blue with Gold "Apple," $170-215.

Automobile

Size:
6 cup, 32 ounces brimful, 4.25" high, 9" wide, Hall No. 3113
Older decorations:
Gold Decorated, Gold "Special," Platinum Decorated, Platinum "Special," Red Kitchenware, solid colors
Newer decorations:
Autumn Leaf, Blue Blossom, Blue Bouquet, Cameo Rose, Cat-Tail, Christmas Tree, Crocus, Little Red Riding Hood, Mexicana, "Orange Poppy," Red Poppy, Silhouette, solid colors, Sun Porch

The Automobile, the Basket, and the Basketball were part of the 1938 line of teapots brought out by The Hall China Company. These new designs were available in Chinese red, Indian red, midnight blue, and jonquil yellow. The Automobile shape won instant favor.

The teapot can be found in a variety of solid colors as well as Gold Decorated. The teapot was also decorated with platinum in the same manner as with the gold. The amount of gold or platinum used can vary from teapot to teapot depending upon the decorator. The Automobile was designed by Leonard Bridley and produced for only a very short time – from June 1938 to January 1939. The bottom marks found are H-3, H-3 with the Gold or Platinum Decorated or Gold "Special" number, and HSQK. The older decorated teapots have a strainer, but the newer ones do not. The Automobile teapot is part of the clever "Novelty" Series, teapots that are shown together later in this book.

China Specialties reintroduced the Automobile in 1992 in newer decorations and colors not previously used. The bottom mark found is China Specialties.

Maroon Automobile, $550-625.

Baltimore

Size:
6 cup, 36 ounces brimful, 4" high without cover, 5" high with cover, 9.5" wide, strainer, Hall No. 124
Older decorations:
#488, Blue Blossom, Early Decals, Gold Decorated, Gold Label, Gold "Special," "Leaf and Vine," Red Kitchenware, Silver Glo, solid colors, "Wild Poppy"
Special treatment:
Metal Clad

In 1935 the Baltimore was available Gold Decorated and in solid colors of black, blue (cobalt), brown, cadet, canary, emerald, green, green lustre, ivory, marine, maroon, rose, and yellow. A gold decorated Baltimore cost $1.15, and the solid colors sold for $1.08 wholesale.

The Baltimore teapot was one of the first teapots decorated with decals. It will be found with a "Minuet" decal on a Warm Yellow teapot with black trim and in ivory with a vase of flowers decal and black trim. Not many of these decorated teapots can be found. The Baltimore is part of the Gold Label line and was available in a variety of colors. In 1964 the Gold Label Baltimore was advertised in maroon with the gold "Nova" decal and sold for $4.95 each. The bottom marks found on the Baltimore are H-3; H-3 and the Gold Decorated, Gold Label, or Gold "Special" number; and HALL incised. It is also found unmarked.

Pink Baltimore, $65-85.

Basket

Size:
6 cup, 32 ounces brimful, 4.125" high without cover, 6.75" high to top of handle, 9" wide, strainer, Hall No. 3114
Older decorations:
Gold Decorated, Gold "Special," Golden Glo, Platinum Decorated, Platinum "Special," Red Kitchenware, solid colors

The Basket was introduced as part of the 1938 fall line of teapots along with the Automobile and Basketball. It was available in Chinese red, Indian red, midnight blue, and jonquil yellow. In some advertisements the Basket was described as "handle over cover" teapot.

The Basket can be found in solid colors, with gold or platinum lining, or with Gold or Platinum "Special" decoration. The bottom mark found is H-3 or H-3 with the Gold or Platinum Decorated or "Special" number. Shown together in the series section of this book are the six "Novelty" teapots.

Canary Basket, $130-160.

Basketball

Size:
6 cup, 40 ounces brimful, 5.5" high without cover, 6.25" high with cover, 8.5" wide, strainer, Hall No. 3117
Older decorations:
Gold Decorated, Gold "Special," Platinum "Special," Red Kitchenware, solid colors
Newer decoration:
Autumn Leaf

The Basketball was introduced in 1938 as the Bull's Eye. This teapot went through several name variations such as the Bull's Eye, Ball Shape, and finally settling on Basketball. It was available in Chinese red, Indian red, midnight blue, and jonquil yellow. The Basketball had a short production life from May 1938 until January 1939.

Chinese Red Basketball, $700-800.

The Basketball can be found in solid colors and with gold or platinum decoration. The bottom marks are H-3, H-3 with the Gold or Platinum Decorated or "Special" number, and HSQK.

National Autumn Leaf Collectors Club reintroduced the Basketball in 1997. In 2000 the Basketball was provided for the East Liverpool Alumni Association in cobalt with gold trim. The bottom marks are NALCC or ELHS Alumni. The newer teapots do not have a strainer. The Basketball is one of six teapots that are shown together as the "Novelty" Series later in this book.

Bellevue

Sizes:
1 cup, 9 ounces brimful, 2.875" high without cover, 3.5" high with cover, 5.5" wide, strainer, Hall No. 150
1.5 cup, 11 ounces brimful, 3.125" high without cover, 4" high with cover, 6" wide, no strainer, Hall No. 150.5
2 cup, 14 ounces brimful, 3.5" without cover, 4" high with cover, 6.375" wide, strainer, Hall No. 155
3 cup, 16 ounces brimful, 3.75" high without cover, 4.75" high with cover, 6.5" wide, strainer, Hall No. 146
4 cup, 24 ounces brimful, 4" high without cover, 4.875" high with cover, 8" wide, strainer, Hall No. 147
6 cup, 32 ounces brimful, 4.625" high without cover, 5.875" high with cover, 8.25" wide, strainer, Hall No. 148

8 cup, 40 ounces brimful, 4.75" high without cover, strainer, Hall No. 149

Older decorations:
Chinese red, Early Gold and Platinum Decorations, "Orange Poppy" (2 cup), solid colors

Newer decorations:
Autumn Leaf (6 cup), Crocus (Green Body - 1 cup)

Special treatment:
Metal Clad (1.5, 2, 3, 4, and 6 cup)

The twelve-sided Bellevue teapot with matching handled and handleless creamers and covered sugars were produced from the early 1920s through the 1980s. In the 1920s the teapot was advertised as "An attractive individual room service for hospitals and hotels. Designed to occupy minimum amount of space on a tray. Also very attractive for individual service in tea rooms." In the 1935 Hall catalog, the one-cup Bellevue was illustrated in twenty-four colors.

Brown 4-Cup Bellevue, $30-45.

A six-cup Bellevue referred to as the "Bartow" is decorated with the Old Gold emblem that was also used on the "Johnson" teapot. The Gold Decorated Bellevue is numbered as part of the Gold Decorated identification numbering system, but it had been dropped from the line by 1935 when the first list was published. The Bellevue teapot can be found with H-2, H-3, H-3 or HALL with the Gold Decorated number, H-4, and HSQK bottom marks.

A one-cup lettuce green Bellevue with a white lid and Crocus decal was sold by China Specialties. In 2003-2004, the Bellevue teapot was made for the National Autumn Leaf Collectors Club. These teapots are marked either China Specialties or NALCC. Bellevue with contrasting covers have been sold through the Hall Closet.

"Benjamin" ("Albert")

Size:
6 cup, 38 ounces brimful, 4.5" high without cover, 5.5" high with cover, 10.5" wide, no strainer

The "Benjamin" was introduced in 1946 as part of the "Victorian" Series. The teapot is found most often in celadon green and less frequently in yellow. The "Benjamin" was available in a variety of gold decorations and is found with or without the H-3 bottom mark. One of the most sought after gold decorations is "Mini-Fleurette," found around the teapot shoulder.

Yellow "Benjamin," $150-180.

"Birch" ("Darby")

Size:
6 cup, 40 ounces brimful, 3.78" high without cover, 5.125" high with cover, 9.875" wide, strainer

In 1947 the "Birch" appeared in an advertisement for the Jewel Tea Company selling for $1.75. The teapot was introduced the year before as part of the "Victorian" Series.

The pastel blue "Birch" teapot came with and without a variety of gold applications. The teapot may or may not have the H-3 bottom mark.

Blue "Birch," $55-65.

Bird Cage

Size:
6 cup, 40 ounces brimful, 5.5" high without cover, 7.5" high with cover, 8" wide, Hall No. 1402

Older decorations:
Gold Decorated, Gold "Special," Red Kitchenware, solid colors

Newer decoration:
Autumn Leaf

The Bird Cage is one of the six "Novelty" teapots that are shown together in the Series section of this book. In late 1939 the Bird Cage was advertised along with the Oval Aladdin and the Melody teapots, and they sold for $1.25 each. They were available in Chinese red, delph blue, green, turquoise, and yellow.

Maroon Bird Cage, $350-400.

In the early 1940s, the Bird Cage could be ordered in a variety of solid and Gold Decorated colors. The gold decoration on the teapot consists of gold lining on the debossed birds and around the spout, top rim of the teapot, and the knob. The various bottom marks found on the Bird Cage are H-3, H-3 with Gold Decorated or Gold "Special" numbers, and HSQK.

The National Autumn Leaf Collectors Club had the Bird Cage produced for its members in 1996. The Bird Cage was made in 1998 for the East Liverpool Alumni Association in ivory and gold. The bottom marks on these teapots are NALCC or ELHS Alumni. The newer Bird Cage teapot has no strainer, and the covers have a solid cover knob rather than an open circle knob.

Boston (knob and sunken cover)

Sizes – Knob Cover:
Miniature 1/5 Salesman Sample
1 cup, 8 ounces brimful, 2.75" high without cover, 3.5" high with cover, 6" wide, Hall No. 19
1.5 cup, 11 ounces brimful, 3" high without cover, 4" high with cover, 6.375" wide, Hall No. 20
2 cup, 14 ounces brimful, 3.25" high without cover, 4.25" high with cover, 6.75" wide, Hall No. 21
3 cup, 20 ounces brimful, 3.5" high without cover, 4.375" high with cover, 7.25" wide, Hall No. 22
4 cup, 28 ounces brimful, 3.75" high without cover, 4.75" high with cover, 7.875" wide, Hall No. 23
5 or 6 cup, 35 ounces brimful, 4" high without cover, 5.25" high with cover, 8.875" wide, Hall No. 24
7 or 8 cup, 40 ounces brimful, 4.5" high without cover, 5.5" high with cover, 9.5" wide, Hall No. 25

Sizes – Sunken Cover:
1 cup, 8 ounces brimful, 2.75" high without cover, 6" wide, Hall No. 9
1.5 cup, 11 ounces brimful, 3" high without cover, 6.375" wide, Hall No. 10
2 cup, 14 ounces brimful, 3.25" high without cover, 6.75" wide, Hall No. 11
3 cup, 16 ounces brimful, 3.5" high without cover, 7.25" wide, Hall No. 12

Older decorations:
Autumn Leaf (2 cup – very limited); Blue Bouquet; Blue Willow (2, 4, and 6 cup); Crocus (8 cup); Early Gold and Platinum Decorations; "Floral Sprig," French Flower; "Gaillardia;" Gold Band; Gold Dot (2, 4, and 6 cups); Gold Decorated; Gold Label; Gold "Special;" Golden Glo (4 and 6 cup); "Green Poppy;" "Mums" (8 cup); "Orange Poppy;" "Pastel Morning Glory;" Red Kitchenware; Red, Ivory, and Platinum; Russet (2 cup); Silver Glo (2, 4, and 6 cup); Sixties Decoration; solid colors; Two Tone; White Bake Ware; "White Rim Band" (1, 1.5, and 2 cup), Wildfire

Newer decorations:
"Antique Rose" (3 cup), Autumn Leaf, "Blue Dresden" (2 cup), Christmas Tree (2-cup sunken cover), "Country Cottage" (3 cup), "Duberry" (2 cup), "Flower Garden" (3 and 8 cup), "Hunt Scene" (3 cup), "Lilac Mist" (3 cup), "New Rose" (3 cup), "No Blue," solid colors, "Summer Song" (3 and 8 cup), "Winter Rose" (3 cup)

Maroon 4-Cup Knob Cover, Boston, $55-65; Weathered Oak 3-Cup Sunken Cover Boston, $45-50.

Special treatments:
Metal Clad (1.5, 2, 3, and 4 cup), Super-Ceram Knob Cover (1.5, 2, 3, 4, and 6 cup), Super-Ceram Sunken Cover (1, 2, and 3 cup)

The Boston teapot is one of the earliest teapots made by The Hall China Company and is still being made today. It comes in seven sizes with a knob cover and in four sizes with a sunken cover. It can be found with numerous bottom marks of H-2; H-3; H-3 with the Gold Decorated, Gold Label, or Gold "Special" number; H-4; HSQK; Tea-O-lator; China Specialties; Modern Antique Concepts; NALCC; or Thornberry. Sugar bowls with covers and creamers are available in the Boston shape.

In 1916, McCormick Tea Company purchased the Boston in green and brown. The seven-cup green Boston was the first Hall teapot carried by the Jewel Tea Company in 1924. Along with the French Light Weight and New York teapots, the Boston was selected in 1920 to make its debut decorated with gold.

When these teapots were introduced at the Pittsburgh Trade Show in 1920, people were amazed to discover that what they thought were "English Decorated Teapots" were not English. They were the advance samples of a line of decorated teapots that were soon to be manufactured in a variety of shapes, sizes, glazes, and decorations comparable with the best-known English teapot manufacturers. In the June 1920 issue of the *Pottery, Glass & Brass Salesman*, "Hall's Teapots are made in a full run of sizes in three distinctive shapes, and may be had in either royal blue, rich green, or brown, with gold decorations by able artists." A variety of gold decorations were tried before settling on one style during the late 1920s. These earlier teapots will be marked with the H-2 bottom mark and widely collectible.

In the 1930s Hall changed the size listed of the Boston teapots from a five-cup to a six-cup and from a seven-cup to an eight-cup teapot. In 1934 Hall produced the eight-cup Boston for the Enterprise Aluminum Company decorated in the Crocus decal, and it will be found with the bottom mark of Tea-O-lator. In 1937 the Boston could be found in velvety blue, mellow Mexican red, and authentic delphinium blue.

The Boston came in a variety of colors and as part of the Gold Decorated, Gold "Special," and Gold Label lines. It was one of the shapes more often used for decals and commercial logos. It was used in the kitchenware lines, by the railroads, airlines, and collectors clubs. In the 1960s the Boston was produced as part of a series in green with a gold fruit decal.

During the early 1970s, Hall changed from making the Boston with a strainer to a free pour. Between the 1970s and 1980s, Thornberry's of Ohio sold the Boston in the "Flower Garden" and "Summer Song" decal with the Thornberry bottom mark. During the 1980s, McCormick Tea advertised the small two-cup Boston for sale in black, cobalt blue, dark green, ivory, marine blue, rose, and sandust for $15.95 each. These are marked on the bottom with McCormick Collection. In the late 1990s, Modern Antique Concept sold the "Antique Rose," "Blue Dresden," "Country Cottage," "Duberry," "Hunt Scene," "Lilac Mist," "New Rose," "Summer Song," and "Winter Rose" decals on Boston teapots. These are marked with Modern Antique Concepts. In 2000 the National Autumn Leaf Collectors Club issued the Boston as a club piece, and it is marked with NALCC. Boston teapots with contrasting covers have been sold through the Hall Closet. In 1999 China Specialties decorated the two-cup Boston in Christmas Tree decoration. It is marked China Specialties.

Boston with Infuser

Size:
2 cup, 12 ounces brimful, 3" high without cover or infuser, 4.25" high with cover and infuser, 4.5" wide, Hall No. 21; infuser 2.375" high

Between 1926 and 1930 Hall advertised the two-cup Boston for use on the railroads. The teapot could be ordered in green or brown with a china or aluminum strainer. Those with china strainers sold for $1.16, and those with aluminum strainers sold for $1.00 wholesale. They have the H-3 bottom mark.

Green Boston with Infuser, ND.

Boston Long Metal Tip Spout (knob and sunken cover)

Sizes – Knob Cover:
1.5 cup, 12 ounces brimful, 3" high without cover, 3.875" high with cover, 6.875" wide, Hall No. MTS-20
2 cup, 14 ounces brimful, 3.125" high without cover, 4.25" high with cover, 7.125" wide, Hall No. MTS-21
3 cup, 16 ounces brimful, 3.5" high without cover, 4.5" high with cover, 7.875" wide, Hall No. MTS-22

Sizes – Sunken Cover:
1.5 cup, 12 ounces brimful, 3" high with cover, 6.875" wide, Hall No. MTS-10
2 cup, 14 ounces brimful, 3.125" high with cover, 7.125" wide, Hall No. MTS-11
3 cup, 16 ounces brimful, 3.5" high with cover, 7.875" wide, Hall No. MTS-12

In the late 1950s Hall started adding metal tip spouts to a wide assortment of their teapots, coffee pots, and beverage pots. The teapots have all the features of the regular pots, plus a bright and protective metal tip spout that minimizes dripping and chipping. The metal tip spout items were advertised as adding sparkle to the table setting and life to the chinaware. There are two styles of metal tip spouts, long and short. They have the H-4 bottom mark and came in a variety of colors. The Boston metal tip spouts were produced through the mid-1990s.

White Sunken Cover and Gray Knob Cover Boston Long Metal Tip Spout, $30-35 each.

Boston Short Metal Tip Spout (knob and sunken cover)

"Steel" Gray "Bowknot," $200-250.

The most common color of the "Bowknot" is pink with and without gold decoration, but it has also turned up in canary and "steel" gray. The teapot is usually marked with H-3, but it will also be found without a bottom mark. Because of the short production, this is one of the hardest in this series to find, especially with gold decoration.

Chinese Red Knob Cover Boston Short Metal Tip Spout, $65-80; Cobalt Sunken Cover Boston Short Metal Tip Short Spout, $50-60.

Sizes – Knob Cover:
1.5 cup, 8 ounces brimful, 2.75" high without cover, 3.5" high with cover, 6" wide, Hall No. MTS-2520
2 cup, 15 ounces brimful, 3.125" high without cover, 4.25" high with cover, 7" wide, Hall No. MTS-2521
3 cup, 19 ounces brimful, 3.5" high without cover, 4.5" high with cover, 7.75" wide, Hall No. MTS-2522

Sizes – Sunken Cover:
1.5 cup, 8 ounces brimful, 3" high with cover, 6" wide, Hall No. MTS-2510
2 cup, 10 ounces brimful, 3.125" high with cover, 7" wide, Hall No. MTS-2511
3 cup, 16 ounces brimful, 3.5" high with cover, 7.75" wide, Hall No. MTS-2512

In 1964 Hall added a short metal tip spout to their Boston line. It could be purchased with either a knob or sunken cover. Metal tip spouts could be purchased on Boston teapots up until the mid-1990s. They came in a variety of colors and will have the H-4 bottom mark.

"Bowling Ball" ("Pepper")

Turquoise "Bowling Ball," $575-650.

Size:
6 cup, 40 ounces brimful, 6.5" high to top of handle, 7.75" wide, Hall No. 3118

The "Bowling Ball" was introduced in July 1938 and produced for a limited time until 1939. This unusually shaped teapot was made for Standard Brands, Inc. and will be found frequently in turquoise. It has been reported to have been made in canary, cobalt, and green lustre; but, this has not been confirmed. Usually the bottom is marked with H-3, but some of the "Bowling Ball" teapots are found not marked. The cover on this teapot is easily dislodged and damaged.

"Bowknot" ("Gladstone")

Sizes:
6 cup, 32 ounces brimful, 4.5" high without cover, 6" high with cover, 8.375" wide, strainer
8 cup, 40 ounces brimful, 4.625" high without cover, 6.5" high with cover, 9" wide, strainer

The "Bowknot" was introduced in 1946 as part of the "Victorian" Series. It is usually found in the six-cup size, but it has been found in an eight-cup as well.

Buffet Hot Water Pot and Teapot

Emerald Buffet Hot Water Pot and Russet Buffet Teapot, $55-65 each.

Sizes – Teapot:
1.5 cup, 11 ounces brimful, 3" high without cover, 4" high with cover, 5.75" wide, Hall No. 248
2 cup, 13 ounces brimful, 3.125" high without cover, 4" high with cover, 5.75" wide, Hall No. 251
3 cup, 16 ounces brimful, 4.5" high without cover, Hall No. 253
Older decorations – Teapot:
French Flower, Russet, solid colors
Special treatments – Teapot:
Metal Clad (1.5 and 2 cup) and Super-Ceram (1.5 and 2 cup)
Size – Hot Water Pot:
1.5 cup, 12 ounces brimful, 4.875" high without cover, 5.875" high with cover, 4.5" wide, Hall No. 250
Older decoration – Hot Water Pot:
Solid colors
Special treatment – Hot Water Pot:
Super-Ceram (1.5 cup)

The Buffet teapot and hot water pot were introduced in 1930 in green or brown. The hot water pot did not have a strainer in the spout; it could be used for tea, coffee, chocolate, cocoa, hot milk, or hot water.

The Buffet teapot can be found in a variety of colors and sometimes found with a different colored cover from the bottom. The two-cup Buffet teapot is still being produced today. A flat-knob cover on a 1.5-cup teapot was made for R. B. Martin and Company with no nibs or notches. The bottom marks are H-3, H-4, and HALL incised. Buffet teapots will be found with and without strainers.

Metal Clad Buffet Teapot, $35-45.

Centennial

Size:
6 cup, 38 ounces brimful, 5.75" high without cover, 7.5" high with cover, 9.125" wide, no strainer, Hall No. 2003

In recognition of their 100th Anniversary in 2003, the Hall China Company introduced the Limited Edition Centennial Teapot. This newly shaped collector's piece was made in six colors, all with 24-carat gold trim and a decorative floral band with a 1903-2003 banner in gold. Production continued through the year, and the production molds for these limited production collector's teapots were destroyed on December 31, 2003. The teapot was made in canary, cobalt, devon cream, forest green, maroon, and platinum blue. The bottom mark for these teapots is shown.

Twenty-four Centennial teapots were made for the East Liverpool Alumni Association auction in placid pink and are marked for the ELHS Alumni. Two of the teapots decorated in Autumn Leaf were made for the out-going and in-coming presidents of the National Autumn Leaf Collectors Club.

Devon Cream Centennial, $95-125.

Hall China President/CEO John Sayle destroys the first Centennial mold.

Bottom mark for the Centennial Teapot

Ceylonator

Size:
6 cup, 32 ounces brimful, 5.75" high without cover and strainer, 7.25" with cover and strainer, 9.5" wide, strainer; infuser 4" high

The Ceylonator was introduced in the 1930s and looks very much like an Albany. However, it has an infuser and the regular Albany cover does not fit the teapot. Robert E. Hall registered the trademark for this teapot. In his booklet, *Golden Tea Tips*, written in the 1930s, he says, "In order that consumers may drink Pure Ceylon Tea, three essential conditions should be fulfilled: (1) They should be able to get 'Pure Ceylon Tea' from their grocers. (2) They should learn the art of preparing a cup of tea. (3) They should employ the proper 'apparatus' for making tea. Each of these conditions is as important as the others, for the best tea can be spoilt easily by being made badly."

He went on to say, "The latest model, known as the 'Ceylonator', which is a combination of the old colonial teapot and the oriental infuser-strainer, is difficult to improve upon. It is, indeed, 'the last word' in tea infusers... It is the 'Ceylonator' (made by the Hall China Co., of East Liverpool, Ohio) that the consumers would be wise to employ to get the very best out of Pure Ceylon Tea, following the rules given." The bottom mark reads, "Robert E. Hall's Registered Trademark, Ceylonator."

Mahogany Ceylonator with Infuser, ND.

Chicago with and without Metal Tip Spout

Teal and White Chicago, $35-40.

Sizes:
1 cup, 7 ounces brimful, 3.1875" high with cover, 6.125" wide, Hall No. 39
1.5 cup, 8 ounces brimful, 3.5" high with cover, 6.5" wide, Hall No. 40
2 cup, 15 ounces brimful, 3.875" high with cover, 6.625" wide, Hall No. 41
3 cup, 17 ounces brimful, 4.5" high with cover, 6.875" wide, Hall No. 42

Sizes – Metal Tip Spout – Long Spout:
1.5 cup, 8 ounces brimful, 3.375" high with cover, 6.25" wide, Hall No. MTS-40
2 cup, 14 ounces brimful, 3.875" high with cover, 6.625" wide, Hall No. MTS-41

Sizes – Metal Tip Spout – Short Spout:
1.5 cup, 9 ounces brimful, 3.25" high with cover, 6.125" wide, Hall No. MTS-2540
2 cup, 10 ounces brimful, 3.875" high with cover, 6.5" wide, Hall No. MTS-2541

Older decorations:
Chinese red, solid colors, "White Rim Band" (1 and 1.5 cup)
Special treatment:
Metal Clad

The Chicago was introduced in the early 1920s and produced until the 1990s. The teapots have strainers, are wide at the bottom, will not tip over, and will stack one upon another. They are excellent for individual service of tea or coffee.

In the late 1950s a new version of the Chicago was introduced with a long metal tip spout. The short metal tip spout was introduced in the mid-1960s. These teapots are found in a variety of colors and have the H-3 or H-4 bottom mark. Chicago teapots may be found with contrasting covers, usually white.

Maroon Long Metal Tip Spout and Green Short Metal Tip Spout Chicagos, $30-35 each.

Chrome Cozy
(Manning Bowman)

Size:
3 cup, 18 ounces brimful, 5.375" high for china pot, 7.25" high for metal cozy to top of knob, 7.25" wide, no strainer, Hall No. 1433

Dark Green Chrome Cozy, $140-160.

The Chrome Cozy was introduced in early 1955. Hall made the vertical paneled teapot to fit inside a felt-lined chrome cozy that has a hinged cover. The cozy insulates the teapot. The teapot is put into the cover from the top, and the chrome cover has slots for the handle and spout. The Manning Bowman Company was a chrome, brass, and copper manufacturer much like Forman Brothers and made the cover. There are some Manning Bowman Chrome Cozy teapots that were made by companies other than Hall.

The most common colors of the Chrome Cozy are dark green, white, and cobalt. The bottom mark on those made by Hall China reads: "A product of Manning Bowman, Meriden, Conn. Made in U.S.A." The cozy cover fits very tight, and it is generally hard to remove in order to clean the teapot or check the bottom mark. Hall China made two additional shapes for the Manning Bowman Company, but these shapes have not been identified.

Cleveland

Size:
6 cup, 32 ounces brimful, 4.75" high without cover, 6" high with cover, 11" wide, strainer, Hall No. 128

Older decorations:
Early Gold and Platinum Decorations, Gold Decorated, Gold "Special," Red Kitchenware, solid colors

The Cleveland was introduced in 1935 in solid colors and gold decorated. The gold decorations on the Cleveland are a series of butterflies around the shoulder with a thin gold band below and above the butterflies, and thin gold lines on the spout, handle, and knob.

In the 1950s and 1960s the Cleveland was usually sold in turquoise with the gold decoration. Bottom marks are H-3, H-3 with the Gold Decorated or Gold "Special" number, HSQK, or no mark at all.

"Colonial" ("Medallion")

Silhouette "Colonial," $75-90.

Size:
8 cup, 64 ounces brimful, 5.75" high without cover, 7.25" high with cover, 10.25" wide, strainer, Hall No. 236S

Older decorations:
"Mums," "Pastel Morning Glory," Silhouette, solid colors

The "Colonial" teapot without a medallion in the band was made in 1933 for the Cook Coffee Company in the Silhouette decal. The teapot is also found in the "Mums" and "Pastel Morning Glory" decorations. The bottom mark found is HSQK. The "Colonial" teapot is similar to the smaller "Medallion" teapot that has a medallion in the band.

The "Colonial" teapot shape was also used for the Enterprise Aluminum Company and made with the Crocus and "Shrub Rose Garland" decals. These pots do not have strainers, and the bottom mark is Drip-O-lator. They were made for use with an aluminum dripper for making coffee or without the drip for tea.

Left:
Turquoise Cleveland, $55-65.

"Columbia"

Size:
6 cup, 35 ounces brimful, 6.5" high without cover, 7.75" high with cover, 9" wide, strainer

Older decorations:
Early Gold and Platinum Decorations

The "Columbia" is a twelve-sided teapot that has been found in brown, cobalt, green, and old rose. It was probably produced in the late 1920s or early 1930s.

The gold stamped emblem and decorations are ornate with gold lining on the handle, spout, around the top of the pot and rim, and on the finial. One of the gold stamped decorations is the same as on the Albany teapot. Other decorations on the "Columbia" include gold striping with a gold floral band or a second gold emblem.

This teapot usually has the H-2 bottom mark and/or HALL incised.

Green with Gold "Lavaliere" Emblem "Columbia," $475-550.

"Connie" ("Victoria")

Size:
6 cup, 32 ounces brimful, 4.25" high without cover, 6" high with cover, 10" wide, no strainer

The "Connie" was introduced in 1946 as part of the "Victorian" Series. It will usually be found in celadon green, but it has also been found in the yellow as shown. A variety of gold treatments were applied to the teapots, but they are more difficult to find. The bottom mark is H-3, but the teapot will be found without any bottom mark.

Yellow "Connie," $140-170.

Counter Service with Spigot and Base

Sizes:
30 cup, 1.25 gallon, 8.25" high without cover, 9.75" high with cover, 15.5" high with stand, 14.5" wide, Hall No. 5030 for the counter service, Hall No. 5031 for the base, Hall No. 5032 for the faucet
60 cup, 2.5 gallon, 10" high without cover, 11.5" high with cover, 18.25" high with stand, 16.75" wide, Hall No. 5060 for the counter service, Hall No. 5061 for the base, Hall No. 5062 for the faucet

Newer decorations:
Autumn Leaf, Blue Blossom, Cameo Rose, Crocus, "Orange Poppy," Red Poppy, Silhouette, solid colors

Hall produced two sizes of counter service beverage pots for use in restaurants, cafeterias, and hotels. Both came with a spigot and sat on a base. The larger pot is frequently found in black or brown with white advertising lettering such as "Hall Fireproof China," "Lipton Tea," "Lipton Iced Tea," "The Long Expected Iced Tea," "Wilkins Tea," and others.

In 1935 the 2.5-gallons counter service was made with "Keeps Hot" lettering, and in 1950 one was marked "Arnholz" and mounted in a metal spring frame. The 2.5 gallons counter service pots were still advertised and available from Hall in the 1990s in a variety of colors. The older counter server had a metal spigot that was replaced by a plastic spigot on the newer pots. The bottom mark will be H-3 or H-4.

The newer decorated counter servers were made in limited numbers by special order and will have China Specialties on the bottom.

Black Counter Server, $475-550.

Cozy Hot Pot

Size:
6 cup, 32 ounces brimful, 5.25" high for china pot, 7" high for metal cozy to top of knob, 9.5" wide, strainer, Hall No. 3330

A Cozy Hot Pot was produced in 1956 for the Forman Family. It has a felt-lined metal cover that fits snugly over the pot with openings on the sides to fit over the handle and spout and insulates the teapot.

The teapot was made in turquoise with a chrome cover, in yellow with a brass cover, and in pink with a copper cover. Matching creamers and sugars with metal covers were available. The Cozy Hot Pot will also be found in black and white with a different style chrome cover. The two styles of covers are shown in the Forman Family section of the book. The bottom mark reads, "Made Exclusively for Forman Family, Inc. by the Hall China Company, U.S.A."

The instructions that came with the Cozy Hot Pot say to remove the insulated top, pour in hot water and drop in a tea bag, put the lid on the teapot, cover with the cozy cover that acts like a blanket, and put a cork plug in the spout. The teapot was available into the late 1970s and early 1980s.

Pink Cozy Hot Pot, $55-65.

Cube

Size:
2 cup, 12 ounces brimful, 3.5" square, 3.5" high, strainer, Hall No. 165
Older decorations:
Chinese red, French Flower, solid colors
Newer decorations:
Autumn Leaf, Blue Blossom, Blue Bouquet, Cameo Rose, Cat-Tail, Christmas Tree, Crocus, Game Bird, Heather Rose, "Orange Poppy," Red Poppy, Silhouette, solid colors

The Cube teapot was first described in a 1926 Hall's catalog as "A unique Teapot that will attract attention in Tea Rooms and Clubs. A square compact shape with sunken cover, a built-in handle, and a spout which is almost unbreakable." Patent Number 1380066 was issued on May 31, 1921, and Patent Number 1599967 on September 14, 1926, to Robert Crawford Johnson of Leicester, England. One of the objectives of the invention of the Cube was to place the spout and handle within the boundaries of the body and to obviate the liability of breakage or injury to the spout and handle. Other companies besides Hall made this teapot shape.

The Cube can be found in a variety of decorations and art glaze colors with the Dec. (decoration) number marked on the bottom in

gold. The bottom mark reads: "The CUBE, Reg. Trade Mark, Reg. No. 693783, Brits Pats 110951 & 258456 AND ABROAD U.S.A. Pat. 1380066-21 and 1599957-26, Cube Teapots Ltd., Leicester."

Blue Spice Cube, $110-135.

A Cube two-ounce handleless creamer and open sugar were available, and Hall also produced a handled Cube creamer in the 1970s. A tray to hold the teapot and creamer was produced. The Cube teapot was last mentioned in a Hall's catalog in the early 1970s; however, it is still being produced upon special request and for China Specialties. The newer decorations will have China Specialties marked on the bottom.

"Damascus"

Size:
6 cup, 40 ounces brimful, 5.25" high without cover, 6.25" high with cover, 9" wide, Hall No. 3204, strainer

The "Damascus" is one of the "Art Deco" series that was introduced in the mid-1930s and was made in blue, olive green, maroon, and yellow colors. The color on the inside of the teapot is the same color as the outside. The "Damascus" will have the H-2 or H-3 bottom mark, and some of the teapots will be found unmarked.

Olive Green "Damascus," $250-300.

"Danielle"

Size:
6 cup, 40 ounces brimful, 5.25" high without cover, 6.25" high with cover, 9.25" wide, no strainer

Blue "Danielle," $195-225.

Another teapot in the 1930s "Art Deco" series is the "Danielle" teapot. Colors of the teapots are blue, olive green, maroon, and yellow. The teapot color is the same on the inside and outside of the teapot. Some of the "Danielle" teapots are not marked, but most have the H-2 or H-3 bottom mark.

"Demi" Teapot
("Morning Teapot")

Size:
3 cup, 22 ounces brimful, 3.375" high without cover, 4.75" high with cover, 7.25" wide, strainer, Hall No. 1393
Older decorations:
Autumn Leaf, Blue Belle with Blue or Pink Flowers, Blue Blossom, Blue Garden, Buttercup with Blue or Yellow Flowers, Fantasy, Golden Glo, Red Kitchenware, solid colors, White Bake Ware, "Wild Poppy"

Chinese Red "Demi" Teapot, $260-310.

The "Demi" Teapot was introduced in the late 1930s. The teapot, along with a matching creamer and covered sugar, are called a Morning Set. The "Demi" Morning Sets were made in several decals and in solid colors. The bottom marks found are H-3 and HSQK. In

a *1940-41 Montgomery Ward* catalog, a bright red "Demi" Teapot was advertised for eighty-nine cents. A Blue Garden Morning Set was listed in a 1941 *Hall China Special Catalog No. 14*.

The "Demi" Teapot was also used as part of the No. 1 Tea Set that consisted of eleven pieces – a teapot, open sugar, creamer, four cups, and four party plates. The set was advertised in Buttercup with blue or yellow flowers and in Blue Belle with blue or pink flowers. The No. 1 Tea Set was advertised in the 1952 *Jewel Tea Company* catalog. The bottom mark on the No. 1 Tea Set is "Hall China, No. 1 Tea Set" followed by the color. In 1958 the "Demi" Teapot was produced in Golden Glo with the H-3 bottom mark.

Denver

Sizes:
Small, 5 ounces brimful, 3.25" high without cover, 4" high with cover, 4.25" wide, strainer, Hall No. 110
1 cup, 7 ounces brimful, 3.75" high without cover, 4.5" high with cover, 4.5" wide, strainer, Hall No. 111
1.5 cup, 9 ounces brimful, 4.125" high with cover, 5" high with cover, 5" wide, strainer, Hall No. 112

The Denver appeared in the early 1920s in green or brown and was made until the mid-1970s. It has a perforated strainer in the spout and has been found with both sunken or knob covers. It was made for individual service for coffee, chocolate, cocoa, hot milk, and hot water. The five-ounce and seven-ounce sizes were recommended for use in hospitals. The Denver was available in a variety of colors and is found with the H-3 and H-4 bottom marks.

Gray Knob Cover and Pewter Sunken Cover Denvers, $30-35 each.

Detroit

Size:
1.5 cup, 13 ounces brimful, 3.125" high with sunken cover, 6.5" wide, Hall No. 60
Older decorations:
French Flower, Pewter, solid colors

The Detroit is another stacking teapot introduced in the early 1920s in green and brown. It has a sunken cover and a wide bottom to allow easy stacking. The Detroit was available in a variety of colors in the Hall catalogs until the early 1970s. The bottom mark is either H-3 or H-4. The teapot had a strainer until the early 1970s.

A knob cover version of the Detroit was decorated by China Specialties and has a bottom mark that reads, "This Hall China Teapot Made Especially for the Dining Car China Collectors Club, Northeastern Chapter. A China Specialties exclusive."

the teapot or pointed down around the body. The teapot with the metal cover is bottom marked with HALL incised, H-3, and "Made Exclusively for Forman Bros. Inc. by The Hall China Co., Hand Decorated." There is a matching creamer and uncovered sugar.

Brown Detroit, $35-40.

Dodecagon with China or Metal Cover

"Chrysler" and Mother of Pearl Dodecagon with Metal Cover, $300-350.

Art Glaze Orange Dodecagon, $200-250.

Size:
6 cup, 32 ounces brimful, 5.5" high without cover, 6.5" high with cover, 9.5" wide, strainer

The Dodecagon is a twelve-sided teapot that has been found with both a china and metal cover. The china cover fits on top of the rim rather than resting inside of the rim. Solid art glaze colors are usually found on this style teapot. The Dodecagon has HALL incised on the bottom.

The teapot has also been found with a metal cover with a tea ball attached to the knob of the cover. This style is normally found with a Mother-of-Pearl body and a decal such as the Chrysler that is shown. The Chrysler decal is found pointed up on the shoulder of

Dohrco ("Irene")

Maroon Dohrco, $70-85.

Size:
2 cup, 12 ounces brimful, 3" high without cover, 3.5" high with cover, 6.75" wide, strainer, Hall No. 2210

The Dohrco teapot was introduced in early 1937 for the Dohrmann Hotel Supply Company. It is found in a variety of colors. The bottom mark is "DOHRCO" with H-3 and Made in USA below. The teapot was distributed on the West Coast where the Dohrmann Hotel Supply Company was located.

Doughnut ("Donut")

Size:
6 cup, 34 ounces brimful, 6.5" high without cover, 7.5" high with cover, 10" wide, Hall No. 3116

Chinese Red Doughnut, $425-475.

Older decorations:
Blue Garden, Crocus, Gold Decorated, Gold "Special," "Orange Poppy," Red Kitchenware, solid colors

Newer decorations:
Autumn Leaf, "Floral," solid colors

The Doughnut is part of the Hall "Novelty" Series of teapots. It appeared in an early 1938 trade journal along with the Football and Airflow. It was described as simulating a doughnut and obtainable in DuPont colors of red, blue, green, or yellow. In 1939 and 1941 the Doughnut was part of the Hall Superior Quality Kitchenware series and sold for $1.50 in Chinese red. It was also available in Indian red, midnight blue, and jonquil yellow (screaming yellow).

The Doughnut can be found in a variety of solid colors, gold decorated with gold lining and with Gold "Special" spout and handle, and in several decal patterns. The bottom marks found are H-3, H-3 or HALL with the Gold Decorated or Gold "Special" number, and HSQK.

Between the 1970s and 1980s, Thornberry's of Ohio sold the Doughnut with the "Floral" decal. The bottom mark is Thornberry. The National Autumn Leaf Collectors Club had the Doughnut produced in white with the Autumn Leaf decal for its members in 1993. It is marked with NALCC. Cobalt, gloss black, hunter green, and light yellow Doughnuts were made in 1993 for Naomi's Antiques of San Francisco. They are marked on the bottom "Made Especially for Naomi's of San Francisco, 1993, Hall, Made in U.S.A." In 1997 the Doughnut was made for the East Liverpool Alumni Association auction in ivory with gold. These are marked with ELHS Alumni.

The Doughnut is currently available in a variety of modern colors from the Hall Closet and is marked H-4 or H-4 above "Classics, HALLCLASSICS.COM, 3116, Made in USA." The Doughnut and other teapots in the "Novelty" series are shown together in another section of this book.

E-Style

Size:
6 cup, 32 ounces brimful, 4" without cover, 5.625" high with cover, 10.75" wide, strainer, Hall No. 4052

Older decorations:
Cameo Rose, Golden Oak, "Pink Rose"

The E-Style teapot was produced in the early 1950s in the Cameo Rose pattern and was available until the early 1970s. The teapot is part of the Cameo Rose E-Style dinnerware set that was sold exclusively through the Jewel Tea Company with a matching creamer and sugar with cover. In 1941, J. Palin Thorley designed the E-Style dinnerware for the Sears, Roebuck and Co.'s Arlington, Fairfax, Monticello, Mount Vernon, and Richmond / Brown-Eyed Susan patterns. Cameo Rose and Golden Oak are the only dinnerware sets that have an E-Style teapot. The bottom mark on the Cameo Rose is HD with "Tested and approved by Mary Dunbar Jewel Homemakers Institute" inside the circle. Some of the teapots will not have a bottom stamp. This style teapot has also been found in other floral decals such as "Pink Rose" and a yellow flower that are not part of any dinnerware set, some with matching creamer and sugar.

Cameo Rose E-Style, $100-125.

Edward Don Open Teapot

White Edward Don Open Teapot, $25-35.

Size:
2 cup, 12 ounces brimful, 4" high, 5.75" wide, no strainer, Hall No. 2856

The Edward Don Open teapot was designed in 1996 exclusively for Edward Don and Company, a national distributor of foodservice equipment and supplies. It comes in white and is currently available in their catalog. The bottom mark reads "Quality DON Ovenware, 12 oz."

Edward Don
Stakups© Teapot

Vanilla Edward Don Stakups Teapot, $20-30.

Size:
2 cup, 12 ounces brimful, 3.5" high without cover, 4.375" high with cover, 7" wide, Hall No. MTS 2571

The Stakups teapot with a metal tip spout was designed in the early 1980s for Edward Don and Company and is still available in their catalog in white. Earlier the Stakups teapot was available in open stock in bone white or Lenox brown. It could be ordered in burnt orange, cadet, green, lemon yellow, lettuce, maroon, and sandust. The cover has a locking tab. The teapot has matching index marks on top of the cover and the body. The bottom mark is "Don STAKUPS© by Hall®."

Edwards with China or
Metal Cover

Size:
6 cup, 32 ounces brimful, 5.25" high without cover, 6.25" high with cover, 9.25" wide, strainer

Rust and Mother of Pearl Edwards with China Cover, ND.

The Edwards teapot was produced for the Forman Brothers, Inc. and has a metal cover with a tea ball attached by chain. A china cover for the Edwards teapot was also available that sits on top of the teapot rim. The teapot is usually found with a Mother of Pearl body and blue, green, or rust on the handle, spout, and around the shoulder of the teapot. The bottom of the teapot has HALL incised; H-3; and "Made Exclusively for Forman Bros. Inc. by The Hall China Co., Hand Decorated, Dec. 711."

"Everson" Ribbed Teapot

Marine "Everson" Ribbed Teapot, $35-50.

Size:
3 cup, 19 ounces brimful, 4" high without cover, 4.75" high with cover, 7.75" wide, Hall No. 5105

The "Everson" Ribbed Teapot was made for the Jewel Tea Company in September 1952 and does not have a bottom mark. It comes in mahogany, marine, and yellow. This teapot is slightly larger and has a strainer. It is similar to the McCormick Ribbed Teapot that comes in gray and does not have a strainer.

Left:
Rust and Mother of Pearl
Edwards with Metal
Cover, $125-150.

Facetation

Facetation Teapot, $25-35.

Size:
3.625" high without cover, Hall No. 4004

The pictured Facetation teapot without its cover is a prototype of the teapot Hall China produced in 1990 for Service Ideas, Inc. of Woodbury, Minnesota. The bottom mark reads "FTP12 Made in U.S.A." We were unable to find a completed production teapot to photograph.

Flare-Ware

Autumn Leaf Flare-Ware, $60-75.

Size:
6 cup, 32 ounces brimful, 4.5" high without cover, 5.5" high with cover, 8.5" wide, no strainer, locking oval cover, Hall No. 1756
Older decorations:
Autumn Leaf, Chestnut, Gold Lace, Gold Lace with Heather Rose, Golden Glo, Mynah, Plain White, Radial, Sunnyvale

The Flare-Ware teapot was introduced in early 1961 by Hall China. It is part of the Modern 61 Flare-Ware series that includes a coffee server, coffee urn, trivet with candle warmer, and serving pieces. The bottom mark reads "Flare-Ware by Hall China, Made in U.S.A."

The most common decorations are the Autumn Leaf, Chestnut, Gold Lace, and Radial. The Autumn Leaf decoration has sometimes been referred to as "Autumn Leaves" to distinguish the decoration from the Jewel Tea Autumn Leaf decoration.

In an advertisement for casseroles lined with Teflon, the Flare-Ware teapot was listed as being available in Mynah, Plain White, and Sunnyvale decorations; however, only teapots in the Sunnyvale decoration have been found.

Flat-Sides Teapot

Apple Green Flat-Sides Teapot, $40-50.

Size:
1.5 cup, 12 ounces brimful, 3.375" high without cover, 3.75" high with cover, 6.25" wide, no strainer, Hall No. 1640
Older decorations:
Golden Glo, solid colors

The Flat-Sides teapot was introduced in the fall of 1961. It was made in a variety of colors and is currently available in the *Hall China Express Catalog* in white. Some of these teapots may be found with contrasting colored covers from the color of the body. Bob Evans Restaurants in Ohio use the Flat-Sides Teapot to serve hot water. The bottom marks used are H-3, H-4, or HALL incised. The body of the teapot has nibs to hold the cover in place.

Football

Sandust Football (China Specialties), $60-70.

Size:
6 cup, 40 ounces brimful, 6.75" high to top of handle, 9.75" wide, Hall No. 3115

Older decorations:
Gold Decorated, Gold "Special," Red Kitchenware, solid colors

Newer decorations:
Autumn Leaf, Blue Blossom, Blue Bouquet, Cameo Rose, Cat-Tail, Christmas Tree, Crocus, Game Bird, Heather Rose, Mexicana, Ohio State, "Orange Poppy," Red Poppy, Silhouette, solid colors, West Virginia

At the early 1938 pottery show, the Football teapot was introduced along with the Airflow and Doughnut teapots. This teapot was designed to look like a football and was obtainable in DuPont colors of blue, green, red, and yellow. The Football has also been referred to as a Spheroid meaning "A body that is an ellipsoid, generated by revolving an ellipse around one of its axes." *(American Heritage Dictionary)* The Football was produced until early 1939.

The Football is found in a variety of solid colors, decorated with gold lining, and decorated as a Gold "Special" with gold lining plus solid gold handles and spout. The bottom marks found on the Football are H-3, H-3 with the Gold Decorated or "Special" number, and HSQK. Shown in the "Novelty" Series section of this book is the Football, along with the other five "Novelty" teapots.

Beginning in 1992 China Specialties reintroduced the Football in solid colors, solid colors with gold lining, and in a limited number of decals. The bottom mark is China Specialties. The older teapots will be found with a strainer, whereas the newer teapots do not have strainers. In 2001, China Specialties decorated a limited number of Hall Football teapots with a space odyssey theme for the Hall Haul group.

French

Maroon 6-Cup French, $50-60.

Sizes:
Teapot with no handle for silver holder
1 cup, 6 ounces brimful, 2.875" high without cover, 3.5" high with cover, 4.25" wide, Hall No. 1690 (90)
1.5 cup, 10 ounces brimful, 3.25" high without cover, 3.875" high with cover, 5.75" wide, Hall No. 1691 (91)
2 cup, 14 ounces brimful, 3.5" high without cover, 4.375" high with cover, 6.75" wide, Hall No. 1692 (92)
3 cup, 18 ounces brimful, 3.75" high without cover, 4.75" high with cover, 7" wide, Hall No. 1692.5 (92.5)
4 cup, 22 ounces brimful, 4.125" high without cover, 5" high with cover, 7.875" wide, Hall No. 1693 (93)
5 or 6 cup, 32 ounces brimful, 4.5" high without cover, 5.5" high with cover, 8.75" wide, Hall No. 1694 (94)

7 or 8 cup, 40 ounces brimful, 5" high without cover, 6" high with cover, 8" wide, Hall No. 1695 (95)
10 cup, 56 ounces brimful, 5.375" high without cover, 6.75" high with cover, 10.125" wide, Hall No. 1696 (96)
12 cup, 62 ounces brimful, 5.75" high without cover, 7" high with cover, 10.875" wide, Hall No. 1697 (97)

Older decorations:
Black Gold (2 cup), Cactus (6 and 8 cup), California Poppy (2 cup), Early Decals, Early Gold and Platinum Decorations, Eggshell Polka Dot (2 cup), Flamingo, French Flower, Gold Dot (2 cup), Gold Decorated, Gold Label (2 and 6 cup), Gold "Special," Golden Glo, Golden Oak, "Leaf and Vine," "Mini-Fleurette," "No Blue," Red Kitchenware (2 and 6 cup), Royal Rose, Russet, solid colors, Sixties Decoration, Springtime, "Wild Poppy"

Newer decorations:
Autumn Leaf (2 cup), Game Bird, Heather Rose

Special treatments:
Metal Clad (6 cup) and Super-Ceram (1.5, 2, 3, 4, and 6 cup)

There are three very similar shapes that will be treated separately – the French, the French Light Weight, and the Infuser/Percolator teapots. The French Light Weight was introduced in the teens, and the Infuser/Percolator teapot appeared in the catalogs in the early twenties. In the late 1930s Hall dropped the French Light Weight and Infuser/Percolator teapots in their advertisement, continuing with the current French style. The French and French Light Weight have the same Hall identification numbers. The same mold was used; however, the French Light Weight was not left in the mold as long as the regular French. This resulted in a thinner, lighter weight teapot.

In 1963 Hall changed the manufacturing numbers for the French teapots from the 90s to the 1690s. At about the same time, the strainers were no long included in the teapot. The bottom marks found on the French shape are H-2, H-3, H-3 with Gold or Platinum Decorated or "Special" number, H-3 or HALL with Gold Label number, H-4, HSQK, and HALL Incised. The 10-ounce and 14-ounce French teapots are both marked as a two-cup teapot.

During the early thirties, the French Light Weight was advertised along with fourteen other teapots as part of Hall's Gold Decorated line. It was decorated with gold French Flowers and gold lining on the handle, spout, around the upper rim of the body, and on the cover. After the French Light Weight was dropped in the late 1930s, the heavier body French was part of the Gold Decorated series that appeared in catalogs through the 1960s. For ordering purposes Hall put together groups of mixed teapots. The French was advertised in black as part of the "Gold Decorated Group 8" in 1956 that consisted of six teapots (six cup in size) and in six colors. In 1957 the French was offered in blue and canary yellow in a "Gold Decorated Group" that consisted of three shapes, five sizes (2, 4, 8, 10, and 12 cup), and six colors.

In the mid-1950s Hall introduced their Gold Label line. The French was advertised in blue turquoise and decorated with gold daisies and had a solid gold handle, knob on cover, and spout. In the sixties the French was part of a series called the Sears or Sixties series. The six-cup French featured a mat black body with a rose decal in gold and was advertised in the *Sears, Roebuck and Co.* catalog. The decal has also been found on a two-cup French.

Lipton Tea Company chose the French shape for their advertising in a series of six colors with the bottom marked "Lipton Teas." The teapots are the same color inside and out and came in black, blue, green, maroon, warm yellow, and yellow. A matching Boston shape creamer and sugar were made in all colors except the maroon to accompany the teapots. The Lipton creamers and sugars are also the same color inside and out.

During 1985 Hall introduced their Hall American Line. The French was one of several teapots chosen to be part of this series. They could be found in standard colors of black, blue, gray, red, tan, and white. Hall also offered over 100 colors for retailers to choose their own. Naomi's Antiques of San Francisco special ordered the six- and eight-cup French in cobalt, orange, and lavender. These teapots are marked with the H-4 bottom mark.

In 1992, the National Autumn Leaf Collectors Club provided the French two-cup for the membership, and the bottom mark is NALCC.

French Light Weight

Brown French Light Weight, $30-35.

Sizes:

Miniature 1/5 Salesman Sample, 3.375" high

1 cup, 6 ounces brimful, 2.875" high without cover, 3.5" high with cover, 4.25" wide, Hall No. 90

1.5 cup, 10 ounces brimful, 3.25" high without cover, 3.875" high with cover, 5.75" wide, Hall No. 91

2 cup, 14 ounces brimful, 3.5" high without cover, 4.375" high with cover, 6.75" wide, Hall No. 92

3 cup, 18 ounces brimful, 3.875" high without cover, 4.75" high with cover, 7" wide, Hall No. 92.5

4 cup, 22 ounces brimful, 4.125" high without cover, 5" high with cover, 7.875" wide, Hall No. 93

5 or 6 cup, 32 ounces brimful, 4.5" high without cover, 5.5" high with cover, 8.75" wide, Hall No. 94

7 or 8 cup, 40 ounces brimful, 5" high without cover, 6" high with cover, 8" wide, Hall No. 95

10 cup, 56 ounces brimful, 5.375" high without cover, 6.75" high with cover, 10.125" wide, Hall No. 96

12 cup, 62 ounces brimful, 5.75" high without cover, 7" high with cover, 10.875" wide, Hall No. 97

Older decorations:

Early Gold and Platinum Decorations, French Flower, solid colors

The French Light Weight teapot is one of the earliest teapots made by The Hall China Company. In 1916 McCormick Tea Company purchased the French Light Weight in green and brown. In early 1920 Hall displayed the Boston, French Light Weight, and New York at the Pittsburgh Pottery Show. These teapots were samples of the Hall line of decorated teapots that they planned to manufacture and begin deliveries on June 1, 1920. When the teapots were distributed later that year, they were advertised in a full run of sizes in royal blue, rich green, or brown, with a variety of gold decorations by able artists.

In September 1920 Hall began a national advertising campaign in *The Literary Digest*, *Good Housekeeping*, and other magazines. Hall's teapots received an approval by the Good Housekeeping Institute. One of the strong selling points in their advertisement in the trade journals was that the teapots were "Next to impossible to break. That is one of the big reasons why the teapots are almost invariably selected by the big hotels, hospitals, and restaurants. They are care-less-waiter-proof." (*Pottery, Glass & Brass Salesman*, November 4, 1920)

In a 1920s *M. Seller & Co.*, Portland, Ore., Seattle and Spokane, Wash. Catalog, the French Light Weight was advertised in two, three, five, and six cups selling from $3.20 to $4.33 depending upon size. The teapots were available in an all-over gold stamped French Flower or with a gold band and line decoration around the center of the teapot. The French Flower stamping was referred to as a gold Japanese floral design.

The French Light Weight was part of a series, along with the Boston and New York that Hall referred to as their China Tea and Coffee Pots. One pot could be used for making coffee, tea, and chocolate made one after the other. With the white inside and smooth surface, no trace of flavor could be retained in the Hall China Pot. The French Light Weight and the French were made from the same mold. The French Light Weight was not left in the mold as long as the French teapot, which resulted in a thinner, lighter weight body.

During the 1920s and 1930s the French Light Weight was decorated in a variety of decals and gold or platinum stamping. It could be ordered in 1935 in the following solid colors: black, blue, brown, cadet, canary, clay, Dresden, emerald, flesh, gray, green, green lustre, ivory, lettuce, lune blue, marine, maroon, orchid, pink, rose, tan, turquoise, violet, and yellow.

Also during the early 1930s, Hall took popular style teapots and decorated them with a decal rather than gold stamping. The five- and seven-cup French Light Weight teapot appeared in both white and warm yellow with a black "Minuet" decal and black lining to the handle, spout, and around the top. By the late 1930s Hall phased out the French Light Weight and the Infuser/Percolator teapots.

The bottom marks found on the French Light Weight are H-2, H-3, HSQK, or HALL incised. On the earlier French Light Weight teapots, the vent hole in the cover will generally be found under the cover handle. This was not always true because the workers have been known to place the vent holes wherever they chose.

Globe

Size:

6 cup, 40 ounces brimful, 5" high without cover, 6" high with cover, 8.75" wide, strainer, Hall No. 1414

Emerald Globe, $135-165.

Older decorations:
Gold Decorated, Red Kitchenware, solid colors

The Globe teapot was introduced in the late 1930s and had a very short production life. It has a tab-locking cover and comes in only one size. The stock color for the Gold Decorated Globe was emerald, and it was decorated with a gold flower on a stem with leaves and gold scalloped lace around the shoulder of the teapot and on the edge of the cover.

In a 1942 catalog the Gold Decorated Globe was available in black, blue, brown, cadet, canary, delphinium, Dresden, emerald, green, green lustre, ivory, marine, maroon, orchid, rose, turquoise, and yellow. The bottom marks found are H-3, H-3 or HALL with the Gold Decorated number, HSQK, or without a mark. The spout of this teapot is easily damaged, and undamaged teapots are hard to find. A teapot similar to the Globe was made in the early 1950s and is called No-Drip.

"Grape" ("Darwin")

White "Grape," $75-90.

Size:
6 cup, 40 ounces brimful, 5.5" high without cover, 7.5" high with cover, 9" wide, strainer, Hall No. 1528
Older decorations:
Bouquet, Game Bird, Gold Band, Harlequin, solid colors

The "Grape" is one of six teapots designed by J. Palin Thorley in the late 1950s. It is part of the Brilliant Series, also known by collectors as the Thorley Series. In 1959 the "Grape" was advertised in black, bright blue, maroon, and white with 22-carat bright gold decoration and brilliants. The "Grape" has also been found in a variety of solid colors and with different decals.

The bottom marks found are H-3 on the solid teapots, HSQK on the decaled teapots, and H-3 or HALL with the Gold Decorated number on those with the gold stipple decoration. Many of the bottom marks will include the Hall identification number.

Hallcraft Century

White Hallcraft Century, $200-225.

Size:
6 cup, 44 ounces brimful, 5.5" high to lower part of rim, 6.75" high with cover, 9.5" wide, no strainer, Hall No. 1582
Older decorations:
Fern, Garden of Eden, Sunglow, White

The Hallcraft Century line was designed by Eva Zeisel and introduced in the mid-1950s. The teapot comes in four decorations and has a locking cover. The Midhurst China Sales Corporation of New York distributed the Hallcraft line. There are creamers and sugars with covers to match the teapots.

The bottom mark reads "Eva Zeisel, Century, Hallcraft, Made in U.S.A. by Hall China Co." There may be an after-market pattern on a teapot in the Flight decal.

Hallcraft Tomorrow's Classic

Hi-White Hallcraft Tomorrow's Classic, $175-225.

Size:
6 cup, 37 ounces brimful, 5.75" high, 8.875" wide

Older decorations:

Arizona, Bouquet, Buckingham, Caprice, Dawn, Fantasy, Flair, Frost Flowers, Golden Glo, Harlequin, Hi-White, Holiday, Lyric, Mulberry, Peach Blossom, Pinecone, Romance, Satin Black, Satin Gray, Spring, Studio 10

Hallcraft Tomorrow's Classic was designed by Eva Zeisel in 1949-1950 for the Midhurst China Company and produced by the Hall China Company in 1951. The teapot was produced in a wide variety of decals with matching creamer and covered sugar. The bottom mark is "Hallcraft by Eva Zeisel."

This teapot is part of the most successful dinnerware line produced by Hall in the modernism design. There may be teapots in Palo Duro, Prairie Grass, Rain Tree, and "Surf Ballet" patterns. Refer to the Eva Zeisel section of this book for further information.

Hollywood

Canary Hollywood, $50-60.

Sizes:

4 cup, 32 ounces brimful, 4.875" high without cover, 6" high with cover, 9.5" wide, strainer, Hall No. 213

6 cup, 38 ounces brimful, 5.25" high without cover, 6.75" high with cover, 10.5" wide, strainer, Hall No. 214

8 cup, 48 ounces brimful, 5.5" high without cover, 6.75" high with cover, 10.625" wide, strainer, Hall No. 215

Older decorations:

Early Gold and Platinum Decorations, Gold Decorated, Gold Label, Gold "Special," Golden Glo, "Leaf and Vine," Mother of Pearl, Red Kitchenware (4 and 6 cup), Silver Glo, Sixties Decoration, solid colors, "Winter Berry"

The Hollywood first appeared in a trade journal advertisement in December 1927. In late 1931 matching creamers and sugars were introduced. From the mid-1930s to the 1960s, the Hollywood was part of the "Gold Decorated Group 8" that consisted of six teapots, six shapes, and six colors. It was most often advertised in chartreuse and decorated with a gold band outlining the shoulder and cover. The teapot shoulder above the band is filled with gold filigree.

The Hollywood is also part of the Gold Label line and was advertised in maroon and ivory. During the 1960s a shiny brown Hollywood was decorated with gold leaves and acorns along with gold lining on the handle, spout, cover, and around the base. The bottom marks found are H-2; H-3; H-3 with the Gold Decorated, Gold Label, or Gold "Special" number; HSQK; and HALL.

Hook Cover

Chinese Red Hook Cover, $240-280.

Size:

6 cup, 40 ounces brimful, 4.625" high without cover, 5.5" high with cover, 9.5" wide, strainer, Hall No. 1420

Older decorations:

Blue Blossom, Gold Decorated, Gold Label, Gold "Special," "Mini-Fleurette," "No Blue," Red Kitchenware, Silver Glo, solid colors

Newer decorations:

Autumn Leaf, Blue Bouquet, Cameo Rose, Cat-Tail, Christmas Tree, Crocus, Game Bird, Heather Rose, Little Red Riding Hood, "Orange Poppy," Red Poppy, Silhouette

Special treatment:

Metal Clad

The Hook Cover was introduced at the January 1940 Pittsburgh Pottery Show. The teapot is sometimes confused with the Parade that also has a hooked cover. The Parade has a patterned body whereas the Hook Cover's body is smooth.

The Hook Cover was part of the "Gold Decorated Group 9" consisting of six styles, a six-cup size, and six colors. The standard Gold Decorated, Gold Label, and Gold "Special" Hook Cover teapot was advertised in cadet. The teapot comes in only one size and is found with H-3; H-3 or HALL and the Gold Decorated, Gold Label, or Gold "Special" number; and HSQK.

In 1994 China Specialties reintroduced the Hook Cover in a variety of decals, and the bottom mark is China Specialties.

Hot Pot (knob and sunken cover)

Size – Knob Cover:

1.5 cup, 9 ounces brimful, 3.625" high without cover, 4.5" high with cover, strainer, Hall No. 2620

Green Sunken Cover Hot Pot, $35-45. (Knob Cover Hot Pot not shown) Reprint from 1964 Hall Catalog.

Size - Sunken Cover:
1.5 cup, 9 ounces brimful, 3.625" high, strainer, Hall No. 2610

The Hot Pot with knob or sunken covers was introduced in 1957 and appears in Hall catalogs from 1959 until 1989. The Hot Pot came in a variety of colors, and the bottom mark is H-3. This Hot Pot is frequently confused with the Hall shape called Teapot.

Iconic Hot Water Pot
and Teapot

Coral Peach Iconic Hot Water Pot, $35-45;
Black Iconic Teapot, $25-30.

Size – Hot Water:
2 cup, 12 ounces brimful, 4.25" high without cover, 5" high with cover, 5.5" wide, no strainer, Hall No. 1505

Size – Teapot:
1.5 cup, 12 ounces brimful, 3.5" high without cover, 4.125" high with cover, 6.25" wide, no strainer, Hall No. 1506

Special treatment:
Super-Ceram

The Iconic Hot Water was introduced by Hall China in the fall of 1955 and remained available until the late 1980s. An Iconic teapot was added in early 1957 and produced through the mid-1990s. The pots are twelve-sided and have different shaped spouts. Matching handled and handleless creamers and handleless sugars were made. The Iconic pieces were available in a variety of colors and have the H-3, H-4, HALL, or Super-Ceram bottom marks.

Illinois

Size:
6 cup, 32 ounces brimful, 4.625" high without cover, 5.75" high with cover, 8.5" wide, strainer, Hall No. 222

Older decorations:
Early Gold and Platinum Decorations, Gold Decorated, Red Kitchenware, solid colors

The Illinois was introduced in the early 1930s. In 1935 the Illinois was available in solid colors and in Gold Decorated under-glaze colors of black, blue (cobalt), brown, cadet, canary, emerald, green, green lustre, ivory, marine, maroon, rose, and yellow. Gold stamping appears around the shoulder and on the cover. This gold stamping pattern is referred to as the "Illinois" and was used as part of the decoration on the "Naomi," Tea for Two Set, Tea for Four Set, Twin-Tee Set, and on the Los Angeles Gold Label teapots.

In 1937 the Illinois was also available in delphinium, orchid, and turquoise. By 1941 the Illinois was dropped from the Gold Decorated line.

Another gold stamping appearing around the shoulders of the Illinois features gold spirals that are referred to as a gold "Nebula." The Illinois teapot is found with the H-3, H-3 or HALL with the Gold Decorated number, and HSQK bottom mark.

Indiana

Marine and Gold Indiana, $320-360.

Size:
6 cup, 32 ounces brimful, 4.375" high without cover, 5.5" high with cover, 9.75" wide, strainer, Hall No. 221

Older decorations:
Gold Decorated, solid colors

The Indiana was advertised in a 1937 *Hall China Revised Special Catalog No. 73* as part of the Gold Decorated line with gold lining and in a variety of colors. The Gold Decorated under-glaze colors were black, blue (cobalt), brown, cadet, canary, delphinium, emerald, green, green lustre, ivory, marine, maroon, orchid, rose, turquoise, and yellow. By 1941 the Indiana was dropped from the Gold Decorated line.

The bottom marks found are either H-3, or H-3 or HALL with the Gold Decorated number. This teapot has been elusive, probably because of a short production run.

Left:
Cobalt Illinois, $240-280.

Infuser/Percolator Teapot
(Older French)

Old Rose Infuser Teapot, ND.

Sizes:
1 cup, 6 ounces brimful, 2.875" high without cover or infuser, 3.75" high with cover and infuser, 4.25" wide, Hall No. 70
1.5 cup, 10 ounces brimful, 3.25" high without cover or infuser, 4.25" high with cover and infuser, 5.75" wide, Hall No. 71
2 cup, 14 ounces brimful, 3.5" high without cover or infuser, 4.625" high with cover and infuser, 6.75" wide, Hall No. 72
3 cup, 18 ounces brimful, 3.875" high without cover or infuser, 5" high with cover and infuser, 7" wide, Hall No. 72.5
4 cup, 22 ounces brimful, 4.125" high without cover, 5.375" high with cover and infuser, 7.875" wide, Hall No. 73
6 cup, 32 ounces brimful, 4.5" high without cover or infuser, 6" high with cover and infuser, 8.5" wide, Hall No. 74
8 cup, 40 ounces brimful, 5.125" high without cover or infuser, 6.5" high with cover and infuser, 8" wide, Hall No. 75

Older decorations:
Early Gold and Platinum Decorations, French Flower, solid colors, "Wild Poppy"

Originally Hall called this teapot the Percolator teapot, but in 1935 they referred to it as the Infuser teapot in their catalogs. In the 1927 *Hall's Vitrified Cooking China Catalog*, the Percolator teapot was advertised in seven sizes in blue, brown, green, or white. They sold for from $1.00 to $1.83 each depending upon size. At an additional cost they could be furnished with gold decorations. The teapot could be used with or without the infuser. The 1- and 1.5-cup sizes were recommended for hospital service.

In 1935 the Infuser teapot was available in under-glaze colors of cadet, canary, cobalt, emerald, lettuce, marine, maroon, orchid, pink, rose, tan, violet, and yellow. In 1937 sea spray, turquoise, and Dresden colors were added to the list of available colors. Decorations found on the Infuser teapot are shown in the Early Gold and Platinum Decorations section later in this book. The bottom marks found will be H-2, H-3, and HALL incised.

The Infuser teapot did not appear in the Hall catalogs after the late 1930s. However, in May 1983 the 1.5- and 2-cup size Infuser teapots were listed in Hall records using the regular French body plus an infuser and special cover to fit.

International

Black and White International, $35-45.

Size:
1.5 cup, 10 ounces, 3.375" high without cover, 4.25" high with cover, 6.5" wide, strainer, Hall No. 2701
Special treatment:
Super-Ceram

The International teapot, with a matching creamer and sugar with no cover, was advertised in the Hall China catalogs from 1964 through the mid-1970s. The International design was advertised as combining beauty and utility. Some of the other International pieces are a coffee pot, two metal tip spout coffee pots, water jug, and bud vase. The lips on the International pieces serve as convenient handles.

The International pieces came in either solid or a two-color combination as shown. The teapot is found with the H-3, H-4, or Super-Ceram bottom mark.

Irvine

Turquoise Irvine,
$240-290.

Size:

3 cup, 9 ounces brimful in largest chamber, 8 ounces brimful in smaller chamber, 3.625" high without cover, 4.25" high with cover, 6" wide, no strainer, Hall No. 3230

The Irvine was made for the Twinspout Pottery Company, Inc. in early 1940 as part of the Teamaster line that includes the Alma, Tea Taster, and Twinspout. The Irvine is a two-chamber teapot, one for tea and the other for hot water. The tea chamber is the larger of the two chambers. The chambers are not marked on the exterior of the teapot as they are on some teapots. The Irvine is similar to the Alma teapot that is also part of the Teamaster line; but the Irvine's handle is square, and the Alma's handle is blended into the body.

The teapot is found in a variety of colors including black, Chinese red, emerald, marine, and turquoise. The bottom mark reads "TWINSPOUT TEAMASTER Patent 2135410 MADE in U.S.A."

"Johnson"

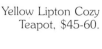

Green "Johnson," $225-250.

Size:

8 cup, 44 ounces brimful, 6" high without cover, 7.5" high with cover, 9" wide, no strainer

Older decorations:

Early Gold and Platinum Decorations, solid colors

The "Johnson" is a ten-sided teapot that has been found in green and cobalt. It was probably produced in the late 1920s or early 1930s. The "Johnson" teapot came in solid colors or with gold stamping. This decoration is similar to the one found on the six-cup Bellevue. Common bottom marks are H-2 or H-3. A decorated "Johnson" is shown in Early Gold and Platinum Decorations later in this book.

Kansas

Ivory and Gold Kansas, $375-425.

Size:

6 cup, 36 ounces brimful, 4.5" high without cover, 5.75" high with cover, 9" wide, strainer, Hall No. 223

Older decorations:

Gold Decorated, Gold "Special," Red Kitchenware, solid colors

The Kansas was advertised in a 1937 *Hall China Revised Special Catalog No. 73* as part of the Gold Decorated line with gold lining and in a variety of colors. The Gold Decorated under-glaze colors were black, blue (cobalt), brown, cadet, canary, delphinium, emerald, green, green lustre, ivory, marine, maroon, orchid, rose, turquoise, and yellow. By 1941 the Indiana was dropped from the Gold Decorated line. Because it was available for a very short time, it is hard to find.

The side of the oval-shaped teapot resembles a heart. The Kansas can be found with H-3, H-3 or HALL with the Gold Decorated or Gold "Special" number, or HSQK.

Lipton Cozy Teapot
("Cozy Cover")

Yellow Lipton Cozy
Teapot, $45-60.

Size:

6 cup, 37 ounces brimful, 5.125" high without cover, 6" high with cover, 7.75" high with aluminum cover, 9.75" wide, strainer, Hall No. 2600

In 1956 the Lipton Cozy Teapot was produced for the Thomas J. Lipton Company. With a Lipton Tea box top and $2.50, one could purchase a cozy teapot. A gold-tone insulated aluminum cover with slots for the handle and spout fits over the teapot. The large handle makes it easy to hold and differs in shape from the Forman Brothers Cozy Hot Pot. The pouring spout was designed to discourage dripping, and the teapot has a built-in strainer to catch the loose tea before pouring into a cup. The bottom mark is H-3, and it has only been found in yellow. See the Lipton section for additional Lipton teapots.

London with and without Metal Tip Spout

Leaf Green London and Pink Orchid Metal Tip Spout London, $35-40 each.

Size:

2 cup, 16 ounces brimful, 3.75" high, 6.5" wide, no strainer, Hall No. 82

Newer decorations:

"Fantasy Dragon," Heather Rose, "Ivy Trellis," solid colors, "Winter Berry"

Size – Metal Tip Spout:

2 cup, 16 ounces brimful, 3.75" high, 6.75" wide, no strainer, Hall No. MTS-2528

The London and London metal tip spout teapots were introduced in the early 1980s. The London is currently available in the *Hall Express Service Catalog* in a variety of colors. The metal tip spout London comes in white and bright white only.

In the late 1980s the London was available in black, cobalt blue, daffodil, lettuce, lune blue, Oxford gray, pink orchid, and maroon. Heather Rose is a decal used by Hall, and the teapot is a later addition to the decal line. "Ivy Trellis" and "Winter Berry" are aftermarket decals. The bottom marks are H-4 or Modern Antique Concepts. "Fantasy Dragon" London was part of a limited dinnerware line and has the H-4 bottom mark.

London Teabob

Brown London Teabob, ND.

Size:

6 cup, 46 ounces brimful, 6.25" high without cover, 7.125" high with cover, 9.75" wide

The London Teabob made for American Teabob Company was introduced in the late twenties or early thirties. It has been found in brown and green. The advertised advantage of the London Teabob was the self-timing feature for brewing the perfect tea. Just fill and start the brewing. The brewing time could be adjusted to suit the tea drinker.

The pieces to the London Teabob are the teapot, a hollow perforated cylinder and airtight float that form a tea basket, and a timing cup. Before brewing tea, the teapot should be warmed with hot water. A level teaspoonful of tea leaves per cup is added to the tea basket, and the basket is joined to the timing cup. Next the warm water is poured out of the pot, and the metal assembly is added to the teapot. Boiling water is then poured into the timing cup. The bottom mark is H-3.

Longaberger®

Red Woven Traditions Longaberger, $125-160.

Size:
6 cup, 45 ounces brimful, 5.25" high without cover, 6.75" high with cover, 10.75" wide, no strainer, Hall No. 4335

The oval Longaberger teapot was available from 1995 to 1998 and was sold as a Hostess Gift at Longaberger basket parties for $59.95.

The teapot has a woven traditions pattern and is decorated with red, blue, green, or holly. Matching creamers and sugars were also made. The bottom mark reads "Microwave * Dishwasher * Oven Safe * Freezer" inside the outer circle with "©LONGABERGER POTTERY, Made in U.S.A." inside a smaller circle. In the center of both circles is a basket weave pattern.

Los Angeles

Chinese Red Los Angeles, $270-310.

Sizes:
4 cup, 28 ounces brimful, 5.125" high without cover, 6.5" high with cover, 8.625" wide, strainer, Hall No. 303
5 or 6 cup, 32 ounces brimful, 5.5" high without cover, 7" high with cover, 9" wide, strainer, Hall No. 304

7 or 8 cup, 40 ounces brimful, 5.875" high without cover, 7.5" high with cover, 9.625" wide, strainer, Hall No. 305

Early decorations:
Early Decals, Early Gold and Platinum Decorations, French Flower, Gold Decorated, Gold Label, Gold "Special," "Mini-Fleurette," Red Kitchenware, Sixties Decoration, solid colors

The Los Angeles appeared in a 1926 Hall catalog available in brown or green in four, five, and seven cup sizes. By 1935 the measurements and bottom marks had changed to four, six, and eight cup. The teapot was available through the 1960s. As advertised in a 1927 trade journal, the proper serving of iced tea requires that the drink should be brewed in a Hall China teapot and the hot tea poured directly into the ice-filled glass. The Los Angeles appeared in a 1928 trade journal that says that for ten years American women have heard through national advertising that good tea requires a Hall China teapot, non-absorbent, non-crazing, and heat retaining.

During the 1930s the Los Angeles was available in solid colors and decorated in gold around the foot and shoulder of the teapot. It was also available in a white with light green-blue overglaze with a floral band on the shoulder with blue trim. In the fifties the Los Angeles was decorated as a Gold Label teapot. The decoration on the teapot was a gold stamping in the Illinois pattern, the same as on the Illinois, "Naomi," Tea-for-Two Set, Tea-for-Four Set, and Twin Tee Set. During the 1960s, a mustard-colored Los Angeles was decorated with a floral band of green leaves. See the Series section later in this book for pictures of the decorations. The bottom marks are H-2; H-3; H-3 or HALL with Gold Decorated, Gold Label, or Gold "Special" number; HSQK; or HALL incised.

Manhattan

Sizes:
3 cup, 16 ounces brimful, 3" high without cover, 4.25" high with cover, 6.5" wide, Hall No. 84
4 cup, 28 ounces brimful, 3.625" high without cover, 5.25" high with cover, 7.625" wide, Hall No. 84.5
5 or 6 cup, 32 ounces brimful, 3.75" high without cover, 5.25" high with cover, 8.75" wide, Hall No. 85
9 or 10 cup, 58 ounces brimful, 4.625" high without cover, 6.5" high with cover, 10" wide, Hall No. 86

Older decorations:
Cactus, "Floral Lattice," Golden Glo, solid colors

In Montgomery Ward's 1931 catalog, the bottom of the French Coffee Biggin was advertised as a teapot and sold for $.83 each. The Manhattan teapot is the bottom and the cover is from the French Coffee Biggin sold as a teapot. The teapot came in Hall's fireproof china brown outside and white inside.

The Manhattan teapot has been found in a variety of colors but has only been found in the Cactus and "Floral Lattice" decals. The solid color teapots have a bottom mark of H-3, and the decorated ones have HSQK.

Cadet Manhattan, $40-50.

When the Manhattan teapot is found, it is hard to tell if it was originally a part of a French Coffee Biggin or was sold as a teapot. In the 1950s and 1960s, the French Coffee Biggin was listed in the Hall catalog, and you could buy the bottom, drip, strainer, and cover separately.

Manhattan Pot (Side-Handled)

Green Manhattan Pot (Side-Handled), $55-65.

Sizes:
1 cup, 7 ounces brimful, 2.5" high without cover, 3.625" high with cover, 4.125" wide to handle, 4" wide to spout, strainer, Hall No. 120
2 cup, 14 ounces brimful, 3" high without cover, 4.75" high with cover, 5.25" wide to handle, 5.875" wide to spout, strainer, Hall No. 121
3 cup, 19 ounces brimful, 3.25" high without cover, 5" high with cover, 5.75" wide to handle, 6" wide to spout, strainer, Hall No. 122
4 cup, 22 ounces brimful, 3.625" high without cover, strainer, Hall No. 123

Older decorations:
Early Gold and Platinum Decorations, solid colors
Newer decoration:
"The Glaze" (1st Anniversary Teapot — 1985)

The Manhattan Pot (Side-Handled) was listed in the Hall China early 1920s catalogs available in four sizes in green or brown. It was listed in the Hall catalogs until the 1970s. Generally the Manhattan Pot (Side-Handled) is found in solid colors, but it has been found with gold decoration. Gold decorations found are bright gold lining or matte gold lining with solid gold handle, spout, and finial on the cover. There are probably more variations of the gold decoration to be found.

In the 1940s the teapot was changed from having a strainer to a free pour. During the 1960s, the two-cup Manhattan Pot (Side-Handled) opening was changed to fit the two-cup French Coffee Biggin drip. The bottom, drip, spreader, and cover of the French Coffee Biggin were sold as separate pieces during the 1950s and 1960s. The bottom marks are H-2, H-3, H-4, or HALL.

McCormick (Bru-O-Lator)

Marine Blue McCormick with Infuser, $90-110.

Sizes:
6 cup, 42 ounces brimful, 5.75" high without infuser and cover, 7.25" high with infuser and cover, 9.125" wide, Hall No. 3023; infuser 3.625" high
6 cup, 36 ounces brimful, 5.5" high without infuser and cover, 6.875" high with infuser and cover, 8.875" wide, Hall No. 5106
Older decorations:
Crocus, Early Gold and Platinum Decorations, French Flower, solid colors
Newer decorations:
Golden Glo, solid colors

In the early 1930s a McCormick teapot with infuser was produced by Hall China in white with green and platinum striping. This McCormick has also been found with an orchid band instead of green. This 44-ounce McCormick teapot was later decorated in solid mahogany or mahogany with a gold medallion.

From 1939 through 1996, a six-cup, 36 ounce, McCormick teapot with infuser was produced. The size of the pot varied in ounces depending upon the age of the mold it was made from. On the spout there is an embossed leaf pointed upward. Colors on the earlier 36-ounce McCormick teapots were turquoise, maroon, brown, light blue, blue turquoise, cascade, and pink. In the 1980s, the 36-ounce teapots were produced in black, canary yellow, cobalt blue, coral peach, Danish white, dark green, gourmet green, marine blue, rose, and Versailles blue.

A collector's 36-ounce teapot and mugs were introduced in 1982. The teapot was white and had a rendition of "Ye Old McCormick Tea House" on the side. The Golden Glo McCormick teapot was introduced in the 1980s with a matching McCormick shape creamer and covered sugar. When production ended in the 1990s, the colors being used were light blue, white, and yellow. The bottom mark on the six-cup infuser teapot is "McCormick & Co., Banquet Teas, Balto" or "McCormick Tea, Baltimore, Md., Made in U.S.A." See the McCormick series later in this book for other teapots made for the McCormick Tea Company.

McCormick Counter Service Teapot

Brown McCormick Counter Service Teapot, $300-350.

Sizes:
1.25 gallon, 10.125" high without cover, 12.75" high with cover, 15.75" wide, Hall No. 5108
2 gallon, Hall No. 5110

In 1940 Hall produced a 1.25-gallon counter service teapot in a shape similar to their six-cup McCormick infuser teapot. The counter service teapot came with a spigot for serving iced or hot tea. A stand for the teapot was not produced. The bottom mark is "Hall, Made in USA." The McCormick Counter Service teapot has also been found with a variety of logos and in black or brown without a logo.

Later, a two-gallon counter service teapot was produced for McCormick. It was advertised in the mid-1980s as a giant teapot. The two-gallon counter service was sold in the McCormick gift shop for $95.00 and available in black with a white logo for McCormick and in maroon without a logo.

McCormick Ribbed Teapot
Size:
3 cup, 18 ounces brimful, 3.875" high without cover, 4.5" high with cover, 7.625" wide, no strainer, Hall No. 5100

Gray McCormick Ribbed Teapot, $25-35.

The McCormick Ribbed Teapot appears in a McCormick Tea Co. advertisement in the early 1950s. The spout of the teapot is drilled and does not have a strainer. The McCormick Ribbed Teapot is similar in shape to the "Everson" Ribbed Teapot and both are found without any bottom stamp. The McCormick Ribbed Teapot has only been found in gray.

McCormick Tea House
Size:
6 cup, 48 ounces brimful, 4.5" high without cover, 5.75" high with cover, 9.875" wide, Hall No. 5107

Golden Olive McCormick Tea House, $70-85.

The McCormick Tea House was commissioned in 1984 and 1985. It was designed to resemble the shape and color of an early English shop. The Tea House will be found undecorated but more often found decorated on both sides as the "Ann Hathaway Cottage." Additional information about the story behind the decal that appears on the Tea House is found in the McCormick series of this book. The bottom mark found is "McCormick Tea, Baltimore, Md., Made in U.S.A."

McCormick – Two Cup
Size:
2 cup, 11 ounces brimful, 3.75" high without cover, 4.75" with cover, 6" wide, Hall No. 5104

Turquoise Two-Cup McCormick, $180-200.

The two-cup McCormick teapot was introduced in the late 1930s. It is usually found in turquoise or green. On the side of the teapot is a large debossed (or raised) "MC." The bottom of the two-cup McCormick is "McCormick, Balto., MD, Made in USA."

Unlike the larger versions of the McCormick, the two-cup does not come with an infuser. It could be used with tea bags. The Bennett Pottery Company made a similar two-cup brown McCormick teapot without the "Mc" emblem on the side.

"Medallion" ("Colonial")

Size:
6 cup, 38 ounces brimful, 5.25" high without cover, 5" high with cover, 8.5" wide, strainer, Hall No. 235

Older decorations:
Red Kitchenware, solid colors

Delphinium Blue "Medallion," $250-300.

The "Medallion" teapot was introduced in the early 1930s. The teapot has vertical lines in a band around the middle of the body with a medallion in the center of the band on both sides of the pot. A similar teapot without the medallion is called the "Colonial."

The six-cup "Medallion" teapot was advertised in the 1935 *Hall China Special Catalog No. 35* as part of the "Lettuce Green Kitchenware" and in the 1937 *Hall China Revised Special Catalog No. 73* as part of the "Delphinium Blue Kitchenware." The "Medallion" teapot can also be found in Chinese red, ivory, and other solid colors. Bottom marks are H-3 and HSQK. Some of the "Medallion" teapots are found without any bottom mark.

Melody

Size:
6 cup, 32 ounces brimful, 5.125" high without cover, 6" high with cover, 9.75" wide, no strainer, Hall No. 1404

Older decorations:
Crocus, Gold Decorated, Gold "Special," "Orange Poppy," Red Kitchenware, solid colors

Chinese Red Melody, $300-350.

In 1939, J. Palin Thorley designed the Saf-Spout teapot and was awarded Design Patent 117855. Later that same year the larger version of the Saf-Spout was released and was given the name Melody by Hall China. In the fall of 1939 the Melody was advertised with an unusually varied selection of Hall's famous teapots. The Oval Aladdin

and the Bird Cage were also advertised. They sold for $1.25 each and came in Chinese red, delph blue, green, turquoise, and yellow. In another advertisement the Melody was described as an "upside-down top hat."

The Melody was added to the Gold Decorated teapot line in 1939. On the Gold Decorated Melody teapot, gold lines run around the rings on the outside of the teapot and on the inside white collar as well as on the handle and cover. The Melody has been found in only two decals. The bottom marks on the Melody are H-3, H-3 or HALL with the Gold Decorated or Gold "Special" number, and HSQK.

Moderne

Size:
6 cup, 35 ounces brimful, 4.875" high without cover, 6.5" high with cover, 10" wide, no strainer, Hall No. 125

Older decorations:
Gold Decorated, Red Kitchenware, solid colors

Lune Blue Moderne, $65-80.

The Moderne teapot appears in a 1935 *Hall China Special Catalog No. 35* in solid colors or Gold Decorated. The gold decoration is on the knob of the cover, the foot, and the throat of the spout. In the 1941 *Hall China Special Catalog No. 14*, the Moderne was advertised in the stock color of canary.

Moderne teapots have been seen in orchid with matte gold trim and art glaze orange with matte gold trim. It is unusual to find art glaze colors used with gold. The bottom marks found are H-3, H-3 or HALL with Gold Decorated number, and HSQK. Some of the Moderne teapots will be unmarked.

"Murphy" ("Peel")

Pastel Blue "Murphy," $55-65.

Size:
6 cup, 32 ounces brimful, 4.125" high without cover, 5.25" high with cover, 9.25" wide, strainer

The "Murphy" teapot is one of the "Victorian" Series teapots produced in the 1940s and 1950s. It is usually found in solid pastel blue, but it has also been found in "steel" gray. The "Murphy" is one of the more elusive in the series to find decorated in gold. The bottom mark is H-3, but the "Murphy" will be found frequently without any marking on the bottom.

Musical

Orchid Musical, $300-350.

Size:
6 cup, 32 ounces brimful, 6.125" high without cover, 7.375" high with cover, 8.25" wide, Hall No. 1341
Older decoration:
Solid colors
Newer decorations:
Autumn Leaf, Blue Blossom, Blue Bouquet, Cameo Rose, Christmas Tree, Crocus, Game Bird, "Orange Poppy," Poinsettia and Holly, Red Poppy, Silhouette

The Musical teapot was produced in the late 1940s in solid colors. In September 1950 it was recast with a stuck-on spout. The *Montgomery Ward* catalogs from 1951 through 1954 advertised the musical teapot. (Whitmyer, 2001, page 257)

The music box fits into a recessed cavity of the teapot and is held in place with a metal over-center spring. It was intended that the music box be removed before washing the teapot to prevent damage to the music box mechanism. Unfortunately this commonly was not done, and the music boxes are rusted and broken. The music boxes played "Tea for Two" and were provided by Thoren's Inc., New Hyde Park, New York. Many of the Musical teapots will be found with a missing bottom spring and music box. A bottom mark of H-3 is sometimes found on the china body underneath the music box.

Since 1997 China Specialties has sold the Musical teapot in a variety of decals. The bottom mark is China Specialties. The older teapots have strainers, but the newer ones do not.

Musical – Rose Petal

Yellow Rose Petal Musical, $45-60.
Size:
8 cup, 40 ounces brimful, 5.5" high without cover, 6.5" high with cover, 9.75" wide, Hall No. 1342

In 1955 Hall China produced a Rose Petal Musical teapot that looks very similar to an English produced teapot. The primary difference is the ridge around the cover opening on the Hall teapot is flat and the English teapot cover opening is wavy. The English style teapot seems to be well marked around the inside bottom rim. Hall musical teapots are not marked or are marked beneath the music box. The Rose Petal Musical is usually found in light blue or yellow.

"Naomi"

Green Decorated "Naomi," $550-625.
Size:
6 cup, 32 ounces brimful, 5.375" high without cover, 6.625" high with cover, 8" wide

Older decorations:
Early Gold and Platinum Decorations, solid colors

The "Naomi" is a six-paneled teapot that is usually found in green but may be found in cobalt or brown. The gold stamping decoration on each panel is called "Illinois." This is the same gold stamping found on the Illinois teapot, Tea for Two Set, Tea for Four Set, Twin-Tee Set, and Los Angeles Gold Label teapot. There is gold lining on the edges of the panels, around the neck, top ridge, and cover. The "Naomi" was probably produced in the late 1920s or early 1930s and is found with the H-2, H-3, or HALL incised bottom marks.

National with and without Metal Tip Spout

Black Metal Tip Spout National and Cascade Super-Ceram National, $35-45 each.

Sizes – with Metal Tip Spout:
1.5 cup, 13 ounces brimful, 3.25" high without cover, 4.25" high with cover, 6.625" wide, Hall No. MTS-1701
2 cup, 15 ounces brimful, 3.5" high without cover, 4.25" high with cover, 6.75" wide, Hall No. MTS-1702
Sizes – without Metal Tip Spout:
1.5 cup, 13 ounces brimful, 3.25" high without cover, 4.25" high with cover, 6.625" wide, Hall No. 1701
2 cup, 15 ounces brimful, 3.5" high without cover, 4.25" high with cover, 6.75" wide, Hall No. 1702
Special treatment – without Metal Tip Spout:
Super-Ceram (1.5 cup) – Hall No. 01701

The National teapots, with and without a metal tip spout, were listed in the Hall catalogs from 1964 through 1973. They were available in green or brown but could be ordered in a variety of colors. These teapots are part of the National Service line that consists of matching coffee pots, handled creamers, open sugar, and table and service items. These pieces have the H-3 or H-4 bottom mark.

During the 1970s, the National teapots were added to the Super-Ceram line. Super-Ceram is a special Hall body that is stronger and denser than the regular body. Super-Ceram items had their own colors and bottom mark.

In the early 1970s, Amtrak chose the stock National items to be used in their dining cars. A special blue color was made for Amtrak and is referred to as Amtrak Blue. The pieces used for Amtrak are either not marked or marked H-4.

Nautilus

Chinese Red Nautilus, $475-550.

Size:
6 cup, 40 ounces brimful, 5.75" high without cover, 6.75" high with cover, 9" wide, Hall No. 1408
Older decorations:
Gold Decorated, Gold "Special," Red Kitchenware, solid colors
Newer decoration:
Autumn Leaf

The Nautilus is one of two seashell style teapots made by Hall, the other being the Surf Side. The Nautilus is reminiscent of a stylized conch seashell and was introduced in 1939 as part of the Gold Decorated line.

The Nautilus can be found in solid colors, Gold Decorated with gold lining, and Gold "Special" with gold lining and gold on the handle, spout, and knob on the cover. The bottom marks found are H-3, H-3 or HALL with the Gold Decorated or Gold "Special" number, and HSQK.

The National Autumn Leaf Collectors Club used the Nautilus in 1998 as a club piece. The teapot was also used for the East Liverpool Alumni Association auction in 1999 and was decorated in ivory with gold trim. The bottom marks found on these two pots are NALCC or ELHS Alumni. Older Nautilus teapots have strainers but newer ones do not.

New York

Chinese Red New York, $175-200.

Sizes:

Miniature 1/5 Scale Salesman Sample

1 cup, 7 ounces brimful, 2.875" high without cover, Hall No. 29

1.5 cup, 11 ounces brimful, 3" high without cover, 4" high with cover, 5.625" wide, Hall No. 30

2 cup, 14 ounces brimful, 3.5" high without cover, 4.125" high with cover, 6.5" wide, Hall No. 31

3 cup, 20 ounces brimful, 3.75" high without cover, 4.25" high with cover, 7.375" wide, Hall No. 32

4 cup, 28 ounces brimful, 4" high without cover, 4.75" high with cover, 7.875" wide, Hall No. 33

5 or 6 cups, 34 ounces brimful, 4.25" high without cover, 5" high with cover, 9" wide, Hall No. 34

7 or 8 cups, 42 ounces brimful, 4.875" high without cover, 5.375" high with cover, 9.25" wide, Hall No. 35

10 cup, 56 ounces brimful, 5" high without cover, 5.875" high with cover, 10" wide, Hall No. 35.5

12 cup, 64 ounces brimful, 5.5" high without cover, 6.25" high with cover, 11" wide, Hall No. 36

Older decorations:

#488, Blue Blossom (6, 10, and 12 cup), Blue Garden (6, 10, and 12 cups), Blue Willow (8 cup), Crocus (2, 4, 6, 8, and 12 cup), Early Gold and Platinum Decorations, Eggshell Lines, "Floral Lattice" (2, 6, and 12 cups), French Flower, Game Bird (2 and 6 cup), Gold Band, Gold Decorated, Gold Dot (2 and 6 cup), Gold Label, Gold "Special," Golden Glo, Golden Oak, Heather Rose, Homewood, Mother of Pearl, "Mums," "Pastel Morning Glory," Red Kitchenware (2 and 6 cup), Red Poppy, RX, Serenade, Silhouette, solid colors, "Wild Poppy" (2, 4, 6, 8, 10, and 12 cups), "Yellow Rose" (4 and 6 cup)

Newer decorations:

Autumn Leaf (4 cup), solid colors

Special treatments:

Metal Clad (1.5, 2, and 3 cup) and Super-Ceram (1.5, 2, 3, 4, 6, and 8 cup)

The New York is one of the earlier teapots made by Hall China and was produced in the largest number of sizes. It was part of their institutional line during the teens and available in green or brown. In 1916 the New York teapot was provided to the McCormick Tea Co.

Along with the Boston and French Light Weight teapots, the New York was chosen to be part of a Gold Decorated line that was introduced at the 1920 Pittsburgh Pottery Show. Buyers at the show were surprised to learn that the teapots were not from England but were made in the United States. This was the beginning of a successful venture into decorated teapots for which Hall became famous. These three teapots were available in several sizes and in royal blue (cobalt), rich green, or brown with gold decorations.

The New York was decorated around the shoulder with a gold stamped pansy border later to be known as Trillium. It was also decorated with a thick gold band and a thinner gold band above and below the thick band. The New York with the bands was advertised as conservative and rich.

Later the Trillium decorated New York would become known as a Gold "Special" with solid gold handle, spout, and knob on cover. There are matching creamers and covered sugars with the gold Trillium design. The New York was part of the Gold Label line and advertised in canary in all sizes and could be ordered in other colors.

Hall introduced the New York in 1985 as part of their Hall American line. The pots could be found in standard colors of black, blue, gray, red, tan, and white. Retailers were able to chose from over 100 additional colors when they ordered items in the Hall American line. Naomi's Antiques of San Francisco ordered the six- and eight-cup New York teapots in cobalt, lavender, and orange. Hall marked all these teapots with the H-4 bottom mark.

The National Autumn Leaf Collectors Club offered its members the New York as a club piece in 1984. There were 536 teapots made, and the bottom mark is NALCC.

The New York teapot was available in nine-sizes and listed in the Hall catalogs until 1989. The two- and three-cup sizes were listed in the catalog through 1996. The New York teapot is found in a wide range of colors and decals. The bottom marks found are H-2; H-3; H-3 or HALL with Gold Decorated, Gold Label, or Gold "Special" number; HSQK; HALL incised; NALCC; and Super-Ceram. New York teapots have strainers except for the six- and eight-cup Super-Ceram.

Newport

Green Newport, $35-50.

Sizes:

5 cup, 34 ounces brimful, 5.75" high without cover, 6.875" high with cover, 9.125" wide

7 cup, 40 ounces brimful, 6" high without cover, 7.25" high with cover, 9.75" wide, Hall No. 1206

Older decorations:

Autumn Leaf (7 cup), Early Decals, Early Gold and Platinum Decorations, Red Kitchenware, solid colors

In 1928 the seven-cup Newport was introduced in rose and cadet blue. In the late 1920s the Jewel Tea Company sold the Newport in green. Because of the popularity of the shape of the Newport teapot, the Autumn Leaf decal was added in 1933 and sold by Jewel. Two years later the Newport was replaced by Jewel with the "Rayed" long-spout coffee - teapot combination. The bottom mark is HSQK.

In 1978 the Newport was reissued in the Autumn Leaf pattern. The 1978 Autumn Leaf decal is slightly different in shape, and the spout of the teapot is trimmed in gold. Some collectors feel that the placement of the vent hole on the cover is critical in telling the age of the Newport. Hall said that the vent hole was placed where the worker in that department happened to put it. The bottom mark on the 1978 Autumn Leaf Newport teapot is HK-Mary Dunbar.

The Newport was used as part of the Gold Decorated line and came in two sizes. It is decorated with a gold bubble band around the shoulder and gold lining on the handle, spout, and cover. The Gold Decorated Newport is numbered as part of the Gold Decorated identification numbering system, but it had been dropped from the line by 1935 when the first list was published.

The Newport is found in solid colors, gold decorated, platinum decorated, and with floral decals. During the 1930s, Hall added to a pink Newport a decal that was of multi-colored flowers in a black pot with the teapot handle, spout, and cover trimmed in black. The bottom marks are H-2, H-3, H-3 or HALL with Gold Decorated number, and HALL incised.

No Drip ("Globe No-Drip")

Gray No Drip, $85-100.

Size:
6 cup, 38 ounces brimful, 5" high without cover, 6" high with cover, 9" wide, Hall No. 1424
Older decorations:
Gold Decorated, solid colors

The No Drip teapot was introduced in the early 1950s and is similar in shape to the Globe teapot. The difference between the two pots is the inverted spout on the No Drip teapot. This teapot has also been called the "Globe No Drip" or "No Drip Inverted Spout." The name given to this teapot by Hall was No Drip.

The teapot is found in solid colors and gold decorated. The decoration is a gold band of flowers around the shoulder rim of the teapot with three semi-circles of flowers below. The No Drip was advertised in cadet, camellia, chartreuse, cobalt, gray, and warm yellow. The bottom marks are H-3, H-3 or HALL with Gold Decorated number, and HALL incised.

No Drip

Golden Glo Sunken Cover No Drip, $50-65; Red Knob Cover No Drip, $35-45.

Sizes:
2 cup, 14 ounces brimful, 3.375" high without cover, 4.625" high with cover, 6.625" wide, Hall No. 2322

3 cup, 16 ounces brimful, 3.5" high without cover, 4.625" high with cover, 6.875" wide, Hall No. 2323
4 cup, 25 ounces brimful, 4" high without cover, 5.25" high with cover, 7.75" wide, Hall No. 2324

White No Drip, $35-40.

The No Drip teapot was introduced in 1973 in three sizes and is currently advertised in the Hall catalog. These teapots should not be confused with the six-cup No Drip, but Hall's official name for both teapots is No Drip. The "no drip" feature of this pot is a small vertical hole in the spout to break the flow of liquid when the pot is tipped back. The teapot is found in a variety of colors and decorations including Golden Glo and with the Club 21 decoration. The bottom mark is H-4.

Ohio

Maroon Ohio, $240-280.

Size:
6 cup, 40 ounces brimful, 4.875" high without cover, 5.75" high with cover, 8.375" wide, strainer, Hall No. 218
Older decorations:
Gold Decorated, Gold Dot, Red Kitchenware, solid colors

The Ohio teapot was introduced in 1930 and discontinued in early 1939. The short production run may be part of the reason this shape teapot is harder to find. The Ohio appears in a 1935 *Hall China Special Catalog No. 35* and the 1937 *Hall China Revised Special Catalog No. 73* in solid colors and gold decorated. The Gold Decorated under-glazed colors were black, blue (cobalt), brown, cadet, canary, delphinium, emerald, green, green lustre, ivory, marine, maroon, orchid, rose, turquoise, and yellow. The decoration is a wide gold band around the shoulder and a gold lacey emblem with streamers below. Another decoration found on the Ohio is Gold Dots around the shoulder of the teapot. The bottom marks are H-3, H-3 or HALL with the Gold Decorated number, and HALL.

Parade

"No Blue" Parade, $300-350.

Size:
6 cup, 40 ounces brimful, 4.875" high without cover, 5.75" high with cover, 9.25" wide, no strainer, Hall No. 1432

Older decorations:
French Flower, Gold Decorated, Gold Label, Gold "Special," Golden Glo, "Mini-Fleurette," "No Blue," Red Kitchenware, Silver Glo, solid colors

The Parade was introduced in the early 1940s and described as having a hook cover that cannot fall off, a sure-grip handle that prevents the hand from slipping, and being perfectly balanced for easy pouring.

During the 1950s and 1960s, the Parade was advertised in canary as a Gold Decorated and Gold Label teapot. As part of the Gold Decorated line, the Parade is decorated with acorns and leaves along the shoulder of the teapot with gold lining. In the Gold Label series, the Parade is decorated with the "Squiggle" decal that is also used on the Aladdin Gold Label teapot. The bottom marks read H-3; H-3 or HALL with Gold Decorated, Gold Label, Gold "Special" number; or HSQK.

Pear

White Pear, ND.

Size:
8 cup, 42 ounces brimful, 5.75" high without cover, 9" high with cover, Hall No. 2516

The Pear teapot was introduced in November 1970 and made for the Carbone Company in white. Even though this teapot was also sold by the Hall Closet at the Hall China factory, it has been hard to find.

Philadelphia

Green Philadelphia, $30-35.

Sizes:
Miniature 1/5 size Salesman Sample
1.5 cup, 10 ounces brimful, 3.5" high without cover, 4.375" high with cover, 5.5" wide, strainer, Hall No. 200
3 cup, 16 ounces brimful, 4.375" high without cover, Hall No. 202
4 cup, 28 ounces brimful, 5" high without cover, 6" high with cover, 7.5" wide, strainer, Hall No. 203
5 or 6 cup, 36 ounces brimful, 5.5" high without cover, 6.625" high with cover, 7.875" wide, strainer, Hall No. 204
7 or 8 cup, 48 ounces brimful, 5.875" high without cover, 7" high with cover, 9.125" wide, strainer, Hall No. 205
10 cup, 52 ounces brimful, 6.125" high without cover, 7.375" high with cover, 8.5" wide, strainer, Hall No. 206

Older decorations:
Blue Willow (5 cup), Early Decals, Early Gold and Platinum Decorations, Gold Band, Gold Decoration, Gold Label, Gold "Special," "Leaf and Vine," Mother of Pearl, Red Kitchenware (3 and 6 cup), Silver Glo, Sixties Decoration, solid colors

Newer decorations:
"Antique Rose" (3, 6, and 8 cup), "Autumn Harvest," Autumn Leaf (4 cup), "Ivy Trellis," "Summer Song"

The Philadelphia is one of the earlier teapots and was available in six sizes from 1.5 cups to 10 cups. As early as 1924 the Philadelphia teapot was shown with a Gold Loop decoration followed by the Gold Bubble decoration in 1928. The 1927 *Sears, Roebuck and Co.* catalog shows a five-cup Philadelphia and matching creamer and sugar in cobalt blue with circles of bright gold and gold traced handles. The teapot sold for $1.98 or the complete set for $3.75.

In the 1930s the Philadelphia appeared with the "Floral Basket" and "Mayflower" decals. In the 1950s the Gold Label series was introduced with the Philadelphia decorated in a gold basket decal with gold lines. In the 1960s Hall introduced a series of teapots with unusual decals. The Philadelphia came in two sizes in blue with a black hearth scene and black trimming. The Philadelphia teapot continued in production until the early 1990s. It will be found with H-2; H-3; H-3 or HALL with Gold Decorated, Gold Label, or Gold "Special" number; H-4; and HSQK.

An Autumn Leaf Philadelphia teapot, creamer, and sugar were offered to the National Autumn Leaf Collectors Club in 1990, and 1,150 sets were made. Thornberry used the "Summer Song" decoration on the Philadelphia teapot in the 1970s, and Modern Antique Concept used the "Antique Rose," "Autumn Harvest," "Ivy Trellis," and "Summer Song" decals in the 1990s. The bottom marks on these teapots are NALCC, Modern Antique Concepts, or Thornberry.

"Philbe"

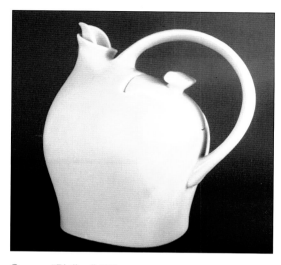

Canary "Philbe," ND.

Size:
5 cup, 30 ounces brimful, 7.625" high to spout tip, 7" wide
Older decorations:
French Flower, solid colors

The "Philbe" is an unusual teapot with a handle over the cover similar to the Airflow. The spout has a catch (collar) that is much like the design of the spout on the Surf Side teapot.

The "Philbe" has the H-3 bottom mark and was also produced without any bottom mark. The "Philbe" has been found in solid colors of cadet, canary, and cobalt; it has also been adorned with the French Flower decoration and a gold spout, handle, and knob on cover.

"Pineapple"

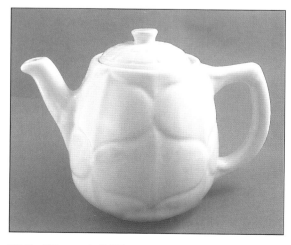

White "Pineapple," ND.

Size:
6 cup, 38 ounces brimful, 5.25" high without cover, 6.25" high with cover, 8.375" wide, strainer, Hall No. 1604

The "Pineapple" with a locking cover was made in the late 1960s exclusively for Dohrmann Hotel Supply Company of California for the Trader Vic restaurant. It was available in white and has the H-3 bottom mark.

Pittsburg

Cadet and White Pittsburg, $35-45.

Size:
2 cup, 14 ounces brimful, 3.25" high without cover, 4.25" high with cover, 7.25" wide, Hall No. 241

The Pittsburg appears in one of the earlier catalogs before Hall China Co. assigned numbers to their products. It was available in green or brown, with and without a strainer. The strainer version was for use when serving tea. The Pittsburg was described in 1927 as being a no-drip, lock-cover teapot with an easy pouring spout designed to prevent dripping, thus keeping the table linen clean, and a cover which is held in place by two nibs, to prevent falling while pouring.

The Pittsburg was available until the mid-1970s in a variety of colors. It was generally sold with a sunken cover, but a knob cover could be specially ordered. It will be found with the H-3, H-4, and HALL incised bottom marks. The Pittsburg have been found with contrasting color covers.

"Plume" ("Disraeli")

Pink "Plume," $55-65.

Size:
6 cup, 36 ounces brimful, 3.75" high without cover, 5.5" high with cover, 9.75" wide, no strainer

The "Plume" is part of the "Victorian" Series. In 1947 it appeared along with the "Birch" in an advertisement for the Jewel Tea Company, selling for $1.75 each.

The teapot will be found in pink with a variety of gold decorations including an all-over gold. See the "Victorian" Series later in this book for examples of gold decorated "Plume" teapots. The bottom mark is H-3, but the teapot is frequently found without any bottom mark.

Plymouth

Size:
2 cup, 12 ounce

Green Plymouth, ND. Reprint from 1927 Hall China Catalog.

The Plymouth is an unusual teapot that was advertised in Hall's 1926 and 1927 catalogs in brown or green. It has not been seen other than in the catalogs.

Portland

Maroon Portland, $35-45.

Sizes:
1.5 cup, 10 ounces brimful, 4.25" high without cover, 5" high with cover, 5" wide, strainer, Hall No. 80
3 cup, 18 ounces, 4.875" high without cover, 6" high with cover, 5.75" wide, strainer, Hall No. 81

The Portland teapot was introduced in the 1920s and could be found in green or brown. It continued being offered in several solid colors, including Pewter, until the late 1980s. This teapot was used for an individual service of tea, coffee, or chocolate. The bottom marks will be either H-3 or H-4. Decorations on the Portland are solid colors with gold lining.

"Radiance" ("Sunshine")

Delphinium "Radiance," $330-380.

Size:
6 cup, 38 ounces brimful, 5.125" high without cover, 7" high with cover, 8.25" wide, strainer, Hall No. 295

Older decorations:
#488, Acacia, "Apple Blossom," "Black Beauty," Cactus, Carrot, Golden Carrot, Golden Clover, "Ivory Beauty," "Parrot Tulip," "Pastel Morning Glory," "Piggly Wiggly," Red Kitchenware, "Shaggy Floral," solid colors, "Stonewall," "Wild Poppy"

The "Radiance" teapot was advertised in a 1935 *Hall China Special Catalog No. 35* in the #488 decal as part of a kitchenware line. In the 1930s and 1940s, it appeared in a large variety of decals and in Chinese red, delphinium blue, and ivory solid colors. It has not been found in a solid color with gold decoration. The bottom mark is HSQK.

The name "Radiance" not only applies to the shape of the teapot, but also to a coffee pot, bowls set, shakers, canister set, and other kitchenware pieces.

"Rayed" ("J-Sunshine")

Autumn Leaf "Rayed," $80-95.

Size:
7 cup, 52 ounces brimful, 6.875" high without cover, 8.25" high with cover, 8.25" wide, strainer, Hall No. 3056

Older decorations:
Autumn Leaf, Crocus

The "Rayed" teapot was introduced in 1935 by the Jewel Tea Company to replace their Autumn Leaf Newport teapot. The "Rayed" teapot is also referred to as the "Long Spout" teapot. It can serve as a seven-cup teapot or four-cup coffee pot. The metal or glass drippers that were added to the teapot when making coffee rather than tea are extremely hard to find. There is a matching creamer and sugar with cover. The teapot does not appear in the Jewel Tea catalogs after 1942.

The "Rayed" teapot was reissued in 1978 by Jewel as a sales award, and only 106 were made. The bottom mark on both teapots is HK-Mary Dunbar. Pictures of the "Rayed" teapot/coffee pot with metal and glass drips are shown in the Coffee Shape section.

A "Rayed" teapot decorated in Crocus has been found and does not have a bottom mark.

Reagan

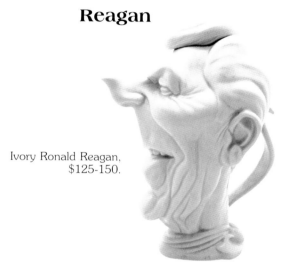

Ivory Ronald Reagan, $125-150.

Size:
6 cup, 44 ounces brimful, 9" high without cover, 9.875" high with cover, 7.25" wide, no strainer, Hall No. 3099

Hall was commissioned to make the Ronald Reagan caricature teapot in 1982. Hall made partial delivery of the teapots, but final delivery of the remaining teapots could not be made because Hall was unable to locate the customer. Subsequently, the remaining Reagan teapots were sold through the Hall Closet. The bottom mark is H-4. This teapot is almost sculpture-like and highly detailed. It might damage easily.

"Regal" ("Dickens")

Left:
Maroon "Regal,"
$125-150.

Size:
6 cup, 34 ounces brimful, 5.875" high without cover, 6.75" high with cover, 9.25" wide, Hall No. 1530

J. Palin Thorley designed the "Regal" in the late 1950s, and the teapot is one of the Brilliant Series. The teapots are found in solid colors and Gold Decorated. In 1959 the "Regal" was available in black, bright blue, maroon, or white with 22-carat bright gold decoration and brilliants. In 1961 the teapot was advertised in apple green.

The bottom marks found are H-3 on the solid colors and H-3 with the Gold Decorated number on those with the gold stipple. Many of the bottom marks will include the Hall identification number.

Rhythm

Lavender Rhythm, $125-150.

Size:
6 cup, 36 ounces brimful, 6.375" high, 8.375" wide, Hall No. 1400

Older decorations:
Gold Decorated, Golden Glo, Red Kitchenware, solid colors

The Rhythm was introduced in 1939 as part of the Gold Decorated line. It was available in a variety of colors, but the advertised color for the Rhythm was yellow. The gold decoration on the Rhythm is a series of gold dots on the upper two drapes of both sides of the teapot. It has the H-3, H-3 or HALL with the Gold Decorated number, or HSQK bottom mark. Earlier Rhythm teapots came with strainers, and the later ones did not.

In 1985 the Rhythm was introduced in the Hall American line. The teapots were available in stock colors of black, blue, gray, red, tan, and white. Retailers could chose their own colors from a palette of over 100 colors. Naomi's Antiques of San Francisco had the Rhythm made in cobalt, orange, and lavender. The later teapots are marked with the H-4 bottom mark.

"Ribbed Band" Hot Water Server and Teapot

White "Ribbed Band" Hot Water Server, $60-80;
Matte Golden Glo "Ribbed Band" Teapot, $125-150.

Size – Hot Water Server:
8 cup, 50 ounces brimful, 8.375" high without cover, 9.5" high with cover, 8.125" wide, no strainer, Hall No. 4522

Newer decorations – Hot Water Server:
"Fruit," Matte Golden Glo, solid colors

Special treatment – Hot Water Server:
Super-Ceram

Size – Teapot:
8 cup, 50 ounces brimful, 5.125" high without cover, 6.25" high with cover, 9.875" wide, no strainer

Newer decorations – Teapot:
"Fruit," Matte Golden Glo, solid colors

There are three pots that are very similar in the "Ribbed Band" design – a water server, teapot, and electric percolator. The bright white hot water server shown is made of Super-Ceram and is marked on the bottom with Super-Ceram. The "Ribbed Band" Hot Water Server has also been found in Golden Glo with the Forman Family bottom mark.

The "Fruit" decal appears on the Forman Adjusto teapot and on the "Ribbed Band" Hot Water Server. The "Ribbed Band" Hot Water Server with the "Fruit" decal was available in 1985 in the Hall Closet. The "Ribbed Band" teapot has only been found in Golden Glo and marked Forman Family on the bottom. It may turn up in other colors. Other Kitchenware pieces in the "Ribbed Band" line have been found.

"Ribbed Globe" ("Fluted Globe")

Size:
6 cup, 32 ounces brimful, 4.5" high without cover, 5.5" high with cover, 8.75" wide, strainer, Hall No. 994

Older decorations:
Russet, Red Kitchenware, solid colors

Chinese Red "Ribbed Globe," $275-325.

The "Ribbed Globe" was introduced in 1935 and advertised as Russet Ware in the *Hall China Special Catalog No. 35*. "This line was named after the color, which was achieved by glazing a piece in Light Russet and then spraying with Dark Russet and refiring." (Duke, *Superior Quality*, page 38). There was probably a short production run in Russet because two years later the teapot and all of the Russet Ware line were available in Chinese red. The "Ribbed Globe" has been found in a deep-violet blue that is probably DuPont blue.

The entire production span of the "Ribbed Globe" was short and ended in early 1939. The bottom mark found is HSQK. The "Ribbed Globe" has noticeable differences to the plain or smooth Globe besides the ribbing. The spout, handle, and cover are also different.

"Ribbed Rutherford" ("Fluted Alton")

Chinese Red "Ribbed Rutherford," $275-325.

Size:
6 cup, 36 ounces brimful, 5.25" high without cover, 6.25" high with cover, 8.625" wide, strainer, Hall No. 995

Older decorations:
Russet, Red Kitchenware, solid colors

The "Ribbed Rutherford" was introduced in 1935 and advertised as Russet Ware in a *Hall China Special Catalog No. 35* and was part of the same line as the "Ribbed Globe." By 1937 the "Ribbed Rutherford" was only available in Chinese red. Production of this teapot style ended in 1939.

The bottom mark found is HSQK. One difference between the "Ribbed Rutherford" and the "Rutherford," besides the ribbing, is the shape of the knob on the cover.

"Royal" ("Eliot")

Ivory with Gold "Royal," $160-190.

Size:
6 cup, 38 ounces brimful, 4.625" high without cover, 6.625" high with cover, 10.375" wide, Hall No. 1532

The "Royal" is part of the Brilliant Series and is found in a variety of colors and with brilliants and 22-carat bright gold decoration. In 1961 the "Royal" teapot was advertised in ivory. The Brilliant Series was introduced in the late 1950s and appeared in catalogs until the end of the 1960s.

The solid colored teapots will have the H-3 bottom mark, and the Gold Decorated ones will have H-3 or HALL with the Gold Decorated number. Many of the bottom marks will include the Hall identification number.

"Rutherford" ("Alton")
Size:
6 cup, 36 ounces brimful, 5.125" high without cover, 6.375" high with cover, 8.5" wide, Hall No. 1295

Russet "Rutherford," $225-275.

Older decorations:
#488, Acacia, "Black Beauty," Cactus, Color Bands, Eggshell Lines, Eggshell Plaid, Eggshell Polka Dot, Eggshell Swag, "Green Poppy," "Mums," "Pastel Morning Glory," Red Kitchenware, Russet, solid colors

The "Rutherford" is very similar in shape to the "Ribbed Rutherford," except for the ribbing and the shape of the knob on the cover. The "Rutherford" was introduced about 1934 and was advertised in a 1935 Hall's special catalog as part of the Buffet Service Set.

The "Rutherford" is found in a large number of decals. Chinese red and Russet are the most common solid colors found. The bottom mark is HSQK.

"Saben"

Black and Silver "Saben," ND.

Size:
6 cup, 36 ounces brimful, 5" high without cover, 6" high with cover, 8.375" wide, Hall No. 1324

The "Saben" teapot, with a matching creamer and sugar, was made in 1953. Saben Silver Company had The Hall China Company make a teapot to be fitted with a silver cover and base to hold the teapot. The teapot is a Boston shape with round handles and spout from one of the "Victorian" Series teapots. The matching creamer and sugar also are fitted with a silver rim for the base.

The "Saben" teapot, creamer, and sugar have the H-3 bottom mark. Hall records indicate that there were additional coffee pots made for Saben, but these pots are yet to be identified.

Saf-Handle ("Sundial")

Lettuce Green Saf-Handle, $95-110.

Sizes:
1.5 cup, 9 ounces brimful, 3" high without cover, 3.5" high with cover, 4.25" wide, no strainer, Hall No. 2090
2 cup, 10 ounces brimful, 3.375" high without cover, no strainer, Hall No. 2091
Older decorations – 1.5 and 2 cup:
Chinese red, solid colors

J. Palin Thorley designed the Saf-Handle teapots and was issued Design Patent 117859 on November 28, 1939. Two sizes of the Saf-Handle teapot shown in the picture were advertised in the Hall China catalogs from 1940 through the mid-1970s. They came in brown and green or could be ordered in a variety of colors. These Saf-Handle teapots are shorter and rounder than the Saf-Handle coffee. The bottom mark is H-3.

Size:
6 cup, 40 ounces brimful, 6.125" high without cover, 7" high with cover, 7.5" wide, strainer, Hall No. 1422
Older decorations – 6 cup:
Blue Blossom, Blue Garden, Fantasy, Gold Decorated, Gold "Special," Red Kitchenware, solid colors

In 1941 the six-cup Saf-Handle was made from the same patent as the smaller version teapots. The Saf-Handle came in solid colors, with gold decoration, and with decals. The standard gold decoration is stylized flowers complimented with gold lining on the spout, handle, pot and cover rims, and knob.

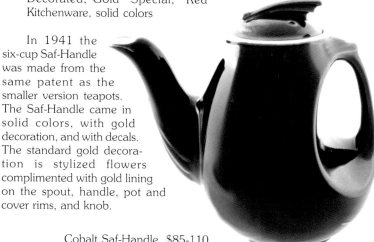

Cobalt Saf-Handle, $85-110.

The six-cup Saf-Handle has a locking tab cover. The bottom marks are H-3, H-3 or HALL with the Gold Decorated or Gold "Special" number, and HSQK.

Saf-Handle is not only the name of the teapot and coffee pot shapes, but numerous other pieces make up the Saf-Handle kitchenware line. Some of the pieces are a batter bowl, casseroles, coffee server, cookie jar, creamer, sugar, syrup, and six-cup teapot.

Saf-Spout (Oval and Round Body)

Sandust Oval and Round Saf-Spouts, $95-110 each.

Size – Oval body:
1 cup, 8 ounces serving size, 11 ounces brimful, 3.25" high without cover, 4" high with cover, 6.5" wide, no strainer, Hall No. 2120

Sizes – Round body:
1 cup, 8 ounces serving size, 11 ounces brimful, 3.25" high without cover, 4" high with cover, 6" wide, no strainer, Hall No. 2110
1.5 cup, 10 ounces serving size, Hall No. 2111
2 cup, 16 ounces serving size, Hall No. 2112

Newer decorations – Round body:
Autumn Leaf, Blue Blossom, Crocus, Game Bird, "The Glaze" (2nd Anniversary Teapot), "Orange Poppy," Red Poppy, Silhouette

The U.S. Design Patent 117855 was awarded to J. Palin Thorley on November 28, 1939, for the design of the Saf-Spout teapots. Design Patents were also issued on that date to Mr. Thorley for the Saf-Spout coffee, covered casserole, and shirred egg dish. One of the distinctive features of the design is the safeguard of the spouts of the teapots and coffee pots that gives all of the items a decidedly different style.

Other Saf-Spout items illustrated in the 1956 Hall catalog are four sizes of creamers and a covered sugar bowl. The pieces were available in green or brown but could be ordered in a variety of colors. The one-cup Saf-Spout was listed through the mid-1970s in the Hall catalog. The two larger sizes were listed in the Hall identification book but were not listed in the catalogs. The bottom mark is H-3 or a circle with Saf-Spout and HALL across the center. The shape of the Saf-Spouts is very similar to the Melody, but the knobs

on the covers are different. The handles on the Melody and the round Saf-Spout are the same; whereas the oval Saf-Spout's handle is different.

The Saf-Spout one-cup teapot was reintroduced by China Specialties in 1995. Prior to this time the Saf-Spout was not produced with a decal. China Specialties refers to this shape as "Baby Melody." The bottom mark on these teapots is China Specialties.

Sani-Grid

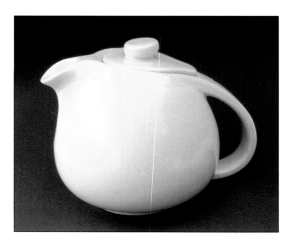

Canary Sani-Grid, $65-85.

Size:
3 cup, 24 ounces brimful, 4.75" high to top of pot, 5.625" wide, strainer, Hall No. 2290
6 cup, 36 ounces brimful, 5.5" high to top of pot, 7.25" wide, strainer, Hall No. 2291

Older decorations:
Gold Decorated, Golden Glo, Mother of Pearl, "No Blue," "Red and White," Rose Parade, Rose White, solid colors, Wildfire

The Sani-Grid teapot appeared with a matching creamer and open sugar in the 1941 *Hall China Special Catalog No. 4* in the Rose Parade and "Red and White" kitchenware line. Also in 1941, the Sani-Grid teapot was added to the Gold Decorated line.

In 1944 the Gold Decorated Sani-Grid was advertised as the perfect teapot for smart afternoon teas. "This lovely Hall teapot is nicely balanced with a symmetrically shaped comfortable handle. Its spout is made with a leaf-retaining grid that is easily accessible for cleaning." (*Pottery, Glass, and Brass Salesman*, April 1944) The gold decoration is a crosshatching on the handle and knob. The bottom marks are H-3, H-3 with the Gold Decorated number, and HSQK.

Sherlock Holmes

Tan and White Sherlock Holmes, $250-300.

Black Glazed Sherlock Holmes,
$250-300.

Don Schreckengost of The Hall China Company designed the Sherlock Holmes teapot in 1987. "This special anniversary edition teapot was inspired by the centennial celebration of Sir Arthur Conan Doyle's first publication of Sherlock Holmes tale in 1887." (The Glaze, January and February 1988, page 13, Elizabeth Boyce)

The Sherlock Holmes will normally be found with the body in Dover white and the deerstalker cover is golden corduroy. There is also a solid black version as shown. At the time of the sale of the teapots, mugs with a Sherlock Holmes decal were available. The bottom mark reads "HOLMES by Hall (in a circle), D.W.B., D.A.S. PORCELAIN, Made in U.S.A."

Short Spout Hot Water Pot
Size:
1.5 cup, 10 ounces brimful, no strainer, Hall No. 189
Special treatment:
Metal Clad

Blue Spice Short Spout Hot Water Pot,
$35-45.

The Short Spout Hot Water Pot is the same as the Tea-for-Two Hot Water Pot but holds two more ounces. Several railroad lines used this shape in their dining cars. The Short Spout Hot Water Pot was available from 1940 through 1996. The bottom marks are H-3 and H-4. Some are found without any bottom mark.

"Side-Handled"
Chocolate Pot

White "Side-Handled" Chocolate Pot, ND.
Size:
1.5 cup, 14 ounces brimful, 5.125" high without cover, 6" high with cover, 5.75" side to handle, 4.75" side to spout, strainer

The white "Side-Handled" Chocolate Pot has recently been found and is marked with the H-3 bottom mark. It has a locking lid.

Solo Tea Set (Hospital Set)
Sizes:
Pot – 1.5 cup, 9 ounces brimful, 3.5" high, 5.5" wide, strainer, Hall No. 315
Creamer – 5.5 ounces, 2.375" high, Hall No. 316
Sugar – 1 ounce, .875" high, Hall No. 317
Newer decorations:
Autumn Leaf, solid colors

The Solo Tea Set is comprised of a stack of teapot, cream, and sugar, thereby occupying a minimum space on a service tray. The creamer serves as the cover for the teapot and the sugar as the cover for the creamer. The set was designed for used in hospitals, thus the original name of Hospital Set. The Hospital Set was available in the Hall catalogs from 1932 through 1964.

Ivory Solo Tea Set (Hospital Set), $80-110.

In 1985 Hall reintroduced the Hospital Set and changed the name to Solo Tea Set. The Solo Tea Set was part of the Hall American line. The sets could be found in standard colors of black, blue, gray, red, tan, and white. Retailers could choose their own colors from a color palette of over 100 colors. Naomi's Antiques of San Francisco ordered a limited number of the Solo Tea Sets in cobalt, orange, and lavender. These newer pots are marked with the H-4 bottom mark.

In 1991 the National Autumn Leaf Collectors Club offered the Solo Tea Set, along with two other pieces, to its members. The bottom mark is NALCC.

St. Louis Chocolate Pot

Platinum Blue St. Louis Chocolate
Pot, $35-45.

Sizes:
1.5 cups, 13 ounces brimful, 4.875" high without cover, 5.5" high
with cover, 4.75" wide, no strainer, Hall No. 130
3 cup, 18 ounces brimful, 5.75" high without cover, 6.25" high with
cover, 5.25" wide, no strainer, Hall No. 131

Older decorations:
California Poppy, Early Gold and Platinum Decorations, solid colors

Newer decorations (3 cup):
Autumn Leaf, Blue Bouquet, Cat-Tail, Crocus, Game Bird, "Orange
Poppy," Red Poppy, Silhouette

Special treatment:
Super-Ceram

In the early 1920s two sizes of the St. Louis Chocolate Pot were
available in green and brown. The pot was described as a covered
pitcher without a strainer in the spout. The cover rests on a small rim
and is held on by two projecting nibs to keep the cover from falling
when pouring. The St. Louis Chocolate Pot is suitable for serving
chocolate, cocoa, hot milk, and hot water. Both sizes of the pot were
available until the early 1990s. A picture of a cobalt St. Louis Chocolate Pot with the Boston standard gold decoration and H-2 bottom
mark was shown in Elizabeth Boyce's article in *The Glaze*, July 1988,
page 8.

The chocolate pot was produced in Super-Ceram in 1967 and
subsequent years. The St. Louis Chocolate Pot will be found in a
variety of colors and was a popular shape for use by railroads and
commercial institutions. In 1994 China Specialties reintroduced the
three-cup St. Louis Chocolate Pot, available in several decals. The
bottom marks found are H-2, H-3, H-4, Super-Ceram, and China
Specialties.

Star

Turquoise Star, $75-90.

Size:
6 cup, 40 ounces brimful, 4.75" high without cover, 6" high with
cover, 9.625" wide, Hall No. 1418

Older decorations:
French Flower, Gold Decorated, Gold "Special," Red Kitchenware,
solid colors

The Star teapot is the same shape as the World's Fair teapot
without the World's Fair debossing. It was introduced in 1939. The
teapot was added to the gold decorated line and advertised as not
only being a practical teapot but also having stunning and modern
lines. The standard gold decoration on the Star is gold stars scattered across the body of the teapot. This teapot derived its name
from the gold decoration used on it.

The Star teapot can be found with silver-overlay decorations.
The bottom marks are H-3, H-3 or HALL with the Gold Decorated
or Gold "Special" number, and HSQK. Some of the solid color Star
teapots will be found without a bottom mark.

"Starlight" ("Tennison")

Size:
6 cup, 40 ounces brimful, 5.125" high without cover, 7.125" high
with cover, 8.75" wide, Hall No. 1534

In the late 1950s the "Starlight" was introduced as part of the
Brilliant Series. It was available in a variety of solid colors and with
brilliants and 22-carat bright gold decorations. In 1961 the "Starlight" was advertised in pink.

The bottom marks found are H-3 for the solid colors and H-3 or
HALL with the Gold Decorated number on those with gold stipple.
Many of the bottom marks will include the Hall identification number.

Lemon "Starlight," $60-75.

Sterling Teapot

White Sterling
Teapot, $25-35.

Size:
2 cup, 12 ounces brimful, 3.5" high with cover, no strainer, Hall No. 3432

The Sterling Teapot with an interlocking cover was made in June 1988 in white for Sterling China Co. There is a companion larger coffee pot.

Streamline

Pink Streamline, $75-100.

Size:
6 cup, 40 ounces brimful, 4.875" high without cover, 6.5" high with cover, 9.125" wide, strainer, Hall No. 3110
Older decorations:
Blue Blossom, Blue Garden, Cactus, Crocus, Fantasy, Flamingo, Gold Decorated, Gold "Special," Meadow Flower, "Mini Fleurette," "Orange Poppy," Platinum Decorated, Red Kitchenware, Silhouette, solid colors, "Spring Blossoms," Wildfire
Newer decorations:
Autumn Leaf, Blue Bouquet, Cat-Tail, Game Bird, Heather Rose, Mexicana, Red Poppy

The Streamline was introduced in the mid-1930s and added to the Gold Decorated line in 1937. The standard gold decoration found on the Streamline consists of gold lines outlining the handle, spout, knob, cover opening, and finial. The cover is delicate, and many are found with the finial glued on or with chips on the extended nibs that hold the cover in place.

The Streamline will be found in solid colors, gold or platinum decorated and with older and newer decorations. The Streamline has also been found in the early gold decoration of "Mini-Fleurette." The bottom marks found on the Streamline are H-3, H-3 or HALL with Gold or Platinum Decoration number, and HSQK.

In 2002 the Streamline was decorated in butternut with gold lining for the East Liverpool Alumni Association. China Specialties reintroduced the Streamline in 2004 in a variety of decals. The bottom marks found on these teapots will be ELHS Alumni or China Specialties.

Super-Ceram Teapot

Size:
1.5 cup, 12 ounces brimful, 3.375" high without cover, 4.125" high with cover, 6" wide, no strainer, Hall No. 4506

Super-Ceram is the Hall China registered trademark for an entirely new type of a super-hard body introduced in the mid-1960s. Super-Ceram items were made to retain heat or cold and to be more resistant to chipping, breaking, and staining.

The teapot shown is called a Super-Ceram teapot after the process used to make it. It was introduced in 1964 and appeared in Hall China catalogs until the late 1980s.

The Super-Ceram teapot could be ordered in 1964 in standard Super-Ceram colors of black, Nile green, pearl, shell, white, or custom ordered with the optional Super-Ceram colors. The teapot was also available in Golden Glo. See the color section for the additional colors. The bottom mark is Super-Ceram.

Surf Side

Chinese Red Surf Side, $280-320.

Size:
6 cup, 44 ounces brimful, 7" high to top of handle, 7.875" wide, strainer, Hall No. 1406
Older decorations:
Gold Decorated, Gold "Special," Red Kitchenware, solid colors

The Surf Side is one of two seashell style teapots made by Hall China in 1939. It was available in solid colors; Gold Decorated with lines outlining the rings of the shell, spout, handle, cover rim, and knob on cover; and Gold Decorated with gold encrusted spout, handle, and knob.

The bottom marks found are H-3, H-3 or HALL with Gold Decorated or Gold "Special" number, and HSQK. The Gold "Special" Surf Side will sometimes be found with a Boston creamer and sugar in matching color and gold.

Left:
Shell Super-Ceram, $35-45.

T-Ball Round

Size:
5 cup, 32 ounces brimful, 4" high without cover, 5" high with cover, 8.25" wide, no strainer, Hall No. 3274

Older decorations:
Gold Label, Red Kitchenware, Silver Glo, solid colors

Black T-Ball Round, $70-85.

The T-Ball Round teapot was introduced in solid colors in late 1948 and made for Bacharach, Inc. of New York. The teapot has one internal chamber and an external pouch on each side for holding teabags. The bottom mark reads: "T-Ball Teapot, Made for BACHARACH by HALL CHINA COMPANY, Patent Applied For." This is all in a large circle with the numbers "3274" below which is Hall's number for the shape of this teapot.

A T-Ball Round teapot has been found with the same gold flower and leaves on its sides that was used on the Airflow teapot. The spout, handle, and knob on the cover are solid gold. The bottom mark on this teapot is H-3 with the Gold Label number below. This makes the thirteenth teapot in the Gold Label Series. The Gold Label T-Ball Round has been seen in black and cobalt.

T-Ball Square

Chinese Red T-Ball Square, $190-230.

Size:
4 cup, 22 ounces brimful, 4" high without cover, 4.75" high with cover, 7.5" wide, no strainer, Hall No. 3275

Older decoration:
Solid colors
Newer decorations:
Autumn Leaf, solid colors

In late 1948 Hall China made an octagonal teapot for Bacharach, Inc. of New York. The teapot is known as the T-Ball Square and has a place on each side to hold a teabag. The teapot was made in solid colors and has the Bacharach bottom mark the same as the T-Ball Round teapot.

In 1985 Hall reintroduced the T-Ball Square along with other teapots in their Hall American line. The standard colors offered were black, blue, gray, red, and tan. Over 100 additional custom colors were offered to retailers to choose from. Naomi's Antiques, an antique dealer in San Francisco, ordered the T-Ball Square in cobalt, orange, and lavender. Other retailers may have ordered the teapot in a special color. These teapots have the H-4 bottom mark.

The National Autumn Leaf Collectors Club offered its members the T-Ball Square in 2000 decorated in the Autumn Leaf pattern. In 2001 the T-Ball Square was made in maroon with gold trim for the East Liverpool Alumni Association auction. The bottom marks on these last two teapots are NALCC and ELHS Alumni. Another T-Ball Square teapot has been found that is slightly smaller than the Hall produced T-Ball Square teapot. The smaller version was not made by Hall.

Tea for Four Set

Sizes:
2 cup, 17 ounces brimful, 4.625" high without cover, 5.125" high with cover, 6.75" wide, strainer, Hall No. 190, Long Spout Teapot; Hall No. 192, Tray
2 cup, 16 ounces brimful, 4.625" high without cover, 5.125" high with cover, 6.75" wide, no strainer, Hall No. 191, Short Spout Water Pot

Gray Tea for Four Set, $70-85.

Older decorations:
Acacia, Early Decals, Early Gold and Platinum Decorations, Red Kitchenware, solid colors, "Wild Poppy"
Special treatment:
Metal Clad

The Tea for Four Set consists of a hot water pot, teapot, and tray. These sets were used in hotels, restaurants, steamships, and railroads. By having the two pots served at one time on a tray, water could be added to the teapot whenever needed without waiting for assistance. The tops on the Tea for Four and the Tea for Two sets are slanted.

The Tea for Four Set will be found in solid colors, with gold decorations, and with decals. The set was offered in the Hall catalogs from 1930 through the mid-1960s. Individual pieces or a complete set could be ordered in a variety of colors. The bottom marks are HALL, H-2, H-3, or HSQK.

Two styles of trays were made for this tea set. Older trays have an opening between the pots whereas the newer ones have a handle lip to help hold the tray when carrying. The teapots will fit either side or direction on the tray.

room table. Some have thought when they found a Tea for Two Set with mixed colors that a marriage of teapot and hot water pot had taken place but that may not be the case.

Naomi's Antiques of San Francisco sold these sets in cobalt, orange, and lavender. These later released teapots have the H-4 bottom mark.

In 1990 the National Autumn Leaf Collectors Club offered the Tea for Two Set to members, and these sets are marked on the bottom with NALCC. Older style trays have a hole between the pots and the newer trays are solid with a handle. The tray holes and handle lip help hold the set while it is transported to the table.

Tea for Two Set

Lenox Brown Tea for Two Set, $55-65.

Sizes:
1.5 cup, 10 ounces brimful, 3.625" high without cover, 4.25" high with cover, 6.875" wide, strainer, Hall No. 185, Long Spout Teapot; Hall No. 187, Tray
1.5 cup, 10 ounces brimful, 3.625" high without cover, 4.25" high with cover, 6" wide, no strainer, Hall No. 186, Short Spout Water Pot

Older decorations:
Early Decals, Early Gold and Platinum Decorations, Golden Glo, Red Kitchenware, solid colors, "Wild Poppy"
Newer decoration:
Autumn Leaf
Special treatments:
Metal Clad and Super-Ceram

The Tea for Two Set was introduced in 1930 and available in the Hall China catalogs through 1996. The sets were available in a variety of colors, and the pieces of the set could be ordered individually. The Tea for Two Sets have slanted tops like the Tea for Four Sets and were used in dining rooms in hotels, restaurants, steamships, and railroads. The bottom marks are HALL, H-2, H-3, H-4, HSQK, and Super-Ceram.

The Tea for Two Set was reintroduced in 1985 as part of the Hall American Line. The standard colors offered were black, blue, gray, red, tan, and white. Additional colors were available; Hall would also develop new colors for the retailer upon request. The mixing and matching of colors with the pieces of the Tea for Two Set were suggested as a way of making a striking presentation on a dining

Tea Taster

Chinese Red Tea Taster, $250-300.

Size:
6 cup, 20 ounces brimful in each chamber, 7" high to top of handle, 9" wide, Hall No. 3232
Older decorations:
Pewter, Red Kitchenware, solid colors

The Tea Taster is one of four teapots in the Teamaster line made for Twinspout Potteries Co., Inc. by Hall China. The Alma, Irvine, Tea Taster, and Twinspout teapots have two compartments, one for tea and one for hot water. There is a built-in strainer only on one side of the teapot, and the teapot handle has a tab on top showing which side has the strainer. The Tea Taster teapot and the Twinspout teapot are similar, but the Tea Taster is oval whereas the Twinspout teapot is round.

The Tea Taster will be found in a variety of colors and with gold decoration. The bottom mark is "TEAMASTER, MADE BY HALL IN U.S.A." Variations of the bottom mark will be found.

In 1985 the Tea Taster was reintroduced as part of the Hall American line. It was available in stock colors of black, blue, gray, red, tan, or white. Retailers could order the teapot in a variety of colors or could order a custom color. The Tea Taster will also be found in cobalt, orange, and lavender – special ordered colors for Naomi's Antiques of San Francisco. The newer teapots will have H-4 or no bottom mark.

Teabagger

Size:
1 cup, 10 ounces brimful, 3.625" high, 4" wide, no strainer, Hall No. 2022

U.S. Patent 2905074 was issued on September 22, 1959, to C. H. Newman, inventor of the Teabagger. The patent's objective for the opening in the cover was to provide a dispenser where the teabag could be conveniently raised above the liquid in the pot. Notice the small knob on the handle to be used to tie the teabag out of the way.

The metal piece that serves as the base, handle, and cover of the teapot reads "Teakoe Teabagger." The bottom mark on the teapot reads: "EKCO – Chicago 39, USA" and "H-3 2022." The "2022" is Hall China's identification number for the item.

This was a short production run for Hall and has only been found in green. In the 1960s the Teabagger shape was advertised in a *Geo. Worthington General Catalog* with a Pyrex™ container.

Green Teabagger, $35-50.

Teapot

Blue Onion Knob Cover Teapot, ND.

Maroon Sunken Cover Teapot, $15-25.

Size:
1.5 cup, 12 ounces brimful, 3.75" high without cover, 4.5" with cover, 4.5" wide, no strainer, Hall No. 2610

Older decorations:
Blue Onion, solid colors

The Teapot with knob cover was introduced in May 1957 and was made for Mayer China Company, Beaver Falls, Pennsylvania. All catalogs show this teapot with a knob cover, but the teapot has recently been available through the Hall Closet with a sunken cover. The teapot is frequently confused with the Hot Pot; however, the handles and spouts are different. The bottom marks are H-3 and H-4.

Teapot Liners ("Red Coach")

Teapot Liners are china bodies that were produced in one or two portion sizes. They were designed with rims around the top and bottom for attaching silver handles and covers. All shapes are unique except for a two-cup French without a handle. Transportation companies, hotels, and clubs purchased the Teapot Liners. They were used for tea, hot water, coffee, and hot chocolate. The bottom marks are usually H-3 and HALL incised. The French has an H-4 bottom mark. Most of the Teapot Liners used on the railroads are referenced in Richard Lunkin's books on railroads. Hall numbers for the various teapot liners have not been correlated with the pictures.

Some companies that made silver covers and handles for the Teapot Liners: Gorham Silver Company, International Silver Company, McAlpin, Pick, Reed and Barton

Prices range from $175-250.

Some of the railroads and clubs that used Hall Teapot Liners: Chicago, Burlington and Quincy; Chicago and Alton; Chicago, Milwaukee, St. Paul; Delaware, Lackawanna, and Western; Detroit Athletic Club; Great Northern; Pullman; Richmond, Fredericksburg, and Potomac; Red Coach; Seaboard Air Line Railroad; Union Pacific; and Southern Pacific

Teapot Metal Tip Spout

Warm Yellow Teapot Metal Tip Spout, $45-60.

Size:
2 cup, 10 ounces brimful, 3.875" high, 6" wide, strainer, Hall No. MTS1601

The Teapot with the metal tip spout was listed in the Hall catalogs from 1964 through 1984. It was available in a variety of colors and is found with the H-3 and H-4 bottom marks.

"Tip-Pot"

Black with Gold Greek Key "Tip-Pot," $220-260.

Size:
8 - 10 cup, 52 ounces brimful, 5.25" high without cover or handle, 7.375" high to top of handle, 9" wide, single chamber, strainer at one end, Hall No. 3334
Older decorations:
Golden Glo, Greek Key, Silver Glo, solid colors

White with Gold Greek Key "Tip-Pot," $220-260.

U.S. Patent 3155284 for a "Dual Swingably Mounted Pot" was issued on November 3, 1964, to Sol Forman and Walter S. Motyka, Brooklyn, and Seymour Sloyer, Lawrence, New York, assignors to Forman Family, Inc., Brooklyn, New York. An objective of the patent was to provide a supporting stand where a pot having a pair of spouts on opposite sides may be tilted in one direction to pour from one spout, or tilted in an opposite direction to pour from the opposing spout. Another objective of this invention was to provide a strong, rugged and durable supported device that would be relatively inexpensive to manufacture, easy to manipulate, attractive in appearance, and yet practical and efficient.

An advantage of this style of teapot was that the pot could be placed in the center of the table and liquid poured to persons sitting on opposite sides. Also, by having the pot on a stand with a pivot, the person doing the pouring would not have to hold a heavy, hot pot while pouring.

There is a built-in strainer only on one side of the teapot. The "Tip-Pot" has a matching creamer and open sugar. The "Tip-Pot" has been found in solid colors of black, canary, and white. The bottom mark reads: "'Tip-Pot', The ultimate in serving hot tea or coffee, 10 Cup, Fire Proof, Hall China, Another Forman Family Product, USA, Pat. Pend."

Twin-Tee Set

Blue Spice Twin-Tee Set, $135-150.

Sizes:
2 cup, 16 ounces brimful, 3.125" high without cover, 4.125" high with cover, 7.25" wide, strainer, Hall No. 180, Long Spout Teapot

2 cup, 14 ounces brimful, 3.125" high without cover, 4.125" high with cover, 6.625" wide, no strainer, Hall No. 181, Short Spout Water Pot; Hall No. 182, tray

Older decorations – Twin-Tee Set:
Early Decals, Early Gold and Platinum Decorations, Red Kitchenware, solid colors

Older decoration – Twin Tea Hot Water Pot:
Blue Willow

Special treatment:
Metal Clad

The Twin-Tee Set consists of three pieces – teapot, hot water pot, and partitioned tray. It was introduced in 1926 and available in the Hall catalogs through 1996. In 1927 the teapot and hot water pot were advertised as having a combined capacity of four cups and came in green or brown.

The tops of the Twin-Tee Set are flat. The older sets may be found in a variety of art glaze colors, solid colors, gold or platinum decorated, and other decorations. The newer sets are found in solid colors. The bottom marks are H-2, H-3, HSQK, or H-4. Two tray styles were provided for this tea set. Older trays have holes between the pots as shown in the picture, and newer ones are solid with a handle lip.

Twinspout

Left:
Turquoise Twinspout,
$90-110.

Size:
6 cup, 24 ounces brimful in each chamber, 6.875" high to top of handle, 9.125" wide, Hall No. 3240

Older decorations:
Chinese red, Golden Glo, solid colors

The Twinspout was made for the Twinspout Pottery Co., Inc., New York, and is part of the Teamaster line. It is similar to the Alma, Irvine, and Tea Taster teapots in that it is divided into separate compartments, one for tea and one for hot water.

U.S. Patent 2135410 was issued to Oscar Ottoson, inventor, on November 1, 1938, for the Twinspout. An objective of the design was for the opening on the tea side chamber to be larger so that tealeaves, teabags, or a tea ball could be put into the chamber more easily.

The Twinspout was available in black, brown, canary, Chinese red, cobalt, emerald, ivory, marine blue, maroon, and turquoise. It may be found in other colors, gold decorated, or with silver overlay. The bottom of the teapot is marked with "TWINSPOUT, TEAMASTER, Pat. 2135410." In 1969 the Twinspout was reintroduced and is marked "INVENTO PRODUCTS."

Wilshire Teapot and Hot Water Pot

Black Wilshire Teapot, $35-50; Marine Wilshire Hot Water Pot, $45-60.

Sizes:

1.5 cup, 10 ounces brimful, 3.375" high without cover, strainer, Hall No. 135

2 cup, 1 ounces brimful, 3.5" high without cover, 3.75" high with cover, 6.5" wide, strainer, Hall No. 136

Size – Hot Water Pot:

1 cup, 10 ounces brimful, 4" high without cover, 4.5" high with cover, 4.875" wide, no strainer, Hall No. 137

The 10-ounce Wilshire teapot and 8-ounce Hot Water Pot were first introduced in the early 1930s followed in 1936 with the two-cup teapot and coffee pot, a two-handled sugar, and three creamers.

The Wilshire line was advertised through the 1970s in the Hall China catalogs and could be ordered in a variety of colors. The bottom marks found on the Wilshire pots are H-3 and H-4.

"Windcrest" ("Bronte")

Lemon "Windcrest," $80-100.

Size:

6 cup, 34 ounces brimful, 4.625" high without cover, 6.125" high with cover, 9.25" wide, Hall No. 1524, Design #6

The "Windcrest" was designed by J. Palin Thorley in the late 1950s and is part of the Brilliant Series. The Brilliant Series teapots will be found in apple green, black, bright blue, lemon, maroon, pink, sky blue, and white. In the 1964 *Geo. Worthington Co. Catalog*, the Brilliant Series was advertised with gold stipple decoration with colored brilliants and selling for $4.95 each. The "Windcrest" was advertised in lemon and will most often be found in that color.

The bottom marks found are H-3 for the solid teapots and H-3 or HALL with the Gold Decorated number on those with gold stipple. Many of the bottom marks will include the Hall identification number. Hall made a plain white "Windcrest" for Carbone in March 1971.

Windshield

Size:

6 cup, 32 ounces brimful, 5.5" high to top of ruff, 6.5" high to top of finial, 8.875" wide, strainer, Hall No. 1412

Older decorations:

Carrot, French Flower, Game Bird, Gold Decorated, Gold Deer, Gold Label, Gold "Special," Golden Carrot, Golden Clover, "Orange Poppy" (locking cover), Platinum Dots, Red Kitchenware, Silver Glo, Sixties Decoration, solid colors

Newer decorations:

Autumn Leaf, Blue Bouquet, Cat-Tail, Crocus, Mexicana, Red Poppy, Silhouette

In June 1941 the Windshield appeared in an advertisement in the *China, Glass, and Lamps* trade journal – "The Attractive HALL Windshield Teapot – The best virtues of traditional and modern design have been combined in this exclusive Hall creation – its prim top reminiscent of a proud Queen Elizabeth stiffly starched ruff while its smooth, flowing lines are strictly in keeping with modern, functional styles. The Hall Windshield Teapot is beautifully gold decorated … crazeproof … stainproof … superior quality … made in America by the world's largest manufacturer of decorated teapots. …"

The Windshield can be found in solid colors and gold decorated. This pot is one of the Gold Label series with a decoration of gold dots. In the 1960s the Windshield was part of a decaled series and can be found in warm yellow with green and white floral decoration around the shoulder and green trim. The bottom marks are H-3 and H-3 or HALL with the Gold Decorated, Gold Label, or Gold "Special" number.

The Windshield was reintroduced in 1999 by China Specialties and is found in a variety of decals. In 2004 the Windshield was made for the East Liverpool Alumni Association auction in ivory with Hall bottom marks placed around the body. The bottom marks on these pots are China Specialties or ELHS Alumni.

World's Fair

World's Fair, $950-1100.

Size:

6 cup, 40 ounces brimful, 4.75" high without cover, 6" high with cover, 9.625" wide, strainer, Hall No. 1416

Left:
Cobalt Windshield,
$80-100.

The year will be either 1939 or 1940.

The visual icons of the 1939-1940 New York World's Fair were the Trylon and Perisphere, which were painted white and lit brightly at night. The Trylon and Perisphere appear in debossed gold on both sides of the World's Fair cobalt teapot that was sold as a souvenir in the Potter's Exhibit. At the 1940 World's Fair, Hall China was one of five pottery firms that participated in an exhibit that included a miniature pottery plant with a tunnel kiln. Exhibitors produced sample souvenir pieces sold at the display.

The Star teapot was also made in the same shape without the World's Fair embossing. The World's Fair teapot has been found without gold decoration or a bottom mark.

Zeisel Kitchenware and Zeisel Kitchenware Side-Handled

Size:
6 cup, 32 ounces brimful, 4.25" high without cover, 5" high with cover, 8.5" wide, strainer, Hall No. 1582
Older decorations:
Casual Living, Tri-Tone
Newer decoration:
"Elena"

Casual Living Zeisel Kitchenware, $85-110.

In October 1954, Eva Zeisel designed a kitchenware shape line that included a six-cup teapot, a side-handled two-cup teapot, and a matching creamer and sugar. The Casual Living decoration on the Zeisel Kitchenware teapot has a seal brown body with several multi-colored lines and circles on a matte-white cover. The Tri-Tone Zeisel Kitchenware Side-Handled teapot has three colors – pink, turquoise, and gray. The turquoise is on one side and pink is on the other side. The two colors overlap to form the gray color. The bottom mark on the Casual Living teapots is H-3 in gold under the cover. The Tri-tone Zeisel Kitchenware Side-Handled has "Made in U.S.A., Tri-Tone, 1581." The Tri-Tone Zeisel Kitchenware has "Made in U.S.A., HALL" on the bottom.

The "Elena" pattern found on the Zeisel Kitchenware teapot was part of a hostess ware set. This teapot will be marked on the bottom with "Hostess Ware" or without a mark.

Size:
2 cup, 18 ounces brimful, 3.5" high without cover, 4.5" high with cover, 5.75" wide to end of spout, 6.5" wide to end of handle, strainer, Hall No. 1581
Older decorations:
Casual Living, Tri-Tone

Tri-Tone Zeisel Kitchenware Side-Handled, $350-400.

Right:
"Orange Floral Bouquet"
"#2 Coffee Shape," $50-60.

Coffee and Beverage Pot Shapes

The coffee and beverage pot shapes are listed in alphabetical order with measurements and capacities. Serving sizes are listed in cups, if known, and capacity in ounces. The measurements were taken from actual pieces of china and cross-referenced with catalogs, brochures, advertisements, and the Hall China mold book. Pots are not included if we did not have a picture. We know that other pots exist based upon Hall China Company records. For example, Hall's records show that a coffee pot was made for the advertising agency representing Folger's Coffee. We think this is a smaller coffee pot, most likely with an advertising decal or Folger's logo. Pre-production samples are not included.

Decorations used on the coffee and beverage pots are listed in two categories and exclude commercial advertising, clubs, and other logos. Demarcation between older and newer decorations is approximately 1970. The newer decorations generally include China Specialties and National Autumn Leaf Collectors Club. We tried to include the date of start of production, date when Hall considered an item no longer available for production, and the company or distributor for whom the pot was made. Special treatments are noted when a pot was made in Super-Ceram or Metal Clad.

Some of the pots have been renamed based upon documentation found in catalogs, advertisements, patents, brochures, or Hall China mold book. If you are unable to locate a coffee pot or beverage pot, check in the Name Cross-Reference in the back. Known bottom marks of the coffee and beverage pots are listed for each shape. Examples of the common bottom marks are shown in the front of the book in the Bottom Marks section. Enterprise Aluminum Company, Eva Zeisel, Forman Family, and Tricolator Company bottom marks are illustrated later in this book. Bottom marks unique to one or two pots are pictured or described with the shape.

"#2 Coffee Shape"

Size:
6 cup, 60 ounces brimful, 7.25" high without lid, 8.75" high with cover, 9" wide, 3.25" diameter opening for drip, Hall No. 3320

In 1950 Enterprise Aluminum Company introduced a coffee pot with fluted edges. Collectors know this coffee pot as the "#2 Coffee Shape." The coffee pot was available with a metal drip and matching creamer and open sugar.

The common decoration is a predominately orange floral on a white body with gold trim. The bouquet consists of a fringed tulip, rose, zinnias, flax, and baby breath. The bottom mark is Drip-O-lator.

#691 All-China Drip

Chinese Red #691 All-China Drip,
$375-450.

Size:
6 cup, 56 ounces brimful without drip, 5.625" high without drip or cover, 11.5" high with drip and cover, 9" wide, 3.75" diameter opening for drip, Hall Nos. 691 and 691X

Older decorations:
#488, Acacia, "Black Beauty," Blue Blossom, Color Bands, Eggshell Plaid, Eggshell Polka Dot, Eggshell Swag, Flamingo, Red Kitchenware, Russet, solid colors, "Wild Poppy"

The #691 All-China Drip was introduced in 1933 for Macy's as a four-piece modern drip pot (bottom body, china drip, china water spreader, and cover). The china drip came with either one or two handles. A version called the #691X was available for use with filter papers instead of the china spreader. Long and short handled china spreaders have been found and are pictured with the "Kadota" All-China Drip.

The #691 coffee pot appears in Hall catalogs between 1935 and 1964. It is found in a variety of decorations, and it is frequently found with color bands of black, blue, green, light green, red, or yellow on an ivory body with platinum trim. It has also been found with a platinum band instead of a color band. The #691 All-China Drip with two handles has been found decorated with color bands, Eggshell Plaid, and Eggshell Polka Dot (red or blue). The bottom mark is HSQK.

The bottom of the #691 has been used by the Enterprise Aluminum Company with a metal drip and china cover and marked Drip-O-lator on the bottom.

Eggshell Plaid #691 All-China Drip, ND.

"Alcony"

Emerald "Alcony," $65-80.

Size:
8 cup, 64 ounces brimful, 6.5" high without cover, 7.75" high with cover, 8.25" wide, 3.75" diameter opening for drip

The "Alcony" coffee pot is usually found in warm yellow or emerald. It may be available in other solid colors, but it has not been found with a decoration. Little is known about this pot. The "Alcony" has the H-3 bottom mark.

Amano Beverage Pot

Size:
2 cup, 14 ounces brimful, 5" high without cover, 6.25" high with cover, 6.75" wide, no strainer, Hall No. 2646

This beverage pot, matching open sugar, and handled creamer are part of the Amano dinnerware line. They appeared in the 1973 through 1989 Hall general line catalogs and were available in Lenox brown or weathered oak. The Amano pieces are marked with the H-4 bottom mark.

Lenox Brown Amano Beverage Pot, $15-25.

Ambassador ("Blossom")

Marine Ambassador, $65-85.

Sizes:
4 cup, 44 ounces brimful, 6.5" high without cover, 8.5" high with cover, 8.5" wide, 3.25" diameter opening for drip

6 cup, 52 ounces brimful, 7" high without cover, 8.75" high with cover, 8.5" wide, 3.25" diameter opening for drip

The Tricolator Company, Inc. advertised the Ambassador in the 1930s for $7.25 with a metal drip. As a special feature, flame pad and matching china tiles were available without additional cost.

The Ambassador came in solid pastel and art glaze colors. It also came decorated in a tan-lustre with a silver floral decoration that is shown in the Tricolator section later in this book. The bottom marks found are Pour Right Tricolator and HALL incised.

"Amory"

Yellow "Amory," $70-85.

Size:
6 cup, 54 ounces, 5.5" high without cover, 7" high with cover, 9.25" wide, 3.5" diameter opening for drip

The "Amory" was advertised in a 1930s Tricolator Company brochure as available in jet-black lustre with colored covers in green, red, white, and yellow. It also came in solid colors of delft, lettuce, marine, Nile green, and yellow.

The cost in the late 1930s for the "Amory" varied from $2.00 to $3.25 depending upon the color and style of metal drip. The bottom is marked with HALL incised and the Tricolator Pour Right mark.

"Andrew" Electric Percolator and Urn

Size – Percolator:
6 cup, 60 ounces brimful, 10" high without cover, 12" high with cover, 8.25" wide
Size - Urn:
7 cup, 64 ounces brimful, 10.75" high without cover, 13" high with cover, 8.5" wide from handle to handle
Older decorations:
Fuji, "Hanging Vine"

The Westinghouse Company sold the "Andrew" electric percolator and urn as individual pots as well as part of a set. Sets included either an electric percolator or urn with a creamer, sugar with cover, and Micarta™ tray. A combined set of the percolator and urn was also available. Westinghouse advertisements list the coffee pot and urn by product number, not by name. Westinghouse purchased china bodies from Hall China Company and added metal and electrical parts and distributed them through their catalogs.

In a 1934 Westinghouse Company catalog, it describes "genuine Hall china with attractive decorations – beautiful companion piece to the finest tableware. Lustrous Micarta tray in black, red, and aluminum – easy to clean, will not chip, crack, burn, peel, or discolor. Corox™ heating element, fuse protected. 400 watts, 115 volts, and miniature plug detachable cord." The advertising goes on to say "many hostesses are using Westinghouse china pots for simplifying the making of cocoa or chocolate" with percolator pump removed.

The bottom mark reads "Westinghouse Fused Type Percolator, Patents 1451755, Made in U.S.A., 400 Watt, Cat. # PF374, Westinghouse Electric and Manufacturing Co., Mansfield Works, Mansfield, OH."

"Arthur"

Size:
8 cup, 82 ounces brimful, 6.25" high without cover, 7.5" high with cover, 10" wide, 4.25" diameter opening for drip
Older decorations:
Crocus; Red, White Accents, and Platinum Trim

The "Arthur" is one of the recently identified coffee pots made by The Hall China Company. The only decorations that have turned up so far are the decaled Crocus coffee pot shown in the picture and a coffee pot with a red body bottom, white accents, and platinum trim. The pot has the HSQK bottom mark.

Crocus "Arthur," ND.

Left:
Fuji "Andrew" Electric Urn, $85-110; Percolator, $65-95.

Autocrat ("Buchanan") Eight-cup – Decorated and Undecorated

Maroon Autocrat, $55-65.

Size:
8 cup, 64 ounces brimful, 6" high without cover, 7.5" high with cover, 9.375" wide, 3.5" diameter opening for cover

In a 1927 Tricolator brochure, the twelve-paneled, eight-cup Autocrat was referred to as the "Tricolator hotel service at home." The coffee pots sold for $5.00 each and came with a metal drip and Tricolator filters. The Autocrat counter service sold for $17.00 and consisted of a heated-by-steam combination. The Autocrat sat on top of the one-gallon aluminum server. A picture of the server is shown in the Tricolator section of this book.

The bottom marks found on the Autocrat are Pour Right Tricolator and/or HALL incised. All Tricolator coffee pots came with a china cover.

During the 1930s the Autocrat coffee pot was available in solid colors and in a variety of decorations. Some of the decorations are shown in the Tricolator section of this book. Tricolator called the six-cup decorated version of this shape the Regent and the six-cup undecorated version Windsor.

Autocrat Jr. ("Buchanan") with Screw Locking Cover

Chinese Red Screw Locking Cover Autocrat Jr., $70-85.

Size:
6 cup, 58 ounces brimful, 5.75" high without cover, 7.25" high with cover, 9.5" wide, 3.75" diameter opening for drip, Hall No. 3101

The twelve-panel Autocrat Jr. was introduced in 1946 with a screw locking cover as shown. The coffee pot has been found in solid colors of Chinese red, ivory, and yellow. Other colors may be available. The Autocrat Jr. was made for the Tricolator Company and has the bottom marks of Pour Right Tricolator and/or HALL incised.

"Baron" ("Rochester")

Size:
8 cup, 76 ounces brimful, 6" high without cover, 7.25" high with cover, 10" wide, 4.25" diameter opening for drip
Older decorations:
Acacia; Red, White Accents, and Platinum Trim

The ten-panel "Baron" coffee is usually found decorated as shown, but it can also be found with black, blue, green, or yellow instead of the red. This pot has also been found decorated in the Acacia pattern that matches a Taylor-Smith-Taylor line of dinnerware. The "Baron" has the HSQK bottom mark.

Red, White Accents, and Platinum Trim "Baron," $65-80.

Basket Weave ("Straw-Weave") Electric Percolator and Urn

Basket Weave Electric Percolator, $100-125; Urn, $125-150.

Size – Percolator:
8 cup, 78 ounces brimful, 11.75" high without cover, 13.5" high with cover, 9" wide, Hall No. 3301
Size – Urn:
8 cup, 76 ounces brimful, 11.5" high without cover, 14.25" high with cover and tall knob, 8.25" wide, Hall No. 3302

The Basket Weave electric percolator, urn, covered sugar, and creamer were introduced in early 1949. Other pieces in the Basket Weave design are a casserole and marmites. The set is most often found in black or white with a gold floral pattern. It has also been found in turquoise and may possibly be found in pink or yellow with small gold flowers. The "Pink and Gray Floral Bouquet" is another pattern found on the Basket Weave items.

Hall made the china pieces and the Forman Family added the metal drips, lids, and electrical components. Note in the picture the different styles of glass knobs for the metal covers. The bottom mark reads "115 Volts, 400 Watts, Cat. No. 400 – FORMAN 4 FAMILY – If percolator fails to heat, remove this base plate and replace fuse." The catalog number for the percolator was 401 and for the urn, 400.

"Basketweave"

Blue "Basketweave," $50-65.

Size:
6 cup, 48 ounces brimful, 5.625" high without cover, 7" high with cover, 10" wide, 3.625" diameter opening for drip

The "Basketweave" coffee pot was made for the Enterprise Aluminum Company and has the Drip-O-lator bottom mark. A metal drip was provided for the "Basketweave" coffee pot by the Enterprise Aluminum Company.

Some of the solid colors that appear on the "Basketweave" Drip-O-lator are blue, orange, white, and yellow. The only decal found on the "Basketweave" so far is called "Wild Rose Floral Garland."

"Bauhaus"

Left:
"June" Flower "Bauhaus," $45-60.

Size:
8 cup, 72 ounces brimful, 6.5" high without cover, 8.25" high with cover, 9.25" wide, 3.75" diameter opening for drip, Hall No. 3167

The "Bauhaus" was introduced in August 1938 for the Enterprise Aluminum Company. It can be found with an ivory body and either the "Jonquil" or "June" Flower decoration. The coffee pot was available until the late 1950s. It is marked on the bottom with Drip-O-lator.

Beacon ("Diver") – Undecorated

Size:
5 cup, 48 ounces brimful, 5.75" high without cover, 7.125" high with cover, 10.125" wide, 3.375" diameter opening for drip

The twelve-panel coffee pot that has been referred to as the "Diver" was actually given three names in the 1930s Tricolator catalog, depending upon whether it was plain or decorated. The undecorated coffee pots are called Beacon or Pekin, and the decorated ones are called Bride. To make it easier for collectors, we have used Beacon for the name of this undecorated coffee pot.

The bottom marks found on the pots are HALL incised and POUR RIGHT. The coffee pot was available in a variety of colors and came with a metal drip and china cover.

Yellow Beacon, $60-75.

"Beaver Falls"

Maroon "Beaver Falls," $55-70.

Size:
8 cup, 80 ounces brimful, 6.5" high without cover, 8" high with cover, 10.25" wide, 4.25" diameter opening for drip, Hall No. 3292

"Beaver Falls" with "Miracle" Electric Drip.

The "Beaver Falls" was introduced in 1940 and was probably named after Beaver Falls, Pennsylvania. It has been found only in solid colors of maroon or delphinium. It may have been available in other colors.

The style of this pot is very similar to the "Daniel" coffee pot that was introduced in 1935, except for the handle. The pot will have an H-3 bottom mark, but it will also be found without a mark.

The "Beaver Falls" was available with a four to eight cup glass drip as shown. An advertisement describes the coffee pot as a "Miracle" fully automatic electric drip coffee maker. The instructions that accompanied the coffee pot say to lift out the electric unit, put the required amount of coffee in the basket, add water, replace electric unit, plug in, turn button on top, and forget it. The "Miracle" will do the rest without any further attention.

Bellevue

Sizes:
1 cup, 10 ounces brimful, 4" high without cover, 4.875" high with cover, 5.375" wide, Hall No. 151
1.5 cup, 14 ounces brimful, 4.75" high without cover, 5.375" high with cover, 5.75" wide, Hall No. 156
2 cup, 18 ounces brimful, 5.375" high without cover, 6.25" high with cover, 5.75" wide, Hall No. 156.25
3 cup, 26 ounces brimful, 6" high without cover, 7" high with cover, 6.5" wide, Hall No. 156.5

Older decorations:
Chinese red, Early Gold and Platinum Decorations, "Orange Poppy" (2 cup), solid colors

Newer decorations:
Autumn Leaf (3 cup), Crocus (green body, 1 cup)

Sandust Two-Cup Bellevue, $15-25.

The Bellevue is one of the earlier coffee pot styles, introduced probably in the late teens by Hall. It is still available in the current catalog. The twelve-paneled coffee pot normally came with a knob cover but could be ordered with a sunken cover. The Bellevue covers are interchangeable and will fit the teapot, coffee pot, individual sugar, and jug. In a 1920s Hall catalog, the Bellevue was advertised as an attractive individual room service item for hospitals and hotels. It was designed to occupy a minimum amount of space on the tray. The Bellevue was suitable for serving cocoa, chocolate, hot milk, and hot water.

The Bellevue was originally made in two sizes – the 10 and 14 ounces in green and brown. By 1935 all four sizes were available in black, blue, cadet, canary, emerald, gray, green lustre, ivory, lettuce, marine, maroon, orchid, pink, rose, tan, violet, and yellow. During the thirties the Bellevue was advertised as part of the Delphinium Blue Cooking Ware line. A limited number of the "Orange Poppy" decaled Bellevue coffee pots have been found and command high prices. Older Bellevue coffee pots have been found in a variety of colors and decorated with gold lining and coin gold (matte) handles, spouts, and knobs. The bottom marks are H-2, H-3, H-4, or HSQK.

"Betty" Electric Percolator and Urn

Cat-Tail "Betty" Electric Percolator, $145-160.

Size – Percolator:
7 cup, 64 ounces brimful, 10.5" high without cover, 12.5" high with cover, 9" wide

Size – Urn:
7 cup, 64 ounces brimful, 10.5" high without cover, 12.5" high with cover, 8.25" wide

Older decorations:
Cat-Tail, "Hanging Vine"

The decals found on the "Betty" electric percolator and urn are described in a Westinghouse Company advertisement as a beautiful modern design that will enhance the finest table service. The Cat-Tail decal shown on the pots matches the Universal dinnerware line. The "Betty" urn features smart, jet-black pendant handles. Westinghouse sold the electric percolator and urn as individual pots as well as part of a set. Sets included a creamer, sugar with cover, and a Micarta tray with either a percolator or urn. A combined set with percolator and urn was also available. Westinghouse used catalog numbers for these items, not a name.

Cat-Tail "Betty" Electric Urn, $160-175.

The Westinghouse Company purchased china bodies from The Hall China Company, added metal and electrical parts, and distributed them through their catalogs. A 1934 Westinghouse catalog says "the lustrous Micarta tray comes in black, red, and aluminum – easy to clean, will not chip, crack, burn, peel, or discolor. Corox heating element, fuse protected. 400 watts, 115 volts, and miniature plug detachable cord."

The bottom mark reads "Westinghouse Fused Type Percolator, Patents 1451755, Made in U.S.A., 400 Watt, Cat. # PF374, Westinghouse Electric and Manufacturing Co., Mansfield Works, Mansfield, OH."

Beverage Pot
(knob and sunken cover)

Sizes – Knob Cover:
2 cup, 14 ounces brimful, 5.375" high with cover, Hall No. 2051
3 cup, 20 ounces brimful, 5.25" high without cover, 6" high with cover, 6.5" wide, Hall No. 2053

Sizes – Sunken Cover:
2 cup, 14 ounces brimful, 5.375" high, Hall No. 2051.5
3 cup, 20 ounces brimful, 5.25" high, 6.5" wide, Hall No. 2053.5

The Beverage Pot came in two sizes and was available from 1971 until the 1990s with a locking knob or sunken cover. It is very similar to the Washington shape coffee pot except for the handle, the cover locking method, and the knob on the cover. Another coffee pot similar to this shape is described under Coffee Pot Metal Tip Spout. The bottom mark is H-4.

Vanilla Beverage Pot, Knob Cover, $30-45. (Beverage Pot, Sunken Cover – Not Shown).

"Bingham" ("Madeline")

Red, White Accents, and Platinum "Bingham," $60-75.

Size:
6 cup, 64 ounces brimful, 5.75" high without cover, 7" high with cover, 10.25" wide, 3.875" diameter opening for drip

In the November 1987 issue of *The Glaze*, this pot was pictured and identified as the "Bingham." In Jeffrey B. Snyder's book, *Hall China*, page 48, the coffee pot is referred to as "Madeline." The coffee pot is decorated similarly to other large Hall coffee pots.

The "Bingham" has been found in green, red, and yellow with white accents and platinum trim. It may have also been available in black or blue. The "Bingham" has the bottom mark of HSQK or Drip-O-lator. It has also been found without a bottom mark.

73

"Bricks and Ivy" – Round and Square Handle

"Orange Floral" "Bricks and Ivy" Round Handle, $40-65.

Size – Round Handle:
7 cup, 60 ounces brimful, 5.75" high without cover, 7.125" high with cover, 10.25" wide, 3.5" diameter opening for drip

Size – Square Handle:
6 cup, 50 ounces brimful, 5.375" high without cover, 7" high with cover, 10.5" wide, 3.5" diameter opening for drip

"Orange Floral" "Bricks and Ivy" Square Handle, $40-65.

These coffee pots have a "Bricks and Ivy" relief decoration on the body, cover, spout, and handle and were made for the Enterprise Aluminum Company. The coffee pots have the Drip-O-lator bottom mark.

They are found in two different sizes with different handle styles: round handle (60 ounces) and square handle (50 ounces). Both shapes are found with an orange floral decal with blue Forget-Me-Nots. The only other known decal found on this shape is "Ivory Beauty."

Bride ("Diver") – Decorated

Acacia Bride, $200-225.

Size:
5 cup, 48 ounces brimful, 5.75" high without cover, 7.125" high with cover, 10.125" wide, 3.625" diameter opening for drip
Older decorations:
Acacia (see Tricolator Section for additional decorations)

The twelve-panel coffee pot that has been referred to as the "Diver" was actually given three names in the 1930s Tricolator catalog, depending upon whether it was plain or decorated. The undecorated coffee pots were called Beacon or Pekin. Decorated "Divers" were referred to as the Bride coffee pots.

The Bride came in various decorations and with platinum lining on ivory bodies with platinum trim. The Bride coffee pots are found with Hall incised and the Tricolator Pour Right bottom mark.

California

Russet California, $45-60.

Sizes:

1 cup, 10 ounces brimful, 4.125" high without cover, 5.125" high with cover, 4.625" wide, Hall Nos. 1800 (100)

1.5 cup, 12 ounces brimful, 4.5" high without cover, 5.5" high with cover, 5" wide, Hall Nos. 1801 (101)

2 cup, 14 ounces brimful, 5.125" high without cover, 6" high with cover, 5.125" wide, Hall Nos. 1802 (102)

2 cup, 16 ounces brimful, 5.125" high without cover, 6.125" high with cover, 5.125" wide, Hall Nos. 1803 (103) (newer cover for Dohrmann Hotel Supply Co.)

Manning Coffee California, $45-60.

The California was introduced in the 1920s and was in production through the mid-1970s. In November 1963 Hall China changed the identification numbers from 100 - 102 to 1800 - 1802. The pot is unique in that it has a strainer behind the spout and a corresponding strainer in the cover flange. It was described as a standard hot water server, but it was also suitable for serving coffee. The bottom marks are HALL incised, H-3, or H-4.

A second version of the two-cup California featuring a locking cover, a redesigned knob, and a heavier spout was made in the early 1960s for the Manning's Coffee Company. It was distributed through Dohrman Hotel Supply Company of California. This coffee pot features Manning's Roasted Coffee around the bottom and a coffee bean and leaves on the side. The Manning's Coffee pot has an H-3 bottom mark.

"Canoy"

Size:

8 cup, 70 ounces brimful, 6.25" high without cover, 7.625" high with cover, 9.875" wide, 3.75" diameter opening for drip

The "Canoy" coffee pot is very similar in shape to the "Corrie" coffee pot. They both have twelve-panels and the same handle shape. The spouts and knobs on the covers, however, are different. The flared section above the ring on top of the panel section of the body is also differently shaped.

The "Canoy" has generally been found in green, but it may show up in other colors. The bottom marks are H-3 and/or HALL incised.

Green "Canoy," $45-60.

Carafe (No Cover)

Black and White Carafe, $25-35.

Size:

2 cup, 15 ounces brimful, 5.25" high, 4" wide, Hall No. 1611

The uncovered Carafe was frequently used for a beverage service of tea, hot water, or coffee by cafeterias, hospitals, and restaurants. It is usually found in white with a black bottom, but it may be found in other colors. Sometimes it came with a paper cover. The bottom marks are H-3 or H-4. The Carafe was distributed from the 1960s through the late 1990s.

"Carrie" ("Connie") with and without All-China Drip

Size:

6 cup, 86 ounces brimful, 5.75" high without cover, 11.5" wide, 4.375" diameter wide for drip, Hall No. 3238

Water container for #3238 pot, Hall No. 3239

Blue Bouquet "Carrie" All-China Drip, ND.

The "Carrie" coffee pot and all-china drip were available in the late 1930s from Hall China. In 1939 the Wilcox Electric Appliance Company of East Liverpool, Ohio, advertised the "Carrie" with a metal drip and electrical heating element. The ad stated, "a fully automatic electric drip coffee maker was available only to Golden Star customers at a special reduced price. Whether you have Golden Star Milk delivered to your door or get it at your favorite grocery store, you can obtain this Fully Automatic Electric Drip Coffee Maker for only $3.95 – you save $2.00. Ask to see it! Buy it on easy terms … pay only $2.50 down and 25 cents a week for the balance! Be the first to enjoy really delicious coffee and benefit by its many extensive advantages. They'll make an inexpensive Christmas gift for your home or for your friends. This offer is limited … during November and December only … throughout the tri-state district (Ohio, Pennsylvania, West Virginia)."

The advertisement continued to say, "Here are 14 features of this unique coffee maker: (1) The only Fully Automatic conventional Electric Drip Coffee Maker on the market today. (2) Can be left plugged in wall socket continuously without damage to drip. (3) Has no switches or thermostats of any kind to get out of order. (4) Not fire hazard. (5) Non burn out element. (6) Water never boils in the water container. (7) Water does not injure the heating unit in any way. (8) Contains no movable parts. (9) Simple in construction. (10) Easy to clean – sanitary. (11) Absolutely fool proof. (12) Simplicity of operation. (13) One of the speediest coffee makers on the market today. (14) Guaranteed for one year against workmanship and defective material. Distributed by Golden Star Dairy … Manufactured by … The Wilcox Electric Appliance Co., Inc."

In the 1950s and 1960s, the "Carrie" all-china drip was part of the Blue Bouquet dinnerware line. The Standard Coffee Company distributed this pattern through their home shopping service across the southern United States. The Blue Bouquet all-china drip appears with the HSQK bottom mark.

The "Carrie" coffee pot without the china drip is found in maroon and black. They will have the H-3 bottom mark or will not have any bottom mark.

"Cathedral" ("Arch")

Daisy Eight-Cup "Cathedral," $50-65.

Sizes:

4 cup, 44 ounces brimful, 4.75" high without cover, 6.125" high with cover, 9.5" wide, 3.625" diameter opening for drip

6 cup, 72 ounces brimful, 6.25" high without cover, 7.75" high with cover, 10.25" wide, 3.75" diameter opening for drip

8 cup, 96 ounces brimful, 6.75" high without cover, 8.625" high with cover, 11.25" wide, 4.375" diameter opening for drip

The "Cathedral" coffee pots are designed with arch-like panels in relief on the pot body. They were made in three sizes for the Enterprise Aluminum Company and have the Drip-O-lator bottom mark. The coffee pots have all been found with variations of a daisy decal.

Left:
Maroon "Carrie," $45-60.

Classic Series™ Beverage Pot Metal Tip Spout

Lenox Brown Classic Series Beverage Pot Metal Tip Spout Set, $45-60.

Size:

2 cup, 13 ounces brimful, 3.25" high without cover, 3.75" high with cover, 7" wide, Hall No. MTS2979

The Metal Tip Spout Beverage Pot is part of the Classic Series line. It was designed to stack easily and in the style of the 1980s. The covers are recessed to allow stacking of the sugar and creamer on top of the pot. The beverage pot cover is an oval-locking cover with index marks while the sugar cover is non-locking. The sugar cover is flat with raised edges to allow the creamer to set on top as shown in the picture. The Classic Series line was available through the mid-1990s in canary, Lenox brown, and a variety of other colors. The pot has the H-4 bottom mark.

"Clayman"

Size:

8 cup, 72 ounces brimful, 5.875" high without cover, 7.375" high with cover, 10" wide, 4.25" diameter opening for drip

The "Clayman" is similar to the eight-cup "Terrace" coffee pot with the exception of the knob on top of the handle. This gave more support to the thumb when pouring coffee. The "Clayman" has been found only in delphinium and has the H-3 bottom mark.

Delphinium "Clayman," $65-80.

Clipper ("Carraway" Long Spout)

Emerald Clipper, $60-75.

Sizes:

2 cup, 16 ounces brimful, 3" high without cover, 3.75" high with cover, 7.625" wide, 3.375" diameter opening for drip, Hall No. 3211

3 cup, 26 ounces brimful, 3.5" high without cover, 4.25" high with cover, 8.25" wide, 3.5" diameter opening for drip, Hall No. 3212

5 cup, 44 ounces brimful, 4.25" high without cover, 5.25" high with cover, 9.97" wide, 3.75" diameter opening for drip, Hall No. 3213

The Clipper coffee pot was made for the Tricolator Co., Inc. in the 1930s. The three sizes of the Clipper could be ordered in solid colors or with decorations on an ivory body. These decorations are shown in the Tricolator section of this book. In the 1930s the Clipper sold from between $2.75 to $4.25 depending upon the decoration and the metal drip. These coffee pots have the Pour Right Tricolator mark and/or HALL incised. The short spout New Yorker coffee pot is similar to the Clipper except for the spout design.

Club

Cadet Club, $45-60.

Sizes:

1 cup, 7 ounces brimful, 3.875" high without cover, 4.5" high with cover, 5.125" wide, Hall No. 160

1.5 cup, 10 ounces brimful, 4.25" high without cover, 4.75" high with cover, 5.5" wide, Hall No. 161

2 cup, 12 ounces brimful, 4.25" high without cover, 5" high with cover, 5.625" wide (Modified lid)

The Club was introduced in the 1920s and available in blue, brown, and green. It was designed with body nibs and a notched cover to prevent the cover from falling off when pouring. The Club also has a wide base to minimize tipping and a free pour spout to simplify cleaning. The Club's size and stability made it ideal for use in men's grills, clubs, dining cars, steamships, cafeterias, and room service. It was suitable for serving coffee, chocolate, cocoa, hot milk, and hot water.

The bottom marks used on this pot are HALL incised, H-3, and H-4. The only non-commercial decoration found on the Club has been a white enamel floral decal on a brown glaze.

Coffee Carafe

White Coffee Carafe, $40-60.

Size:

10 cup, 84 ounces brimful, 10.5" high without cover, 11" high with cover, 9.5" wide

The Coffee Carafe was designed by Ernest Sohn and came in both the smooth and ribbed body. The smooth body carafes are marked H-3, whereas the fluted-body Doric Coffee Carafe is marked Ernest Sohn Creations. The only decoration other than hand painting found on the smooth Coffee Carafe is Gold Dots. Some of the carafes are found with a warmer and candleholder. They have locking covers that have been found with ceramic and metal cover knobs.

Coffee Pot Metal Tip Spout

White Knob Cover and Maroon Sunken Cover Coffee Pot Metal Tip Spouts, $25-40 each.

Sizes – Knob Cover:

1 cup, 10 ounces brimful, 4" high without cover, .4.75" high with cover, 5.625" wide, Hall No. MTS-2550

1.5 cup, 14 ounces brimful, 4.625" high without cover, 5.375" high with cover, 6.25" wide, Hall No. MTS-2551

2 cup, 20 ounces brimful, 5.25" high without cover, 6" high with cover, 6.625" wide, Hall No. MTS-2553

3 cup, 30 ounces brimful, 6" high without cover, 7.125" high with cover, 7.625" wide, Hall No. MTS-2554

Sizes – Sunken Cover:

1 cup, 10 ounces brimful, 4" high without cover, 5.625" wide, Hall No. MTS-2550.5

1.5 cup, 14 ounces brimful, 4.625" high without cover, 6.25" wide, Hall No. MTS-2551.5

2 cup, 20 ounces brimful, 5.25" high without cover, 6.625" wide, Hall No. MTS-2553.5

These pots are essentially identical in shape to the Beverage Pot shown earlier in this book except that these have a metal tip spout. The Coffee Pot Metal Tip Spouts were introduced in 1979 and available until 1996. Depending upon the Hall catalog, these pots have been referred to by several names. Initially they were called Beverage Pot Metal Tip Spout. Later the Hall catalogs changed the name to Coffee Pot Metal Tip Spout. Then on one of Hall's product sheets, it was called a Washington. The later Hall catalog refers to them as the Coffee Pot Metal Tip Spout. These pots are free pour and have a knob or sunken locking cover. The bottom mark is H-4.

Coffee Princess / Coffee Queen / Coffee Empress

Sizes:

4 cup, 36 ounces brimful, 3.375" high without cover, 4.25" high with cover, 9.5" wide, 4.25" diameter opening for drip, Hall No. 3219

6 cup, 46 ounces brimful, 3.5" high without cover, 4.5" high with cover, 10.375" wide, 5" diameter opening for drip, Hall No. 3220

8 cup, 66 ounces, 4.125" high without cover, 5" high with cover, 11.25" wide, 5.5" diameter opening for drip, Hall No. 3221

Lune Blue Coffee Empress, $35-50.

This series of Tricolator Co., Inc. coffee pots was introduced in the early 1950s. They came with a stylized metal drip. Original packing that came with these coffee pots known as the Royal Family Series refers to the four-cup size as the Princess, the six-cup size as the Coffee Queen, and the eight-cup as the Empress. (Whitmyer, 2001, page 342).

In an advertisement in the November 1951 issue of *Living for Young Homemakers*, the award winning Tricolator coffee maker was offered in six smart decorator shades of Addison gray, cherry red, citron yellow, lune blue, oyster white, and willow green. The pot was advertised as the perfect bridal gift for the bride and perfect coffee for the groom. The coffee pots have also been found in black and may be found in other colors. The bottoms are marked Tricolator Products and/or H-3.

Coffee Urn – Drip-O-Lator

48-Cup Drip-O-lator Glossy Black Coffee Urn, $175-225.

Sizes:

18 cup, warmer 3.5" high, coffee container 8.375" high, drip 5.25" high, total 17.875" high, Hall No. 1056

48 cup, warmer 5.25" high, coffee container 9.75" high, drip 6" high, total 23" high, Hall No. 1054

Enterprise Aluminum Company provided two sizes of commercial urns. The forty-eight-cup urn was introduced in 1934, and the eighteen-cup was introduced in 1936. Hall China provided the vitrified glossy black china coffee container to which Enterprise Aluminum Company provided the brewing basket and heating element.

In a 1940-41 Montgomery Ward catalog, the coffee urn was advertised as easy to use with no bags, sieves, or filter papers. In addition to an electrical burner, natural or artificial gas burners with a Tomlinson gauge were available for the forty-eight-cup urn. The bottom mark is H-3, and both styles are found with a Drip-O-lator label on the heating units.

with a visible Coffelator bottom mark on an unglazed bottom. The embossed bottom mark reads "Patented Coffelator Co., It's In The Bag, Reg. U. S. Pat. Office, Newark, N.J., U.S.A."

Colonial Blue Coffelator, $150-175.

"Colonial" ("Medallion") All-China Drip

Silhouette "Colonial" All-China Drip, ND.

18-Cup Drip-O-lator Glossy Black Coffee Urn, $175-225.

Coffelator

Size:
6 cup, 64 ounces brimful, 5" high without cover, 6.25" high with cover, 9.75" wide, 4.125" diameter opening for drip, Hall No. 5028

The Coffelator Company commissioned Hall China in 1939 to make this coffee pot using their design. Hall was not the exclusive maker of this style of coffee pot for Coffelator. According to an advertisement referenced in Harvey Duke's *HALL 2*, page 38, the Coffelator was available in six colors: Chinese red, colonial blue (cobalt), delphinium, emerald, tangerine, and yellow ivory. The coffee pot may be found in other colors. The Coffelators produced by Hall will be found in the high-white clay used in their manufacture and

Size:
6 cup, 52 ounces brimful, 5.25" high without drip or cover, 11" high with drip and cover, 8.25" wide, 3.625" diameter opening for drip, Hall No. 88S

In 1933 the "Colonial" All-China Drip was made in Silhouette for the Hellick Coffee Company of Easton, Pennsylvania. The bottom mark is HSQK. The Silhouette "Colonial" All-China Drip was advertised in a Hellick Coffee Co.'s *Home Service News*. "For those who prefer a stoneware or china coffee-pot. Matches our other items in the same ware. And the lower section can be used as a tea-pot. Two items in one."

A customer would earn 125 advertising credits for the purchase of the Hall China Dripper. A matching creamer and covered sugar were also advertised in the catalog, and a customer was awarded forty points for the purchase.

The "Colonial" style is similar to the "Medallion" style but without a medallion in the band around the pot.

"Colonial" ("Medallion")

Crocus "Colonial," $85-100.

Size:
8 cup, 64 ounces brimful, 6" high without cover, 7.25" high with cover, 10.25" wide, 3.75" diameter opening for drip, Hall No. 236X

Older decorations:
Crocus, "Shrub Rose Garland"

The free pour "Colonial" coffee pot was introduced in the early 1930s and made for the Enterprise Aluminum Company. It is an eight-cup coffee pot made for use with a metal drip top. The "Colonial" coffee pots are found with the Drip-O-lator bottom mark.

The "Colonial" style is similar to the "Medallion" style but without a medallion in the band around the pot.

"Colonial Tall" ("Medallion")

"Green Poppy" "Colonial Tall," $180-220.

Size:
10 cup, 80 ounces brimful, 7" high without cover, 8.625" high with cover, 9.625" wide, 4.5" diameter opening for drip, Hall No. 89X

Older decorations:
"Green Poppy," "Mums," Silhouette

The "Colonial Tall" coffee pot was introduced in the early 1930s. It is an ten-cup coffee pot made for use with a metal drip top. The "Colonial Tall" coffee pots are found with the Drip-O-lator, HSQK bottom marks, or without a bottom mark.

The "Colonial" style is similar to the "Medallion" style but without a medallion in the band around the pot.

"Corrie"

Yellow "Corrie," $60-75.

Size:
4 cup, 44 ounces brimful, 5" high without cover, 6.25" high with cover, 8.75" wide, 3.75" diameter opening for drip

The "Corrie" is a twelve-panel coffee pot that has been seen in canary, orchid, stock green, and warm yellow. Other colors are probably available. The bottom mark is HALL incised and/or H-3. The Warm Yellow "Corrie" has Dec. T-142 on the bottom representing the matte art glaze color number. The pot has not been found with decal decorations.

Cube

Indian Red Art Deco Cube, $110-130.

Size:
2 cup, 11 ounces brimful, 4.25" high, 3" diameter, Hall No. 167

The Cube coffee pot was introduced in 1928, two years after the Cube teapot. It is taller than the teapot and was made under the same patent as the Cube teapot. Other companies besides Hall made this shape coffee pot. The Cube coffee pot was listed in a Hall's catalog until the mid-1970s.

The Cube coffee pot is found in a variety of colors; many of them are matte art glaze colors with and without trim. The bottom mark reads: "The CUBE, Reg. Trade Mark, Reg. No. 693783, Brits Pats 110951 & 258456 AND ABROAD U.S.A. Pat. 1380066-21 and 1599957-26, Cube Teapots Ltd., Leicester." The Hall-produced Cube coffee pots have HALL impressed on the bottom. Matching creamer, sugar, and trays were also available.

"Daniel" ("Rickson")

Red Poppy "Daniel," $40-55.

Size:
8 cup, 80 ounces brimful, 6.375" high without cover, 7.875" high with cover, 10.125" wide, 4.125" diameter opening for drip, Hall No. 3092

Older decorations:
Red Poppy, "Mums," solid colors, "Tulip"

The "Daniel" coffee pot and matching creamer and sugar were introduced in 1935 in Red Poppy. The pieces were made for the Grand Union Company and will have HSQK for the bottom mark.

Available in two sizes, the "Daniel" is also advertised in a 1940-41 Montgomery Ward catalog with a glass dripper and heating element. The pot is described as an automatic electric drip coffee maker. All that was necessary to make coffee was to add the coffee grinds, cold water, and plug in the coffee pot. When the water had

Automatic Electric Drip Coffee Maker

Perfect French Drip Coffee $5.45 6-cup
• Perfect Coffee from COLD Water in Six to Ten Minutes
Ⓚ All you do is measure coffee, pour in cold water and plug it in. When coffee has dripped through, current shuts off. Serve from Ivory Hall China pot (heat-proof). Upper bowl crystal clear glass. Instructions, cord, plug. Any 110-120-volt A.C. or D.C. *App. by Underwriters.* Ship. wts. 7 lbs. and 8 lbs.
86B4875—30-oz. (6 6-oz. cups)$5.45
86B4876—48-oz. (8 6-oz. cups) 6.45

dripped through, the current would shut off. Then the hot coffee is served in a Hall China "Daniel" coffee pot. We have not found more than the one size "Daniel." The ounces listed in the measurements are brimful and do not allow space for the drip that takes up the upper third of the pot body.

The "Daniel" has been found in "Mums" and "Tulip" decals without a bottom mark. In 1940 the "Daniel" was made with a revised handle and referred to by collectors as the "Beaver Falls."

"Dart" ("Russell")

"Pink Rose" "Dart," $65-80.

Size – Enterprise Aluminum Company:
8 cup, 66 ounces brimful, 6.5" high without cover, 7.5" high with cover, 8.125" wide, 3.625" diameter opening for drip, Hall No. 3036

Size - Forman:
8 cup, 64 ounces brimful, 6.625" high without cover, 7.25" high with cover, 8.25" wide, 3.75" diameter opening for drip, Hall No. 3036

Older decorations:
Enterprise Aluminum Company – "Pink Rose"
Forman Family Company – Fuji, solid colors

Fuji "Dart," $60-75.

The "Dart" has three flutes on each side of the coffee pot and was first made for the Forman Family, Inc. in the early 1930s. It was available in solid colors or with the Fuji decal. The bottom mark is Forman Family.

In the 1950s the shape was also used by the Enterprise Aluminum Company and distributed with the "Pink Rose" decal. These pots will have the Drip-O-lator bottom mark. There are matching creamers and sugars for the "Dart" coffee pots.

"Dave"

Lettuce "Dave," $80-95.

Size:
3 cup, 26 ounces brimful, 3.5" high without cover, 4.75" high with cover, 7.25" wide, 3.375" diameter for drip

The "Dave" is a collector-named coffee pot that was produced for the Tricolator Company. It comes with a locking screw cover as shown. It is found in a variety of solid colors but has not been found with a decal decoration. Other sizes may have been produced. The bottom marks are Tricolator Pour Right and HALL incised.

"Deca-Flip"

Size:
8 cup, 88 ounces brimful, 5.75" high without cover, 7.125" high with cover, 11.75" wide, 4.125" diameter opening for drip

Red, White Accent, and Platinum Trim "Deca-Flip," $65-80.

The "Deca-Flip" is a ten-paneled coffee pot and was introduced during the late 1930s. It is usually found in the color combinations shown and has a bottom mark of HSQK. The white, red accents, and platinum trim "Deca-Flip" is referred to as the inverse version. "This inverse version has been found in an original box that indicates it was a premium for the Cook Coffee Co. (Whitmyer, Margaret and Kenn, 2001, page 308)

The "Deca-Flip" has a tab mark on the cover. This coffee pot is confused with the "Perk." One of the major differences between the two pots is the plain handle on the "Perk."

White, Red Accent, and Platinum Trim "Deca-Flip," $70-85.

"Deco"

Crocus "Deco," ND.

Size:
6 cup, 68 ounces brimful, 5.125" high without cover, 6.25" high with cover, 10.75" width, 3.5" diameter opening for drip

There is very little known about the "Deco" coffee pot. It has only been found with the Crocus decal. There are three ribs around the shoulder, cover, and three steps on the round handle. Most Crocus decorated pots are trimmed with platinum; however, this one only has the decal. The "Deco" is found without a bottom mark.

Demi Coffee Pot

Blue Belle Demi Coffee Pot, $90-110.

Size:
4 cup, 26 ounces brimful, 6.375" high without cover, 7.5" high with cover, 6.875" wide, strainer, Hall No. 3322

Older decorations:
Blue Belle with Blue or Pink Flowers, Buttercup with Blue or Yellow Flowers, Christmas Tree, Golden Glo, Holly, Silver Glo, solid colors, White Bake Ware

Other treatment:
Metal Clad

The Demi Coffee Pot was introduced in 1951, modeled after the Enterprise Aluminum Company coffee pot known by collectors as the "#2 Coffee Shape." The Demi server was used as part of a coffee set that was advertised in the 1952 Jewel Tea catalog along with the No. 1 Tea Set. The coffee set consisted of eleven pieces – a coffee server, open sugar, creamer, four cups, and four party plates. The set was called the No. 2 Coffee Set and advertised with coin gold lines and traces furnished in Buttercup with blue (Dec. 80-B) or yellow (Dec. 80-Y) flowers and in Blue Belle with blue (Dec. 80-B) or pink (Dec. 80-P) flowers. The bottom mark is "Hall China, Set No. 2" followed by the color and flower.

The Demi Coffee Pot was used in the Christmas dinnerware lines and was decorated with a Christmas Tree or Holly decal. The bottom mark on these coffee pots is HD.

Later the Demi Coffee Pot was available as part of the White Bake Ware line, and also in Golden Glo and Silver Glo. The bottom mark on the Golden Glo Demi Coffee Pot is "Golden Glo, H-3, Warranted 22 Carat Gold." The Silver Glo may not be marked.

"Devon"

Size:
8 cup, 74 ounces brimful, 5" high without cover, 6.5" high with cover, 11.5" wide, 3.625" diameter opening for drip

The "Devon" is usually found in ivory without decoration, but it has been found with an after-market decoration of roses and gold trim. The "Devon" is usually found without a bottom mark.

Ivory "Devon," $70-85.

"Drape" ("Swathe")

Size:
6 cup, 62 ounces brimful, 5.125" high without cover, 6.75" high with cover, 11.125" wide, 3.75" diameter opening for drip

The "Drape" was made for the Enterprise Aluminum Company and has the Drip-O-lator bottom mark. The design is suggestive of the Parade teapot but with a different cover and much larger. It is usually found in white with the mini-floral decal along the top ridge.

"Mini-Floral" "Drape," $40-60.

"Duse"

Size – Enterprise Aluminum Company:
6 cup, 58 ounces brimful, 7.625" high without cover, 8.5" high with cover, 8.375" wide, 3.5" diameter opening for drip, Hall No. 3026

Size – Forman Family, Inc.:
6 cup, 48 ounces brimful, 7.25" high without cover, 8.25" high with cover, 8.5" wide, 3.625" diameter opening for drip, Hall No. 3026

Older decorations:
Enterprise Aluminum Company – solid colors, "Yellow Tulip"
Forman Family, Inc. – "Apple Blossom," Fuji, solid colors

"Yellow Tulip" "Duse," $65-80.

The "Duse" was first introduced for the Forman Family, Inc. in 1933. It is found with the "Apple Blossom" or Fuji decals trimmed in black, and the coffee pot has the Forman Family bottom mark.

In 1950 the Enterprise Aluminum Company used the same shape, and the coffee pot has the Drip-O-lator bottom mark. It has been found in solid colors and with the "Yellow Tulip" decal. There are matching creamer and sugar for both the Drip-O-lator and the Forman coffee pots.

"Apple Blossom" "Duse," $70-85.

"Dutch" with China and Metal Cover

"Christopher" "Dutch," $125-150.

Size:
6 cup, 48 ounces brimful, 5.875" high without cover, 7.625" high with cover, 10.5" wide, 3.625" diameter opening for drip

Older decorations:
"Christopher," "Chrysler," "Eden Bird," Fuji, "Oriental Butterfly" (See Forman Section for additional decorations)

"Oriental Butterfly" "Dutch," $125-150.

The "Dutch" is an eight-sided coffee pot made for the Forman Family. It is similar to the Bride coffee pot, but the china cover on the "Dutch" fits on top of the pot rather than inside the rim. The "Dutch" also comes with a metal cover with a basket rather than a china cover. It is interesting that the pot is marked on the bottom with Drip-a-Drop Coffee, yet it has a strainer like the teapots. There is a matching creamer and covered sugar.

The bottom mark reads, "Drip-A-Drop Coffee Pot made by Forman Bros. Inc., Brooklyn, N.Y., Patent 1,792,218."

E-Style All-China Drip

Mount Vernon E-Style All-China Drip, $100-125.

Size:
6 cup, 64 ounces brimful, 5.75" high without drip or cover, 11.5" high with drip and cover, 10.125" wide, 3.875" diameter opening for drip, Hall No. 1464

The E-Style All-China Drip was designed by J. Palin Thorley, introduced in early 1942, and available through the 1950s. It was sold through Sears, Roebuck, and Co. as a matching piece to the Mount Vernon Granitone dinnerware and is trimmed in gold. The matching creamer and sugar were sold with the all-china coffee as a set for $4.65. The coffee pot has not been found in any other decoration. The bottom mark is shown.

Eastern

Green Eastern, $15-25.

Size:
1 large cup, 9 ounces brimful, 3.875" high without cover, 4.5" high with cover, 5" wide, Hall No. 48

The Eastern beverage pot was available from the 1920s through the mid-1970s. There is no strainer in the spout, and the Eastern pot is suitable for serving coffee, chocolate, cocoa, hot milk, or hot water. It is usually found in green or brown and has the H-3 or H-4 bottom mark.

Edward Don Beverage Pot

Bone White Edward Don Beverage Pot, $20-35.

Size:
1.5 cup, 12 ounces brimful, 4.625" high, Hall No. 5279

The Edward Don Beverage Pot is part of the Euro Classic line introduced in early 2000. The pot was designed exclusively for Edward Don and Company, a nation-wide distributor of foodservice equipment and supplies. It currently comes only in bone white.

Edward Don Stakups
Metal Tip Spout

Size:
2 cup, 16 ounces brimful, 4.625" high without cover, 5.375" high with cover, 6.875" wide, Hall No. MTS-2572

The metal tip spout Edward Don Stakups beverage pot was introduced in late 1980 and could be used for tea, coffee, or hot chocolate. It was made exclusively for Edward Don and Company. The beverage pot was available in black, bone white, burnt orange, cadet, green, lemon yellow, Lenox brown, lettuce, maroon, and sandust. The bottom mark reads Don Stakups© by HALL®.

Left:
Black Edward Don StakUps
Metal Tip Spout, $20-35.

Electrodrip All-China Drip

"Floral Garland" Electrodrip, $150-175.

Size:
6 cup, 56 ounces brimful, 7.375" high without drip or cover, 12.75" high with drip and cover, 8.5" wide, 3.625" diameter opening for drip, Hall No. 1460

Hall China started production of this style coffee pot in 1941. The coffee pot style was marked as discontinued in 1958 in Hall's records. Hall China made the body, cover, water container, and spreader for Robeson Rochester of Rochester, New York. The bottom of the body of the coffee pot has a ridge to lock into a metal heater. The metal heater bottom reads: "Robeson Rochester Corp.; Rochester, NY. Royal Rochester, Pat. Appld. for; Electrodrip; Cat. No. 10996-A, C3; 110-120; 100W." This pot is almost identical to a pot produced for Robeson Rochester Corp. by Fraunfelter, having the "Fraunfelter" or "Ohio Potteries" bottom mark. Fraunfelter owned Ohio Potteries.

In August 1941, the same cover, spreader, body style without heater, and water container minus lugs were used for the Jewel Tea Company and called the "Jordan" All-China Drip coffee pot.

Electromatic Coffeemaker ("Big Boy")

Maroon and Platinum Trim Electromatic Coffeemaker, $35-45.

Size:
8 cup, 94 ounces brimful, 5.5" high without cover, 6.75" high with cover, 10" wide, 4.5" diameter opening for drip

Maroon and Platinum Trim Electromatic Coffeemaker with Electric Drip, $75-95.

The Electromatic has only been seen in maroon with platinum trim and has the HSQK bottom mark. The Electromatic Coffeemaker is frequently found with a metal basket attached to an Electromatic heating unit. Ads for the Electromatic Coffeemaker say, "Scientifically designed instrument heats water drop by drop – thereby making sure that every drop is just the right temperature as it passes through the coffee grounds." Another advantage is that the method is "Economical … You get all the rich flavor from the coffee, giving you more coffee per pound … better flavor … perfect every time. Convenient … Put your Electromatic right on the table; it makes your coffee while you're making toast. Or your husband can plug it in when he starts to shave and have piping hot coffee when he's finished." In February 1942, Patent No. 2272471 was issued to Earl M. Miller, inventor of the heating element.

Encore ("Crown" and "Wilson") – Undecorated

Brown with White Knob One-Gallon Encore, $45-60.

Sizes:
8 cup, 58 ounces brimful, 5.5" high without cover, 7.25" high with cover, 8.875" wide, 3.625" diameter opening for drip
1 gallon, 130 ounces brimful, 7" high without cover, 8.75" high with cover, 12.375" wide, 5" diameter opening for drip

Two sizes of the Encore coffee pot were made by Hall China for the Tricolator Company in the twenties. Collectors have referred to these pots as the "Wilson" and the "Crown."

In the Tricolator catalogs, these undecorated coffee pots are referred to as Encore, and the decorated pots are referred to as Erie. Both sizes of the Encore have the patented Tricolator spout. The larger Encore coffee pot has recesses around the bottom, whereas the smaller one does not.

The larger Encore is shown in a Tricolator catalog with a large metal drip that will work with any drip coffee pot. Tricolator Company called the drip mechanism the Crown.

The Encore has been found in black, brown, cobalt, and green with the upper half of the knob in white. The bottom marks are HALL incised, H-3, or Tricolator. This same coffee pot without the patented Tricolator spout is referred to as the "Wilson."

Erie ("Crown" or "Wilson") – Decorated

Sizes:
8 cup, 58 ounces brimful, 5.5" high without cover, 7.25" high with cover, 8.875" wide, 3.625" diameter opening for drip
1 gallon, 130 ounces brimful, 7" high without cover, 8.75" high with cover, 12.375" wide, 5" diameter opening for drip

In the 1930s the Tricolator Company advertised an Erie coffee pot that was a decorated version of the Encore. The only three known decorations are the French Flower, a potted flower, and a floral decoration shown in the Tricolator section of this book. The Erie has the Tricolator bottom mark.

French Flower Erie, ND.

White Ever Fresh, $65-80.

Ever Fresh Coffee – Short

Size:
6 cup, 42 ounces brimful, 5.375" high, 5.5" wide, Hall No. 1405

The Ever Fresh Coffee Pot is one of two coffee pots produced for the Wood Manufacturing Company in September 1981. Koenig Coffee Company, Cincinnati, Ohio, produced "Ever Fresh" coffee. The coffee pot has only been found in white with the letters "EF" on the side. The Ever Fresh Coffee Pot has a locking cover. The bottom mark is H-4.

White Ever Fresh, $65-80.

Ever Fresh Coffee – Tall

Size:
8 cup, 64 ounces brimful, 7.5" high, 8.25" wide, Hall No. 1403

The Ever Fresh coffee pot with a locking cover was made in May 1981 for the Wood Manufacturing Company. The coffee pot has only been found in white with the letters "EF" on the side and the H-4 bottom mark. Koenig Coffee Company, Cincinnati, Ohio, produced "Ever Fresh" coffee.

"Five Band" ("Banded") – Partial Tab Cover

Size:
8 cup, 78 ounces brimful, 6.125" high without cover, 7.5" high with cover, 12.625" high with glass drip and cover, 10.75" wide, 3.875" diameter opening for drip

Older decorations:
Crocus, Silhouette with and without glass drip

This "Five Band" coffee pot is referred to as having a partial tab cover since the knob on the cover does not go across the entire cover. It is similar to the "Five Band 'D' Handle," but the opening for the drip is smaller and the handle has a flat top. The partial tab cover "Five Band" coffee pot does not have a strainer. The bottom mark found is HSQK.

This coffee pot will be found with and without the glass drip. The aluminum heater with the glass drip reads, "Electric Automatic Coffee Brewer, Mfg'd. by R. W. Pinckney Inc. Chicago, 625 Watts, Pat. No. 2215837, 110 Volts, A.C. Only, Do not immerse in water." The patent for the coffee maker was issued on September 24, 1940, to Robert W. Pinckney, Elmhurst, Illinois. As cold water placed in the drip passed through the heating element, the water temperature was raised to boiling temperature before passing over and through the coffee grounds. Essentially the water passed through the grounds one drop at a time.

Silhouette "Five Band" – Body and Cover, $60-70; with Glass Heater, $200-250.

"Five Band" ("Banded") Carafe

Chinese Red "Five Band" Carafe, $300-325.

Size:
8 cup, 68 ounces brimful, 7.25" high without cover, 8.75" high with cover, 7.625" wide

Older decorations:
Red Kitchenware, solid colors

The "Five Band" Carafe is part of the "Five Band" kitchenware line that Hall China introduced in 1935. The carafe is found in solid colors and with the bottom mark of HSQK.

"Five Band 'D' Handle" ("Banded")

Blue Bouquet "Five Band 'D' Handle," $80-100.

Size:
8 cup, 74 ounces brimful, 6.25" high without cover, 7.5" high with cover, 10.5" wide, 4.25" diameter opening for drip

Older decorations:
Blue Bouquet, Cactus, Silhouette

There are two styles of the "Five Band" coffee pot. They were both introduced in the late 1930s. Notice that the cover on the "Five Band 'D' Handle" coffee pot has a knob on the cover that extends the full width of the cover. Also note that the handle on the "Five Band 'D' Handle" is round, whereas the partial tab cover "Five Band" has a resting place for the server's thumb. The pot is classified as a coffee pot, but it has been found with and without a strainer. This goes against the general rule that only teapots have strainers. The bottom mark is HSQK.

Flare-Ware Coffee Server

Size:
15 cup, 104 ounces brimful, 7.75" high without cover, 9.5" high with cover, 11.125" wide, Hall No. 1755

Older decorations:
Autumn Leaf, Gold Lace, Heather Rose with Gold Lace, Radial

The Flare-Ware Coffee Server was introduced in 1961 by Hall China as part of the "Modern 61" series. The coffee server came complete with a brass warmer including a candle. The bottom mark is "Flare-Ware by HALL CHINA, Made in US.A." The Autumn Leaf (Autumn Leaves) pattern found on the Flare-Ware pieces differs from the one used by the Jewel Tea Company.

Gold Lace Flare-Ware Coffee Server, $40-55.

Flare-Ware Coffee Urn

Size:
15 cup, 96 ounces brimful, 7.5" high without cover, 8.875" high with cover, 7.5" wide, Hall No. 1759

Older decorations:
Autumn Leaf, Gold Lace, Radial

The Flare-Ware Coffee Urn came complete with a faucet, trivet, candleholder, and candle. It was produced in the 1960s by Hall China. The bottom mark is "Flare-Ware by HALL CHINA, Made in U.S.A." The Autumn Leaf (Autumn Leaves) is not the same as the decoration used on the Jewel Tea Company products.

Autumn Leaf Flare-Ware Coffee Urn, $60-75.

Flared Tabletop
Beverage Pot

Size:
2 cup, 14 ounces brimful, 5" high without cover, 5.625" high with cover, 5.625" wide, Hall No. 836

The Flared Tabletop Beverage Pot was introduced in 1989 and available in the Hall catalogs through 1996. It was available in black, bone white, cascade green, cobalt blue, daffodil, lune blue, maroon, oxford gray, and pink orchid. It is found with the H-4 bottom mark. A matching sugar packet holder and two sizes of open creamers were available.

Forman Carafe

Size:
6 cup, 52 ounces brimful, 9.125" high, 5.5" wide

Black with Greek Key Forman Carafe, $45-55.

Left:
Bone White Flared Tabletop
Beverage Pot, $30-45.

This carafe was made for the Forman Family, Inc. and has been found with a metal cover and metal stand that holds a candle warmer. The Carafe has been found in black, pink, turquoise, white, and yellow solid colors and with the Greek Key decal. The bottom mark is Forman Family.

Black with Greek Key Forman Carafe with Stand, $55-70.

Four-Matic (4-Matic)
Electric Percolator

Size:
6 - 8 cup, 80 ounces brimful, 10.5" high without cover, 11.25" high with cover, 9.5" wide, Hall No. 5205

The Four-Matic (4-Matic) Electric Percolator was made for the Forman Family in black, pink, turquoise, white, or yellow solid colors and with the Greek Key decal and in Silver Glo. The percolator was sold with a creamer, sugar, and tray. The creamer and sugar have slide-on and slide-off metal covers. The matching pieces for the pink came in solid copper, for the turquoise in chromium, and for the yellow in solid brass. The bottom mark reads "115 Volts, 400 Watts, Cat. No. 400 – FORMAN 4 FAMILY – If percolator fails to heat, remove this base plate and replace fuse." The coffee pot was also sold with a Hall China bottom plate rather than the Forman bottom plate.

Yellow Four-Matic (4-Matic) Electric Percolator, $65-85.

French Coffee Biggin
(French Drip Coffee Maker)

Two-Tone Citron and Mahogany Six-Cup French Coffee Biggin, $85-110.

Sizes:
3 cup, 16 ounces brimful, 3" high without cover, 7.75" high with drip and cover, 6.5" wide, Hall No. 84
4 cup, 28 ounces brimful, 3.625" high without cover, 5.25" high with cover, 7.625" wide, Hall No. 84.5
5 or 6 cup, 32 ounces brimful, 3.75" high without cover, 9.875" high with drip and cover, 8.75" wide, Hall No. 85
9 or 10 cup, 58 ounces brimful, 4.625" high without cover, 11.5" high with drip and cover, 10" wide, Hall No. 86

Older decorations:
Blue Blossom (2 cup), Blue Garden (4 cup), "Floral Lattice" (2, 6, and 10 cup), French Flower, Golden Glo (all sizes), Matte Gold (10 cup), Red Kitchenware, Russet, solid colors, Two-Tone (4, 6, and 10 cup), White Bake Ware (all sizes), "Wild Poppy" (3, 4, and 6 cup)

The French Coffee Biggin was introduced in 1930 in the three, five, and nine-cup sizes. The Hall China catalog says, "These All China Drip Coffee Biggins brew clear, delicious coffee by the drip method. Fine grain steel cut coffee is placed (one tablespoon for each cup) in the biggin. The china spreader is then put in place and vigorously boiling water poured slowly into the biggin. The resultant cups of coffee are free from the injurious acids present in boiled coffee." The coffee pot advertised consisted of two sections, cover fits both top and bottom. The upper section had a fine drainer and water spreader.

In 1935 the French Coffee Biggin could be ordered in blue, cadet, canary, emerald, lettuce, marine, maroon, orchid, pink, rose, tan, violet, and yellow. The coffee pot was shown listed in the 1937 Hall China special catalog in the Delphinium Blue Cooking Ware section.

In the early fifties the coffee pot was shown on the Two-Tone and Famous White Bake Ware Hall Product Sheets. Filter papers were listed along with the French Coffee Biggin in the 1956 catalog. The coffee pot last appeared in a 1964 Hall catalog. It was advertised as a drip pot providing from three to ten cups, and could be used in the kitchen, or to dramatize coffee preparation and service in the dining room. The bottom marks found are H-3, HSQK, or without any mark.

"Gardiner" ("Corydon")

Size:
6 cup, 32 ounces brimful, 5.75" high without cover, 11.25" high with cover, 7.5" wide

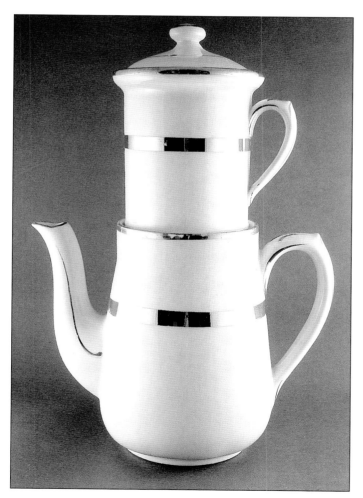

White and Platinum Trim "Gardiner"
Coffee Pot, $160-200.

The "Gardiner" coffee pot is an unusual style drip-coffee pot that has been found in brown, cobalt, green, or white with platinum trim. The coffee pot has the H-2 bottom mark. Around the rim of the drip that fits inside the bottom reads "The Gardiner Co., Inc., New Orleans, U.S.A., Patd. Aug. 30, '21, Others pending." U.S. Patent 1389299 was issued on August 30, 1921, for a drip-coffee pot to Edwin Samuel Gardiner, New Orleans, Louisiana.

An objective of the design was to provide a drip coffee pot that made it easy to adjust to the thickness of the coffee grounds by using perforated disks. Two of the disks were placed in the drip, then the coffee, and then two more disks were placed above the coffee. Boiling water was then poured into the drip portion of the coffee pot. The design allowed for easy cleaning of the parts after the coffee was made.

"Gibson" Electric Percolator and Urn

Size – Percolator:
8 cup, 72 ounces brimful, 11.875" high without cover, 12.5" high with cover, 8.75" wide

Fuji "Gibson" Electric Urn, $80-95; Percolator, $70-85.

Size – Urn:
8 cup, 72 ounces brimful, 11.25" high without cover, 14.25" high with cover, 8.75" wide

Older decorations:
"Apple Blossom" (two variations), Fuji, "Oriental Butterfly," "Tree of Life"

Hall China Company made the china bodies for the electric coffee urn and percolator. Forman Family, Inc. added the electrical components and lids. This style coffee pot and urn were probably made in the mid-1930s. The "Gibson" electric percolator and urn came with matching creamer and covered sugar.

Note in the picture the grooved arches across the body, and that the coffee and urn have different glass knobs in the metal covers. The bottom mark reads: "115 Volts, 150 Watts, Chromium Plated Ware, Forman Bros., Inc., Brooklyn, New York, To avoid damage to heating unit – Do not set article in water."

Great American
("Golden Key")

"Orange Poppy" Great American, $50-65.

Size:
9 cup, 86 ounces brimful, 6.5" high without cover, 9.625" high with cover, 10.25" wide, 3.625" diameter opening for drip, Hall No. 3072

Older decoration:
"Orange Poppy"

The Great American coffee pot, with matching creamer and covered sugar, was produced for the Great American Tea Company in the mid-1930s. The bottom mark is HSQK. Two years later the S-Handle coffee pot replaced the Great American coffee pot.

A Great American style coffee pot with "a profusion of beautiful, delicate lavender flowers and gold trim" was reported in the March 1987 issue of *The Glaze*. This decal and "Orange Poppy" are the only two that are known.

Hallcraft
Tomorrow's Classic

Hi-White Hallcraft Tomorrow's Classic, $125-175.

Size:
6 cup, 41 ounces brimful, 8.75" high, 6.875" wide

Older decorations:
Arizona, Bouquet, Buckingham, Caprice, Dawn, Fantasy, Flair, Frost Flowers, Harlequin, Golden Glo, Hi-White, Holiday, Lyric, Mulberry, Peach Blossom, Pinecone, Romance, Satin Black, Satin Gray, Spring, Studio 10

Hallcraft Tomorrow's Classic was designed by Eva Zeisel in 1949 for the Midhurst China Company and produced by the Hall from 1951 through 1958. The coffee pot was produced in a wide variety of decals with matching creamer and covered sugar. The bottom mark is "Hallcraft by Eva Zeisel."

The only decorations for this coffee pot that were specifically attributed to Eva Zeisel are the Hi-White, Satin Gray, and Satin Black. A coffee pot has been found in the after-market decoration of "Surf Ballet." Additional coffee pots may be found in Palo Duro, Prairie Grass, and Rain Tree decorations. Refer to the Eva Zeisel section for further information.

Heirloom

Size:
8 cup, 56 ounces brimful, 7" high without cover, 9.5" high with cover, 9.125" wide

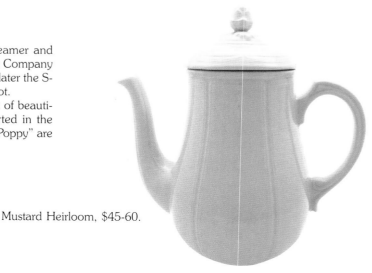

Mustard Heirloom, $45-60.

Older decorations:
Christmas, Colonial White, solid colors

The Heirloom coffee pot, with matching creamer and covered sugar, was patterned after a French ironstone design and introduced in the mid-1950s by the Midhurst China Company. Heirloom coffee pots were available in blue, two shades of green, mustard, pale pink, and white. The coffee pot is part of a dinnerware set and has the Hallcraft Heirloom bottom mark. Some of the pieces will be found unmarked.

In the 1960s Hall used the Heirloom shape for the Liberty Hall coffee pot made for the Block China Company. The coffee pot was available in Colonial White. The bottom mark is a circle with a bee in the center and around the outside is "Liberty Hall Ironstone made in America." The Colonial White Heirloom has also been found with the H-4 bottom mark.

A unique Christmas decal was used on the Heirloom coffee pot, creamer, and sugar; and the set was sold at the Hall Closet.

Hi-Tech™ Metal Tip Spout Beverage Pot

White Hi-Tech Metal Tip Spout Beverage Pot, $30-45.

Size:
1.5 cup, 16 ounces brimful, 3.75" high without cover, 4.25" high with cover, 7" wide, Hall No. MTS-2940

In 1981 Hall China created Hi-Tech tableware, designed exclusively for ABC Affiliated Distributors, Inc. The beverage pot and matching handled creamer and open sugar were available for delivery in bone white and Lenox brown. These items could be special ordered in other colors. The bottom mark is the H-4 in a large circle with Hi-Tech, 1981 below and ABC Triple Checked Approved. The trademark for Hi-Tech was first used in July 1981 and registered in October 1985. It is still an active trademark.

Hot Beverage Pot – Tray Service

Size:
1.5 cup, 14 ounces brimful, 3.125" high without cover, 3.75" high with cover, 6.125" wide, Hall No. 1740

The Hot Beverage Pot was designed for use in the food service industry to conserve tray space and to provide portion control. It was advertised for use in college dining rooms, hospitals, cafeterias, and other large buffet style dining facilities or where the food was served on a tray.

Sky Blue Hot Beverage Pot – Tray Service, $30-45.

The Hot Beverage Pot and matching covered creamer were available in bone white, sky blue, spring green, and sunlight yellow. The bottom mark is H-4. Note the mark on the cover of the Hot Beverage Pot to indicate the location of the locking tab on the inside of the cover.

"Hoyt R"

Matte Art Glaze Green "Hoyt R," $60-75.

Size:
8 cup, 72 ounces brimful, 6.875" high without cover, 8.25" high with cover, 10.5" wide, 3.625" diameter opening for drip

The ten-panel "Hoyt R" is very similar in shape to the Norfolk made for Tricolator, except the "Hoyt R" has a rounded bottom and is larger. It is found in matte art glaze colors with ceramic tiles but may also be found in other solid colors. The bottom marks are H-3 and/or HALL incised. This pot has not been found with decals.

Iconic

Iconic, $30-45. Reprint from a 1964 Hall Catalog

Size:
2 cup, 12 ounces brimful, 4.5" high, Hall No. 1509 (changed to 15 ounces in 1994)

The Iconic coffee pot was introduced in 1964 and available through 1994. It could be ordered in a variety of colors with matching handled and handleless creamers and handleless sugars. The Iconic coffee pot does not have a strainer. The bottom marks found are H-3 or H-4.

"Imperial" ("Clover") with and without All-China Drip

Black and White "Imperial," $50-65.

Size:
8 cup, 64 ounces brimful, 4.75" high without cover or drip, 6" high with cover and without drip, 10.5" high with drip and cover, 10.25" width, 3.75" diameter opening for drip

The "Imperial" without the all-china drip was made for the Tricolator Company in the 1930s. It was available in solid colors, black with a white lid as shown, and with floral decals on an ivory body. The bottom mark is Tricolator. See the Tricolator section for the decals.

The "Imperial" All-China Drip was made a few years later and comes in several solid colors. The all-china drip on the "Imperial" is the same style as the one used on the "Jordan" coffee pot. At first it was thought that this was a marriage of parts, but too many have

showed up for them to not have been made for each other. The bottom mark on the all-china drip "Imperial" is H-3 and/or HALL incised.

Marine "Imperial" All-China Drip, $250-300.

International with and without Metal Tip Spout

Sizes:
1.5 cup, 10 ounces brimful, 3.875" high without cover, 4.25" high with cover, 6.75" wide, Hall No. 2703
2 cup, 14 ounces brimful, 4.75" high without cover, 5.5" high with cover, 7" wide, Hall No. 2704

Size – Modified:
2 cup, 14 ounces brimful, 4.75" high without cover, 5.5" high with cover, 7" wide, Hall No. 1904

Black International and White with Green Cover Modified International, $30-45 each.

1.5 cup, 10 ounces brimful, 4.5" high with cover, Hall No. MTS-1903
2 cup, 14 ounces brimful, 5.5" high with cover, Hall No. MTS-1904

The two sizes of the International coffee pot were available from 1962 through the mid-1970s in the Hall China catalogs. They could be ordered in green or brown colors that Hall carried in stock. The International items could be special ordered in any of the twenty-five other colors listed in the catalogs. Matching pieces in the International line are a teapot, open sugar, handled creamer, water jug, and a bud vase. The bottom marks are H-3 and H-4. There are two styles of the International, one with a wavy front and back collar edge and the other with straight collar edges.

"Jerry" ("Monarch")

"Floral Lattice" "Jerry," $45-60.

Size:
6 cup, 56 ounces, 5.625" high without cover, 7.125" high with cover, 9.5" wide, 3.75" diameter cover for drip

The "Floral Lattice" decal shown on the "Jerry" is the same that appears on the "Floral Lattice" kitchenware pieces. On the other side of this coffee pot is the flowerpot part of the decal. The "Jerry" is also found with red around the lower bottom of the pot and red on the cover ridges with the rest of the pot and cover being white. This coffee pot was made for the Enterprise Aluminum Company with a Drip-O-lator bottom mark.

"Jordan" All-China Drip
Size:
5 cup, 56 ounces brimful, 6.75" high without drip or cover, 10.75" high with drip and cover, 8.25" wide, 3.75" diameter opening for drip, Hall No. 1461
Older decorations:
Autumn Leaf, Crocus, Morning Glory, Rose Parade, Serenade, solid colors, "Wild Poppy," "Yellow Rose" ("Jordan" top and Kadota All-China Bottom)

The "Jordan" All-China Drip was introduced in 1942 in the Autumn Leaf pattern for the Jewel Tea Company. The coffee pot was patterned after the Electrodrip All-China Drip made for Robeson Rochester Corporation.

"In order to bring out the maximum flavor, yet use less than the usual amount of coffee to brew a cup of normal strength, and also to implement the government's request to conserve coffee and to eliminate the use of metal, Jewel introduced, in 1942, the Hall All-China five-cup capacity maker, No. 325. It was the first reference made to the pattern by name, exclusively Autumn Leaf Pattern." (Miller, 1994, page 189). The bottom mark on the Autumn Leaf "Jordan" All-China Drip is HD-Mary Dunbar.

This pot has also been used with a variety of decals. The bottom marks found are H-3 or HSQK. The upper section of the "Jordan" all-china drip and cover were used with the "Imperial" and "Kadota" coffee pot bottoms.

Rose Parade "Jordan" All-China Drip, ND.

"Kadota" All-China Drip

Homewood "Kadota" All-China Drip, $110-135.

Size:
6 cup, 58 ounces brimful, 5.5" high without drip or cover, 10.5" high with drip and cover, 9.25" wide, 3.75" diameter opening for drip, Hall No. 1463

Older decorations:
Blue Bouquet, Crocus, "Floral Lattice," Homewood, "Parrot Tulip," Serenade, Silhouette, "Stonewall," Tulip, Wildflower, "Yellow Rose" ("Kadota" bottom with "Jordan" all-china drip)

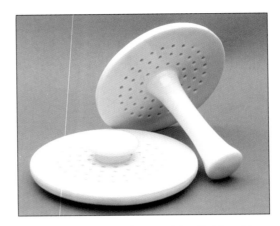

Long and short spreaders used in all-china drips.

The "Kadota" All-China Drip is found in a variety of decals. The coffee pots were made for Hall's kitchenware line and for the Enterprise Aluminum Company. Depending upon the decal, the bottom marks are HSQK or Drip-O-lator. The Tulip "Kadota" All-China Drip is found with gold trim and marked HSQK, but the same pot with the Tulip decal and without gold trim is marked Drip-O-lator. Two different styles of spreaders came with the all-china drips. Some of the all-china drips were sold without spreaders for use with filter papers.

"Kadota"
Large Coffee Base

"Pink and Gray Floral Bouquet" "Kadota"
Large Coffee Base, $45-60.

Size:
8 cup, 68 ounces brimful, 5.875" high without cover, 7.125" high with cover, 9.75" wide, 4" diameter opening for drip

Older decorations:
Golden Oak, "Pink and Gray Floral Bouquet," Springtime, "Yellow Rose"

The "Kadota" large coffee base is a larger version of the bottom part of the "Kadota" All-China Drip. The coffee pot pictured has the HSQK bottom mark. An all-china drip has not been seen to match this size and style coffee pot bottom.

"Lassitter"

Size:
8 cup, 58 ounces brimful, 6.5" high without cover, 8.5" high with cover, 9.5" wide

The twelve-panel "Lassitter" has generally been found in butterscotch or green, but it may show up in other colors. The bottom mark is H-3.

Green "Lassitter," $45-60.

"Lewis"

"Three Poppies" "Lewis," $40-55.

Size:
6 cup, 62 ounces brimful, 5.5" high without cover, 6.75" high with cover, 10.5" wide, 4.5" diameter opening for drip

The "Lewis" coffee pot was made for the Enterprise Aluminum Company and has the Drip-O-lator bottom mark. A metal drip was used with the pot. "Three Poppies" is the only decal found thus far.

"Lotus"

"Impatiens" "Lotus," $40-55.

Size:
6 cup, 52 ounces brimful, 4.375" high without cover, 6.875" high with cover, 9.75" wide, 3.5" diameter opening for drip

The "Lotus" coffee pot was made for the Enterprise Aluminum Company and has the Drip-O-lator bottom mark. A metal drip was used with the pot. "Impatiens" is the only decal found thus far on the "Lotus."

"Medallion" ("Colonial") All-China Drip

Size:
6 cup, 52 ounces brimful, 5.375" high without drip or cover, 11" high with drip and cover, 8.25" wide, 3.625" diameter opening for drip, Hall No. 88

Older decorations:
Red Kitchenware, solid colors

The "Medallion" All-China Drip was advertised in the 1935 Hall catalog and identified as a "Drip Coffee." It was available in green or brown; but, for an additional cost, the all-china drip could be ordered in black, blue, cadet, canary, emerald, gray, green lustre, ivory, lettuce, marine, maroon, orchid, pink, rose, tan, violet, and yellow. Filter papers were to be used with the coffee pot.

The "Medallion" All-China Drip also appeared in a 1935 *Hall China Special Catalog No. 35* in lettuce green. Two years later the coffee pot was listed as part of the Delphinium Blue Kitchenware pattern with white glaze inside the pieces. Chinese red was added to the kitchenware line, and the "Medallion" All-China Drip will be found in this color. The bottom marks are H-3 or HSQK.

"Meltdown"

Size:
8 cup, 80 ounces brimful, 5.75" high without cover, 7.5" high with cover, 10.75" wide, 4.25" diameter opening for drip

Older decorations:
#488; Crocus; "Mums;" Red, Ivory or White Accents, and Platinum Trim

The "Meltdown" is found in the color combination shown and in several decals. It may be found with other colored bottoms, such as black, blue, green, or yellow. The bottom mark on the colored bottom "Meltdown" is Drip-O-lator. A matching red and white with platinum trim creamer and sugar set has been found marked with HSQK. The decaled pieces will have either Drip-O-lator or HSQK bottom marks.

Red, White Accents, and Platinum Trim "Meltdown," $50-65.

Left:
Lettuce Green "Medallion" All-China Drip, $250-300.

Million Dollar Coffee Pot

Marine Million Dollar Coffee Pot, $150-180.

Size:
8 cup, 64 ounces brimful, 6.125" high without cover, 8.5" high with cover, 9.75" wide, 4" diameter opening for drip, Hall No. 5021

In late 1939 the Million Dollar coffee pot was produced exclusively for the F. S. Martin Company of Chicago, Illinois. It has been found in canary, Chinese red, delphinium, emerald, green lustre, Indian red, and marine. The cover has a locking double verge as shown. The coffee filter is cloth attached to a metal frame, making it a reusable filter. The bottom mark is "Million Dollar Coffee Pot – designed and distributed exclusively by F. S. Martin, 1832 Belmont Ave., Chicago." The prices found marked on the bottom have ranged from $1.95 to $7.95. A variation of the bottom mark is an upside-down triangle with Million Dollar Coffee and the price inside.

"MJ" Electric Percolator

"Old Garden Rose" "MJ" Electric Percolator, $85-100.

Size:
8 cup, 74 ounces brimful, 10.625" high without cover, 11.5" high with cover, 8.5" wide, Hall No. 5200

Older decorations:
Autumn Leaf, Bouquet, "Bronze Rose," "Coat of Arms," Game Bird, Gold Deer, Hunting Dog, "Ohio State Seal," "Old Garden Rose," "Pink and Gray Floral Bouquet," RX

After the Porcelier Manufacturing Company of South Greenberg, Pennsylvania, went out of business in 1954, Hall purchased the electrical components for making the electric coffee percolators. They were first introduced in 1957 in the Autumn Leaf decal and discontinued in 1969. Later Ernest Sohn Creations of New York distributed some of the pieces. The "MJ" Electric Percolator is found in several decals. The coffee pot was designed to keep the coffee at the perfect brewing temperature. The bottom reads "Use on AC only, Do not immerse in water, The Hall China Co., East Liverpool, Ohio, 115V, 450W."

National with and
without Metal Tip Spout

Sizes:
1.5 cup, 16 ounces brimful, 4.25" high without cover, 5.25" high with cover, 6" wide, Hall No. 1703 and No. MTS-1703
2 cup, 16 ounces brimful, 4.75" high without cover, 5.5" high with cover, 6.375" wide, Hall No. 1704 and No. MTS-1704

The National coffee pots were listed in the Hall catalogs from 1964 through 1973. They were available in green or brown but could be ordered in a variety of colors. These coffee pots are part of the National Service line that consists of matching teapot and table and service items. Matching handled creamers came in three sizes, and the open sugars came in two sizes. These pieces have the H-3 or H-4 bottom mark.

In the early 1970s Amtrak chose the stock National items to be used in their dining cars. The blue color was especially made for Amtrak and is referred to as Amtrak Blue. The pieces used for Amtrak are either not marked or marked H-4.

White Metal Tip Spout National and Amtrak Blue National, $35-50 each.

New Yorker ("Carraway" Short Spout)

Emerald New Yorker, $60-75.

Sizes:
2 cup, 18 ounces brimful, 3" high without cover, 3.75" high with cover, 6.75" wide, 3.375" diameter opening for drip, Hall No. 3216
3 cup, 24 ounces brimful, 3.25" high without cover, 4.125" high with cover, 7" wide, 3.375" diameter opening for drip, Hall No. 3217
5 cup, 44 ounces brimful, 4.25" high without cover, 5.25" high with cover, 8.625" wide, 3.875" diameter opening for drip, Hall No. 3218
9 cup, 76 ounces brimful, 6.125" high without cover, 7" high with cover, 9.5" wide, 4.125" diameter opening for drip

In the 1930s the Tricolator Company introduced the New Yorker coffee pot at the same time as the Clipper coffee pot. The two coffee pots are very similar in shape with the main difference being the shape of the spout. The Clipper has a long spout, and the New Yorker has a short spout.

The New Yorker coffee pot came in several solid colors and decals. See the Tricolator section for pictures of the decorations. The same floral decal was available on all sizes of the pot. During the 1930s the New Yorker sold for between $2.25 to $4.25 each depending upon the decoration and drip. The New York will have the Pour Right Tricolator mark and/or HALL incised.

"Nolte"
Size:
8 cup, 68 ounces brimful, 6.75" high without cover, 8.875" high with cover, 9.875" wide

The twelve-panel "Nolte" has an H-3 bottom mark and has been found in green and tan.

Green "Nolte," $45-60.

Norfolk ("Hoyt")

Matte Art Glaze Yellow Norfolk, $65-80.

Size:
6 cup, 64 ounces, 6.625" high without cover, 8.25" high with cover, 11" wide, 3.75" diameter opening for drip

Tricolator gave different names to this style coffee pot to distinguish between solid or decorated. The names were Norfolk and Sheridan. The advertisement found does not indicate which name applies to which, thus Norfolk was selected.

The twelve-panel Norfolk is very similar in shape to the "Hoyt R," but the "Hoyt R" is larger and has a rounded bottom. The Norfolk has the Tricolator bottom mark, whereas the "Hoyt R" has the H-3 bottom mark.

The Norfolk is found decorated and in matte art glazes with ceramic tiles. Some of the decorations are shown in the Tricolator section of this book.

"Norse" ("Everson")

"Piggly Wiggly" "Norse," ND.

Size:
8 cup, 80 ounces brimful, 6.875" high without cover, 8" high with cover, 10.625" wide, 4.25" diameter opening for drip
Older decorations:
"Piggly Wiggly," "Yellow Rose"

The "Norse" coffee pot is more often found in the "Yellow Rose" decal with matching creamer and covered sugar. These pieces are marked with HSQK.

The "Norse" coffee pot with the "Piggly Wiggly" decal is marked on the bottom with the Drip-O-lator bottom mark and was made for the Enterprise Aluminum Company.

"Orb"

Size:
8 cup, 76 ounces brimful, 6.5" high without cover, 7.25" high with cover, 10.25" wide, 3.5" diameter opening for drip, Hall No. 3162

The "Orb" coffee pot was made for the Enterprise Aluminum Company in August 1937 and has the Drip-O-lator bottom mark. The round style coffee pot was patterned after the shape of the "Sash" coffee pot but without the band found on the "Sash."

"Panel"

Size:
6 cup, 74 ounces brimful, 6.25" high without cover, 7.75" high with cover, 9.5" wide, 3.75" diameter opening for drip, Hall No. 3176

The "Panel" coffee pot was introduced in late 1939 for the Enterprise Aluminum Company. It has only been found with variations of the decal shown – two or three potted flowers. The bottom mark is Drip-O-lator.

"Potted Flowers" "Panel," $40-55.

Panther ("Ritz")

Size:
6 cup, 64 ounces brimful, 6" high without cover, 8.25" high with cover, 10" wide, 3.625" diameter opening for drip, Hall No. 3018

The Panther or Stag coffee pot was made for the Tricolator Company in 1932. It has been found with a regular and a screw locking cover. Tricolator gave the same coffee pot different names to distinguish the solid or decorated coffee pots and those with a screw locking cover. The advertisement found does not indicate which name applies to which, thus Panther was selected.

The Panther has been found in several solid colors, color combinations, and decorations with silver trim. The color combinations came in a solid jet-black lustre body with a colored tile and cover in

Left:
"Bird of Paradise"
"Orb," $45-60.

blue, green, red, white, or yellow with a black knob. Some of the decorations are shown in the Tricolator section of this book. The Panther has the Tricolator bottom mark, but some are found with HALL incised or H-3.

Yellow Panther, $60-75.

"Perk" ("Deca-Plain")

Size:
6 cup, 64 ounces brimful, 5" high without cover, 6" high with cover, 11.5" wide, 3.875" diameter opening for drip

Older decorations:
"Parrot Tulip;" "Pastel Morning Glory;" Red, White Accents, and Platinum Trim; "Texas Rose;" "Tulip"

The ten-panel "Perk" was available from the late 1930s through the 1950s. The "Perk" has the HSQK bottom mark. The coffee pot also came in green and white accents with platinum trim and matching sugar and creamer. These pieces have the Drip-O-lator bottom mark.

The "Perk" is sometimes confused with the "Deca-Flip" coffee pot. One of the major differences between the two pots is the plain handle on the "Perk." The Cook Coffee Company used the "Perk" with the "Tulip" decal as a premium. Fraunfelter made a coffee pot of similar design and "Tulip" decal that has sixteen panels.

"Texas Rose" "Perk," $45-60.

"Petal"

"Sutter's Gold" "Petal," $50-65.

Sizes:
4 cup
6 cup
8 cup, 78 ounces, 6.5" high without cover, 7.625" high with cover, 11" wide, 4.375" diameter opening for drip

The "Petal" has a debossed rose vine around the upper rim of the pot and flower petals around the lid and the body of the pot. The coffee pot has diagonal lines around its lower portion.

The "Petal" was made for the Enterprise Aluminum Company and has Drip-O-lator as a bottom mark. The decal resembles the "Sutter's Gold" flowering shrub.

The coffee pot comes in three sizes with the two smaller sizes being the hardest to find.

Plaza
("Ansel" / "Suzannah")

Size:
6 cup, 60 ounces brimful, 5.75" high without cover, 6.75" high with cover, 10.25" wide, 3.5" diameter opening for drip

The sixteen-panel Plaza Tricolator was made in a variety of matte art glaze colors and has been found in a tan-lustre with gold striping. This decoration is shown in the Tricolator section.

Matte Art Glaze Nile Green Plaza, $100-125;
Matching Tile, $40-60.

The Plaza coffee pots were also available in ivory with a color combination of blue, green, or red polka dots. In the 1930s the coffee pot sold for $7.50 and included a beautiful matching colored china tile and a packet of 100 filters with directions.

The coffee pot came with a metal drip with a capacity of from four to nine cups. The bottom will have HALL incised and the Tricolator Pour Right mark.

"Radiance" ("Sunshine") All-China Drip

Size:
6 cup, 56 ounces brimful without cover, 5.5" high without drip and cover, 11.625" high with drip and cover, 8" wide, Hall No. 89 (All China); Hall No. 89X (Metal Top Drip)

"Wild Poppy" "Radiance" All-China Drip, $375-425.

Older decorations:
#488, Acacia, Golden Clover, "Parrot Tulip," "Pastel Morning Glory," Red Kitchenware, solid colors, "Stonewall," "Wild Poppy"

The "Radiance" All-China Drip was introduced in the early 1930s as a "Decorated Kitchen Set Coffee Biggin." It was produced for use with and without filter papers.

In 1933 the "Radiance" All-China Drip was made for the Cook Coffee Company for use with a metal drip top. In the Hall China 1937 special catalog, the "Radiance" All-China Drip was listed in the #488 decal and also furnished in delphinium blue. They sold for $25.00 a dozen wholesale.

The coffee pot has been found in numerous other decals. The "Radiance" All-China Drip coffee pot was discontinued in the late 1950s. The bottom mark found is HSQK.

"Ralston"

Green "Ralston," $45-60.

Size:
8 cup, 54 ounces brimful, 6.5" high without cover, 8.875" high with cover, 9.875" wide

The twelve-panel "Ralston" has the Tricolator spout and an H-3 bottom mark. It is usually found in stock green. The shape of this coffee pot is similar to the "Lassitter," which does not have the Tricolator spout.

"Rayed" ("J-Sunshine")

Sizes:
8 cup, 68 ounces brimful, 7.375" high without cover, 9" high with cover, 8" wide, 4.25" diameter opening for drip, Hall No. 3058
10 cup, 94 ounces brimful, 8.375" high without cover, 10" high with cover, 8.5" wide, 4.375" diameter opening for drip, Hall 3052

Autumn Leaf "Rayed," $65-75.

Older decorations:
Autumn Leaf, "Tulip"

The "Rayed" coffee pot was introduced with an open drip in late 1936 exclusively for the Jewel Tea Company in the Autumn Leaf pattern. Because the cover did not fit the drip, a different dripper was designed that could be used with the cover. During the early 1940s, a glass dripper was sold to replace the metal one which had become unavailable because of wartime restrictions on aluminum. In 1953 a round warmer to fit either the "Rayed" coffee pot or the casserole was introduced. A larger size of the coffee pot was introduced in the thirties to fit the West Bend aluminum dripper. Matching creamer and sugar were introduced in 1936 and produced for a short period of time. The bottom mark found is HD-Mary Dunbar. A "Rayed" coffee pot has been found decorated in "Tulip" with gold trim and no bottom mark.

"Rayed"
("J-Sunshine" Long Spout)

Autumn Leaf "Rayed" with glass drip, ND.

Size:
4 cup, 52 ounces brimful, 6.875" high without cover, 8.25" high with cover, 8.25" wide, Hall No. 3056
Older decoration:
Autumn Leaf

The Jewel Tea Company introduced the "Rayed" teapot in 1935. It can serve as a seven-cup teapot or four-cup coffee pot. Metal or glass drippers were added to the teapot when making coffee rather than tea, and the drippers are extremely hard to find. There is a matching creamer and sugar with cover. The teapot does not appear in the Jewel Tea catalogs after 1942. The bottom mark is HK-Mary Dunbar.

Autumn Leaf "Rayed" with metal drip, $275-325.

Regent ("Buchanan") – Decorated

Size:
6 cup, 44 ounces brimful, 5.25" high without cover, 7" high with cover, 9.125" wide

"Floral Bouquet" Regent, $125-150.

The six-cup decorated "Buchanan" was advertised as the Regent in a 1930s Tricolator catalog. The six-cup undecorated was called the Windsor, and the eight-cup solid or decorated was called Autocrat. The Regent has been found in other decorations that are shown in the Tricolator section. The bottom mark found is Pour Right Tricolator and/or HALL incised.

"Ribbed Band"
Electric Percolator

Size:
6 cup, 60 ounces brimful, 10.5" high without cover, 11.5" high with cover, 9" wide, Hall No. 4525

There are three pots that are very similar in the "Ribbed Band" design – a water server, teapot, and electric percolator. The electric percolator has a locking cover and is marked on the bottom, "Use on AC only; Do not immerse in water; UL; The Hall China Co.; East Liverpool, Ohio; Cat. No.; 115V; 450W." The "Ribbed Band" electric percolator and the matching water server have been made of Super-Ceram and are bright white.

White "Ribbed Band" Electric Percolator, $75-90.

Roosevelt ("Blaine")

Size:
6 cup, 54 ounces brimful, 6" high without cover, 7.75" high with cover, 10.25" wide, 3.5" diameter opening for drip

The twelve-panel Roosevelt was advertised in a 1930s Tricolator catalog in a variety of solid colors such as cadet, emerald, and warm yellow and in solid matte art glaze colors.

Nile Green Roosevelt, $70-85.

A variety of metal drips from Tricolator could be purchased for the Roosevelt. Samples of the metal drips are shown in the Tricolator section of this book. The bottom mark found will be Pour Right Tricolator with HALL incised.

"Rounded Terrace"
("Step Round")

"Floral Rose" Six-Cup "Rounded Terrace," $40-55.

Sizes:
2 cup, 24 ounces brimful, 4" high and has no cover, 6.5" wide, 3.625" diameter opening for drip
4 cup, 40 ounces brimful, 4.75" high without cover, 5.875" high with cover, 8.125" wide, 3.625" diameter opening for drip, Hall No. 3084
6 cup, 66 ounces brimful, 5.75" high without cover, 7" high with cover, 9.5" wide, 3.75" diameter opening for drip, Hall No. 3085
Older decorations:
"Floral Rose," "Pasture Rose," "Pink and Gray Floral Bouquet," "Rambling Rose," Wildflower

The "Rounded Terrace" coffee pot was introduced in 1935 and was referred to as the "bulge bottom" coffee pot by the Hall China Company. It is very similar in shape to the "Terrace" except for the bulge. The two-cup pot is sometimes referred to as a jug and has a metal drip with a metal cover; the medium-sized pot has a lid that fits over the top rim of the pot; and the larger pot has a lid that fits inside the top rim. The bottom mark is Drip-O-lator. A different style metal drip is found for each size coffee pot.

Green Lustre Royal Park, $70-85.

Wildflower Two-Cup "Rounded Terrace," $35-45.

S-Handle

"Rambling Rose" Four-Cup "Rounded Terrace," $40-55.

Wildfire S-Handle, $65-80.

Royal Park ("Lincoln")

Size:
6 cup, 40 ounces brimful, 6.625" high without cover, 8" high with cover, 8.5" wide, 3.25" diameter opening for drip

The twelve-panel Royal Park was produced for the Tricolator Company in the late 1930s. The footed base attached to the coffee pot was advertised as giving it remarkable rigidity and beautiful contour.

The Royal Park was available in solid colors. The coffee pot sold for $4.75 complete, including a packet of 100 filter wafers with directions. The bottom mark is Tricolator.

Size:
9 cup, 81 ounces brimful, 6.625" high without cover, 7.375" high with cover, 9.125" wide, 3.875" diameter opening for drip, Hall No. 3075
Older decorations:
"Orange Poppy," Wildfire with and without glass drip

In 1936 the S-Handle coffee pot was made to replace the Great American coffee pot for the Great American Tea Company. Metal drips were normally used for making coffee, but a glass drip has been found for the Wildfire coffee pot. The bottom mark is HSQK. Matching creamers and sugars in this shape were not made.

Saf-Handle ("Sundial")

Vanilla Saf-Handle, $95-110.

Sizes:

1 cup, 10 ounces brimful, 3.875" high without cover, 4.5" high with cover, 4" wide, Hall No. 2100

1.5 cup, 12 ounces brimful, 4.25" high without cover, Hall No. 2101

The Saf-Handle shape coffee pot with a locking cover was introduced in the late 1930s. Joseph Palin Thorley was issued U.S. Design Patent 117859 on November 28, 1939, for the design of the Saf-Handle coffee pot and teapot. The two sizes of the Saf-Handle coffee pot appeared in the Hall catalogs from 1940 through the mid-1970s.

The coffee pots were available in a variety of colors including canary, Chinese red, cobalt, green, Indian red, maroon, and marine. The bottom mark is H-3 on most of the Saf-Handle coffee pots, and HSQK on the Chinese red pots.

Saf-Handle ("Sundial") Coffee Server

Size:

5 pints, 84 ounces brimful, 7.75" high without cover, 8.75" high with cover, 8.75" wide, Hall No. 2108

Older decorations:

Blue Blossom, Blue Garden, Fantasy, Red Kitchenware, solid colors

The Saf-Handle coffee server was produced beginning in the late 1930s or early 1940s. A 1941 Hall special catalog shows the Saf-Handle Coffee Server in both the Blue Blossom and the Blue Garden decals. The cover turns ninety degrees to lock into place. The bottom marks are H-3 and HSQK.

Chinese Red Saf-Handle Coffee Server, $500-550.

Saf-Spout

Sizes:

1 cup, 8 ounces serving size, 12 ounces brimful, 4.125" high without cover, 5" high with cover, Hall No. 2115

1.5 cup, 10 ounces serving size, Hall No. 2116

2 cup, 16 ounces serving, Hall No. 2117

Vanilla Saf-Spout, $95-110.

On November 28, 1939, the U.S. Design Patent 117855 was awarded to J. Palin Thorley for the design of the Saf-Spout coffee pot. Four sizes of creamers and a covered sugar bowl were illustrated in the 1956 Hall catalog. The pieces were available in green or brown but could be special ordered in a variety of colors. The Saf-Spout items were listed through 1964 in the Hall catalogs. The bottom mark is H-3. The one-cup Saf-Spout coffee pot has been the easiest size to find.

The Saf-Spout was made in the early 1960s for the Manning's Coffee Company. This coffee pot features Manning's Roasted Coffee around the bottom and a coffee bean and leaves on the side. The Manning's Coffee pot has an H-3 bottom mark.

Manning Coffee Saf-Spout, $95-110.

Sanka and Sanka Embossed Coffee

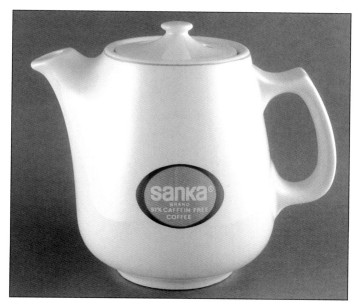

White Sanka, $30-45.

Size – Regular:
2 cup, 12 ounces brimful, 4.125" high without cover, 4.625" high with cover, 5.375" wide, Hall No. 1891
   Sizes – Sanka Debossed:
1 cup, 12 ounces brimful, 3.875" high without cover, 4.75" high with cover, 5.625" wide, Hall No. 1895
2 cup, 16 ounces brimful, 4.625" high without cover, 5.5" high with cover, 6.375" wide, Hall No. 1896

Lenox Brown Embossed Sanka, $30-45.

The white Sanka coffee pot and matching coffee cups were introduced in the early 1970s. The bottom mark is critical in identifying whether this coffee pot and coffee cups were made by Hall China or one made in Japan. The bottom mark reads "Made Expressly for Sanka Brand Decaffeinated Coffee, Furnished by Minners and Co., Inc., Hall China."

The Lenox brown embossed Sanka coffee pots were introduced in 1983 and will have H-4 or H-4, Made in U.S.A. and the identification number on the bottom. The embossed Sanka coffees were also made in white.

"Sash"

Size:
8 cup, 76 ounces brimful, 6.5" high without cover, 7.25" high with cover, 10.5" wide, 3.5" diameter opening for drip, Hall No. 3158

The "Sash" was introduced in July 1937 for the Enterprise Aluminum Company. The coffee pot will be found with a red, blue, or green band and also found with white stars scattered along the colored band.

The bottom mark is Drip-O-lator. Later that year the "Orb" coffee pot was made in the same round shape without the band.

Red and White "Sash," $85-100.

"Scoop"

Size:
6 cup, 62 ounces, 5.375" high without cover, 7.25" high with cover, 10.125" wide, 4.5" diameter opening for drip

The "Scoop" was made for the Enterprise Aluminum Company and has Drip-O-lator as a bottom mark. It is found with either the "Brand" decal that is shown or with the Wildflower decal that is also used on other Enterprise Aluminum Company coffee pots.

"Brand" "Scoop," $50-65.

Seawinds Beverage Pot

Size:
2 cup, 14 ounces brimful, 3.75" high without cover, 4.875" high with cover, 6.25" wide, Hall No. 3385

Hall China made accessory pieces in the late 1980s for Corning Inc., Corning, New York. A beverage pot, creamer, open sugar, shakers, and vase were made to match the Pyroceram® Expressions® Collection made by Corning. The patterns were Metallic Gold, Blue Flair, Kabuki, Royal Flair, Elegant Harmony, Whispering Mist, Classic Ebony, and Cordon Blanc. The beverage pot came in bone white, bone white with Addison gray lines or coral peach and jade lines or maroon and gray lines. It also came in the solid colors of Addison gray, jade green, and coral peach. The Seawinds Beverage Pot appears in Hall China catalogs from 1989 to the present and was available in the Hall Closet. The bottom mark is H-4, and some will be unmarked.

Bone White with Addison Gray and
Maroon Lines Seawinds, $30-45.

Size:
1 quart, 8.75" without cover, 9.75" high with cover

Pictured is a prototype of a carafe made for Service Ideas in 1990. Hall China made the body of the carafe and a plastic cap and metal rim were added. The cap screws on and off to allow for easy cleaning. The bottom mark is unknown. This was a short production run when Service Ideas replaced their ceramic carafes with plastic ones.

Sterling Coffee Pot

White Sterling Coffee Pot, $30-45.

Size:
2 cup, 15 ounces brimful, 4.625" high with cover, No. 3432

The coffee pot pictured is a prototype of the one made in June 1988 exclusively for Sterling.

Service Ideas Carafe

Left:
Rose Pink Service
Ideas Carafe, ND.

"Steve"

Marine "Steve," $65-80.

Sizes:

3 cup, 20 ounces brimful, 3" high without cover, 4.25" high with cover, 7.625" wide

5 cup, 30 ounces brimful, 4" high without cover, 5.375" high with cover, 8.125" wide

The "Steve" coffee pot was made for the Tricolator Company. It has been found in two sizes and in both solid colors and decorated. The screw-locking cover is similar to other locking covers used on Tricolator coffee pots. The bottom mark is Tricolator Pour Right. See the Tricolator section later in this book for a decorated "Steve" coffee pot.

Super-Ceram Coffee Pot

Size:

1.5 cup, 12 ounces brimful, 4.5" high without cover, 5.25" high with cover, 5.75" wide, Hall No. 04509

Super-Ceram is the Hall China registered trademark for an entirely new type of a super-hard body introduced in 1961. Super-Ceram items were made to retain heat or cold and were more resistant to chipping, breaking, and staining.

The coffee pot shown is called Super-Ceram after the process used in making it. It was introduced in 1964 and appeared in Hall China catalogs until the late 1980s. The Super-Ceram coffee pot could be ordered in 1964 in standard Super-Ceram colors of black, Nile green, pearl, shell, white, or custom ordered with the optional Super-Ceram colors. The Super-Ceram Coffee Pot was also available in Golden Glo. The bottom mark is Super-Ceram.

Gray Super-Ceram Coffee Pot, $20-35.

"Sweep"

"Modern Tulip" "Sweep," $40-55.

Size:

6 cup, 62 ounces, 5.125" high without cover, 6.75" high with cover, 11.125" wide, 3.75" diameter opening for drip

The "Sweep" was made for the Enterprise Aluminum Company and has the Drip-O-lator bottom mark. A metal drip was available for use when making coffee. The "Modern Tulip" and Wildflower are the only decals that are found on this coffee pot.

"Target" ("Bullseye")

"Dutch Couple" "Target," $40-55.

Size:

6 cup, 72 ounces, 5.25" high without cover, 7.25" high with cover, 10.5" wide, 3.75" diameter opening for drip

The "Target" coffee pot was made for the Enterprise Aluminum Company and has the Drip-O-lator bottom mark. The coffee pot came with a metal drip. The coffee pot has been found with both the "Dutch Couple" and "Windmill" decals. The same decal appears on both sides or a combination of the two decals was used.

"Terrace" ("Step Down")

Homewood Eight-Cup "Terrace," $60-75.

Sizes:

2 cup, 24 ounces brimful, 4" high and has no cover, 6" wide, 3.625" diameter opening for drip, Hall No. 3065

6 cup, 64 ounces brimful, 5.375" high without cover, 7.125" high with cover, 10.25" wide, 4.5" diameter opening for drip, Hall No. 3064

8 - 9 cup, 78 ounces brimful, 6.5" high without cover, 8" high with cover, 9.5" wide, 4.125" diameter opening for drip, Hall No. 3062

Older decorations – 8 cup:

#488; Acacia; Blue Bouquet; Blue Garden; Crocus; "Gaillardia;" Gold Band; Gold Label; Heather Rose; Homewood; "Mums;" "Pastel Morning Glory;" Red Kitchenware; Red, Ivory Accents, and Platinum Trim; Serenade; Silhouette

"Shrub Rose Garland" Two-Cup "Terrace," $30-45.

The "Terrace" coffee pot was introduced in 1934 and available in several sizes. The eight-cup coffee pot is found in a wide assortment of decals to go with dinnerware and kitchenware patterns made by Hall China and are marked HSQK. Many of the "Terrace" coffee pots were made for the Enterprise Aluminum Company and are found with the Drip-O-lator bottom mark. A variety of metal drip styles were used with the "Terrace" coffee pot. Note that the small "Terrace" is shown with a metal drip and cover. It did not come with a china cover.

During the mid-1950s the eight-cup "Terrace" coffee pot was chosen to be a part of the Gold Label series. The bottom mark is HSQK on these pots.

The six-cup "Terrace" that is shown has not been proven to have been made by Hall, even though the Drip-O-lator bottom mark is the same as used on other items made by Hall China. The same coffee pot has been found with a green emblem on the side.

White and Green Trim Six-Cup "Terrace," $45-60.

"Terrace" ("Step Down")
All-China Drip

Size:

4 cup, 40 ounces brimful, 5 - 8.75" high, 5.25" diameter, 10" high for use with filter papers, Hall No. 3121

Green "Terrace" All-China Drip, $175-200.

Older decorations:

Blue Garden; Crocus; Red Kitchenware; Red, White Accents, and Platinum Trim; solid colors; "Wild Poppy"

The four-cup all-china "Terrace" was introduced in 1935 and available in the Hall catalogs through 1964. It came for use with filter papers or with a china dripper. The drip coffee pot was advertised as being used in the kitchen or to dramatize coffee preparation and service in the dining room.

The bottoms of the coffee pot are HALL incised, H-3, or HSQK. The all-china "Terrace" coffee pot has also been found in black, emerald, or yellow with ivory accents and platinum trim.

"Trellis"

Art Glaze Blue "Trellis," $65-80.

Size:

6 cup, 56 ounces brimful, 5.625" high without cover, 7.125" high with cover, 10.375" wide, 3.625" diameter opening for drip, Hall No. 3144

The "Trellis" has been found in ivory and art glaze colors of blue, green, orange, red, and yellow. It may be found in additional solid colors. It will also be found with a "Floral Bouquet" decal on a white body. The coffee pot was made for the Enterprise Aluminum Company and has the Drip-O-lator bottom mark. The "Trellis" was advertised in solid ivory with a six-cup metal drip for $.79 in the 1937 Sears, Roebuck, and Co. catalog.

Trieste Beverage Pot

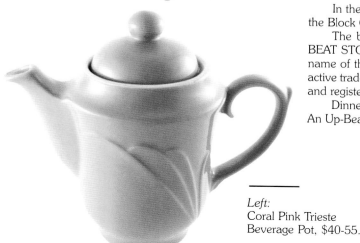

Left:
Coral Pink Trieste
Beverage Pot, $40-55.

Sizes:

2 cup, 12 ounces serving

3 cup, 15 ounces serving, 18 ounces brimful, 5.25" high without cover, 6.125" high with cover, 7.25" wide

This beverage pot was made in June 1988 as a companion piece for the Sterling China Company Trieste dinnerware line. It came in two sizes and in white and coral pink. The bottom mark is H-4, and some will be unmarked.

Up-Beat Beverage Pot
(Block China)

Watusi Up-Beat Beverage Pot, $65-80.

Size:

6 cup, 52 ounces, 7.625" high without cover, 8" high with cover, 8.625" wide, 4.875" diameter

Older decorations:

Folk Song, Impressions, Toccata, Watusi

In the 1960s Hall China made the Up-Beat dinnerware line for the Block China Company. It came in four patterns.

The bottom mark is a bee inside a circle surrounded by UP-BEAT STONEWARE, Made in America, Block China Co., and the name of the pattern is below the circle. The bee in the circle is the active trademark and was first used by Block China in October 1962 and registered in July 1963.

Dinnerware pieces have been found in the Nocturne pattern. An Up-Beat Beverage Pot may have been produced in this pattern.

"Viking" ("Bell")

Size:
8 cup, 80 ounces brimful, 6.25" high without cover, 7.125" high with cover, 10" wide, 3.875" diameter opening for drip, Hall No. 3148

Older decorations:
"Bird of Paradise," Cactus, Flamingo, "Flower Pot"

Cactus "Viking" with Arch Cover, $60-75.

Flamingo "Viking" with Mesa Cover, $50-65.

In late 1936 the "Viking" coffee pot was made for the Enterprise Aluminum Company, and the bottom mark is Drip-O-lator. A matching creamer and sugar was made in 1937. Note that the coffee pot came with two different style covers. The Mesa cover has ridges like on the upper body of the coffee pot and has a flat top on the handle, and the Arch cover is a curved upper surface. The cover on the sugar matches the Mesa cover. A variety of metal drips were available. The "Viking" has been found in ivory or white body.

Washington
(knob and sunken cover)

Ivory Knob Cover Washington and Warm Yellow Sunken Cover Two-Cup Washington, $25-35 each.

Sizes – Knob Cover:
1 cup, 7 ounces brimful, 3.75" high without cover, Hall No. 49 1/2
1.5 cup, 9 ounces brimful, 3.625" high without cover, 4.125" high with cover, 5.625" wide, Hall No. 50 1/2
2 cup, 14 ounces brimful, 4.625" high without cover, 5.25" high with cover, 6.375" wide, Hall No. 51 1/2
6 cup, 32 ounces brimful, 6" high without cover, 6.75" high with cover, 8" wide, Hall No. 53 1/2
12 cup, 64 ounces brimful, 7.25" high without cover, 8.25" high with cover, 9.375" wide, Hall No. 54 1/2
15 cup, 75 ounces brimful, 8.5" high without cover, 9.25" high with cover, 10" wide, Hall No. 55 1/2

Special treatments – Knob Cover:
Metal Clad and Super-Ceram (1.5, 2, 6, and 12 cup)

Sizes – Sunken Cover:
1 cup, 8 ounces brimful, 3.5" high, 5.375" wide, Hall No. 49
1.5 cup, 10 ounces brimful, 3.625" high, 5.625" wide, Hall No. 50
2 cup, 14 ounces brimful, 4.625" high, 6.375" wide, Hall No. 51

Special treatment – Sunken Cover:
Super-Ceram (1.5 and 2 cup)

Older decorations:
Black Gold (15 cup), Blue Garden, Blue Willow (2 cup), Early Gold Decorated, "Floral Lattice" (6, 12, and 15 cup), French Flower, Golden Glo, Heather Rose (2 and 6 cup), Oyster White and Red Cooking China (15 cup), "Pastel Morning Glory" (15 cup), Red Kitchenware, solid colors, Springtime, White Bake Ware (15 cup), "White Rim Band" (2 cup), "Wild Poppy" (2 and 12 cup)

Newer decoration:
Autumn Leaf (12 cup)

The Washington coffee pot was introduced in the late teens in green or brown with knob or sunken covers. It did not have a strainer and was suitable for coffee, chocolate, cocoa, hot water, and hot milk. The Washington came in six sizes and is still available in the Hall catalogs in the two- and six-cup sizes. The coffee pot comes in a variety of colors and decorations. In October 1954 a round warmer was made to go along with the twelve-cup Washington and especially made for the Jewel Tea Dining Room. The bottom marks one the Washington coffee pots are H-2, H-3, H-4, and HSQK.

In 1985 Hall reintroduced the Washington coffee pot along with teapots in their Hall American line. The standard colors offered were black, blue, gray, red, and tan. Over 100 additional custom colors were offered to retailers to choose from. Naomi's Antiques, an antique dealer in San Francisco, ordered the Washington coffee pot in cobalt, orange, and lavender. Other retailers may have ordered the coffee pot in a special color. These coffee pots have the H-4 bottom mark.

The National Autumn Leaf Collectors Club offered its members the Washington coffee pot in 1999 decorated in the Autumn Leaf pattern. The bottom mark is NALCC.

"Waverlet" ("Crest")
Sizes:
4 cup, 48 ounces brimful, 4.875" high without cover, 7" high with cover, 9" wide, 3.75" diameter opening for drip

6 cup, 64 ounces brimful, 5.75" high without cover, 7.875" high with cover, 9.75" wide, 3.875" diameter opening for drip

8 cup, 84 ounces brimful, 6.5" high without cover, 9" high with cover, 10" wide, 4.375" diameter opening for drip

Older decoration:
"Minuet"

The "Waverlet" is very much like the "Waverly" coffee pot. The "Waverlet" has a short spout and a dome-shaped cover. It was made for the Enterprise Aluminum Company and has the Drip-O-lator bottom mark.

"Minute" "Waverlet," $45-60.

"Waverly" ("Crest")
Sizes:
4 cup, 48 ounces brimful, 4.875" high without cover, 6.125" high with cover, 8.5" wide, 3.7625" diameter opening for drip

6 cup, 64 ounces brimful, 5.75" high without cover, 7" high with cover, 10.625" wide, 3.625" diameter opening for drip

Older decorations:
"Jonquil" Flower, "June" Flower, "Minuet," "Mini-Fleurette," "Tulip," "Yellow Rose"

The "Waverly" was made for the Enterprise Aluminum Company and has the Drip-O-lator bottom mark. The differences between the "Waverly" and the "Waverlet" coffee pots are the length

of the spout and the style of cover. The "Waverly" has a longer spout and a knob on the cover that looks like a crest. A larger size is probably available for this pot the same as there is for the "Waverlet."

"Tulip" "Waverly," $45-60.

"Wellman"
Size:
8 cup, 68 ounces brimful, 6.875" high without cover, 8" high with cover, 10.625" wide, 3.75" diameter opening for drip

The "Wellman" coffee pot was made for the Tricolator Company and has the Pour Right bottom mark. It is found in brown, Chinese red, green, marine, and yellow. It may be found in other colors.

Yellow "Wellman," $60-75.

"Wicker"

"Shrub Rose Garland" "Wicker," $40-55.

Size:
6 cup, 50 ounces brimful, 5.25" high without cover, 6.625" high with cover, 10.25" wide, 3.625" diameter opening for drip

The "Wicker" coffee pot was made for the Enterprise Aluminum Company and has a Drip-O-lator bottom mark. It is most often found in the "Shrub Rose Garland" decal. An unusual decoration found on the "Wicker" was the Red Poppy decal with a red cover.

Wilshire

Size:
1.5 cup, 13 ounces brimful, 4.5" high without cover, 5.125" high with cover, 5.5" wide, Hall No. 138

The twelve-ounce Wilshire coffee pot was introduced in 1936, along with the fourteen-ounce teapot, a two-handled sugar, and three creamers. The Wilshire line was advertised through the 1970s in the Hall China catalogs and could be ordered in a variety of colors. The coffee pot will be found with the H-3 or H-4 bottom marks.

Turquoise Wilshire, $30-45.

"Wilson"

Size:
6 cup, 58 ounces brimful, 5.5" high without cover, 7.25" high with cover, 8.875" wide, 3.625" diameter opening for drip

The six-cup undecorated "Wilson" coffee pot is similar to the "Encore" coffee pot made for Tricolator. The "Wilson," however, does not have the Tricolator spout and has H-3 for the bottom stamp. It comes in brown or black with a white knob.

Brown with White Knob "Wilson," $35-50.

Windsor ("Buchanan") –
Six-cup Undecorated

Size:
6 cup, 44 ounces brimful, 5.25" high without cover, 7" high with cover, 9.125" wide

The six-cup undecorated "Buchanan" was advertised as the Windsor in a 1930s Tricolator catalog. The six-cup decorated "Buchanan" was called the Regent, and the eight-cup solid and decorated "Buchanan" was called the Autocrat.

The Windsor was available in delft, ivory, Ming red, Nile green, or yellow. The coffee pot was available in additional colors at a later date. The bottom mark found is Pour Right Tricolator and/or HALL incised.

Coral Pink Windsor, $60-75.

Early Gold and Platinum Decorations

In 1920 Hall started adding gold decorations to its line of teapots being sold to distributors, retailers, hotels, and restaurants. The gold decorations were gold lining; gold lining with gold stamping; or gold lining, gold stamping, and gold handles, spouts, and finials. Several variations of gold decoration were designed for each teapot style, and some of the gold decorations were used on more than one teapot style. The most popular gold decorations on a given teapot style went on to form the Gold Decorated series of teapots. These gold decorated teapots were well received by the public and supported Hall's claim to be the largest maker of gold decorated teapots in the world. The pictures in this section show the range of early gold and platinum decorations found on teapots produced between 1920 and the early 1930s. Most of these will have the H-2 bottom stamp.

It is interesting that the teapots in production between 1920 and 1930 that were not included in the Gold Decorated series were the Bellevue, "Columbia," "Johnson," "Naomi," and Newport. The Bellevue and Newport teapots were assigned color and shape numbers for reordering, but they had been dropped from the Hall China published order forms before 1935. The "Columbia," "Johnson," and "Naomi" teapots have an H-2 or H-3 bottom stamp but have not been found in the Hall mold book. They were apparently considered by Hall to be discontinued by the time the mold book was produced.

Five-cup teapots decorated with platinum rather than gold are rarely found. This may have been because the platinum products were not as bright as the gold products. A French teapot with platinum French Flower stamping and platinum handle, spout, and finial has been found, indicating some early work with platinum decorations. A variety of platinum decorations were used on the Tea for Four Sets, Tea for Two Sets, and Twin-Tee Sets.

The teapots and coffee pots on which decorations appeared are listed below the pictures. The year of the first advertisement found for a decoration has been noted.

Known decals not shown are the "Floral" on the "Columbia," the "Gold Sprig" on the Boston, and the "Hollyhock" on the Newport and Twin-Tee Set.

"Art Nouveau" Twin-Tee Set, $200-230.

"Band and Lace" Los Angeles, $85-100.

Advertisement appeared in 1926.

"All Over Daisy" New York, $150-175.

Other shape: Boston.

"Band and Lines" New York, $85-100.

Other shapes: Boston and French.
Design variations: Band and Upper Line or Band and Lower Line.
Advertisement appeared in 1921.

Bubble New York, $125-150.

Other shapes: Cleveland, Newport, and Philadelphia.
Advertisement appeared in 1923.

"Band and Lines with Gold Handle, Spout, and Finial" New York, $85-100.

Burbick New York, $425-475.

Boston Standard Gold Decoration on a Washington, $100-125.

Other shapes: Boston, Infuser, and St. Louis Chocolate Pot.
Advertisement appeared in 1920.

Burbick New York, $425-475.

Other shape: Philadelphia.

"Elizabethan Bouquet" Philadelphia, ND.

Other shape: McCormick.

French Flower (Gold) Boston, $190-225.

Other shapes: Cube, Detroit, French Light Weight, Infuser, New York, Washington.

Advertisement appeared in 1920, and the decal was called "gold Japanese floral."

"Emblem" Bellevue, $575-650.

Other shape: "Johnson."

French Flower (Platinum) French Light Weight, ND.

"Gold Blossom" French, ND.

"Floral Vine" Twin-Tee Set, $325-350.

"Gold Frize" French, $200-225.

Other shapes: Boston, New York.

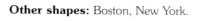

"Gold Lined" Manhattan Pot (Side-Handled),
$75-100.

Other shape: Two-Cup Bellevue Teapot.

"Hollywood Standard Gold Decoration"
Hollywood, $70-85.

Advertisement appeared in 1927.

"Gold Mini-Floral with
Matte Gold Band"
Infuser, $125-150.

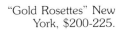

"Gold Rosettes" New
York, $200-225.

"Illinois" Tea for Two Set, $100-125.

Other shapes: Illinois, "Naomi," Tea for Four Set, Twin-Tee Set.
Advertisement appeared in 1926.

"Gold Trim"
French, $125-150.

"Golden Renaissance" Twin-Tee Set,
$200-250.

"Japoneske" Twin-Tee Set, $200-250.

Other shape: Newport.

"Lavaliere" "Columbia," $475-550.

"Mini-Fleurette" Los Angeles, $150-175.

Other shape: French (See Decorations section for additional teapots).
Advertisement appeared in 1928.

Loops Philadelphia, $150-175.

Other shape: New York.
Advertisement appeared in 1924.

"Nebula" Illinois, $175-200.

Other shape: Two-Cup Bellevue Coffee Pot.

"Matte Gold Trim" Manhattan Pot (Side-Handled), $75-100.

"Nouveau" Philadelphia, $125-150.

Other shapes: French Light Weight, St. Louis Chocolate Pot.

"Palm" Philadelphia, $275-300.

Other shapes: French Light Weight (cobalt blue with green rather than gold), Infuser, New York.

"Posey" Twin-Tee Set, $200-250.

Other shape: Newport.

"Palm Tree" French Light Weight, ND.

"Snow Flake" New York, $175-200.

Other shape: Infuser.

"Platinum Garden" Twin-Tee Set, $200-250.

Other shape: Newport.

"Spider Web" Twin-Tee Set, $250-300.

Other shape: Newport.

"Sponge Gold" Los Angeles, $100-125.

"Trailing Aster" Boston, $200-225.

Other shape: St. Louis Chocolate Pot.

"Sycamore" French Light Weight, $125-150.

"Trillium" New York, $65-75.

Advertisement appeared in 1920.

"Victorian Swag" Twin-Tee Set, $250-300.

"Tiled Band and Flowers" French Light Weight, $150-175.

Other shape: Infuser.

"Wreath" French, $150-175.

Early Decals

In about 1926 Hall China started limited production of teapots with decals requested by customers. The "Minuet" decal was used on the Baltimore, French, and Philadelphia teapots. This decal was later used on the Enterprise Aluminum Co. Waverlet and Waverly coffee pots. The "Leaf and Vine" decal was used on a blue Baltimore teapot in the early years but later appears in other colors and on other style teapots as shown in the Decorations section of this book. The Baltimore, Los Angeles, Newport, and Philadelphia teapots appear in a wide variety of floral decals. An assortment of floral decals was used on the Tea for Two, Tea for Four, and Twin-Tee Sets. This may have been because hotels, restaurants, and tearooms were the main purchasers.

Hall greatly expanded its use of decals after the beginning of the production of the dinnerware patterns in 1936. Hall China did not develop a decal shop but used decals from commercial shops or those supplied by a customer.

Pictured below are decals used by Hall from between 1926 and the introduction of Hall's dinnerware and kitchenware decals. These teapots were generally marked with the H-2 bottom mark. Additional teapot shapes on which the decoration appears are listed with the pictures.

"Black Garden" Twin-Tee Set, $190-240.

"Chintz" Twin-Tee Set, $150-175.

"Alexander" Twin-Tee Set, $175-200.

"Chintz" Tea for Two Set, $150-175.

Other shape: Tea for Four Set.

"Daisy and Poppy" Twin-Tee Set, $325-350.

"Floral Basket" Newport, $225-250.

Other shape: Philadelphia.

"Daisy and Poppy" Tea for Two Set, $325-350.

Other shape: Tea for Four Set.

"Floral Fan" Baltimore, $200-250.

"Leaf and Vine" Baltimore, ND.

"Floral Band" Los Angeles, $125-150.

"Mayflower" Philadelphia, $125-150.

"Minuet" Five-Cup French, $150-175.

Other shapes: Baltimore, Seven-Cup French, Philadelphia.

"Pansy" Twin-Tee Set, $150-175.

"Sanford" Twin-Tee Set, $200-250.

"Perzel" Twin-Tee Set, $175-200.

"Tulip and Carnation" ("Walsh") Tea for Four Set, $300-350.

Other shape: Tea for Two Set (Came with decaled panel and all-over decal).

"Art Deco" Series

The "Adele," "Damascus," and "Danielle" are the three teapots that make up the series referred to by collectors as the "Art Deco" Series. The teapots were distributed in the mid-1930s in blue, olive green, maroon, and yellow colors. The colors seem to be unique to this series of teapots. The color is considered an "all over color" as the inside of the teapot is the same color as the outside. The bottom stamps are H2 or H3, but some of the teapots will not have any bottom stamp. The teapots have not been reported with any gold or decoration.

Olive Green "Damascus," $250-300; Blue "Danielle," $195-225; Maroon "Adele," $250-275.

"Novelty" Series

At the 1938 Pittsburgh Pottery Show, the Airflow, Doughnut, and Football were introduced. Later that year at the New York Pottery Show, Hall introduced the Automobile, Basket, and "Bull's Eye," available in Chinese red, green, Indian red, jonquil yellow, and midnight blue. The Bird Cage was introduced at the February 1939 pottery show. The automobile shape won instant favor as a novelty and both the basket and bull's eye shapes were praised for their beautifully simple design. "Streamlined, dynamic, rhythmic, styled with the same smart lines that make the modern auto a joy to behold. Available in all the colors that are in demand," quotes the writer in the December issue of *China, Glass, and Lamps*. The article also states, "A variety of shapes in a selection of colors that make the rainbow droop in dismay. Decorated with breath-taking beautiful gold ornamentation. Include these novelty teapots in your display for young people, for old people with young ideas; in fact, for everyone who likes the sleek lines of modern style."

The Automobile and Football teapots were reissued in 1992 by China Specialties in a variety of solid colors with platinum trim or gold. The Doughnut was reissued in 1993 in white with the Autumn Leaf decoration for the National Autumn Leaf Collectors Club. A limited number of Doughnuts in cobalt, gloss black, hunter green, and light yellow were made for Naomi's Antiques in San Francisco in 1993. The East Liverpool Alumni Association auctioned eighteen ivory with gold Doughnut teapots in 1997. The Doughnut in a variety of colors is sold through the Hall Closet. In 1995 the National Autumn Leaf Collectors Club distributed the Bird Cage teapot in Autumn Leaf. Twenty-four ivory with gold Bird Cage teapots were auctioned in 1998 for the East Liverpool Alumni Association. In 2000 the East Liverpool Alumni Association auctioned twenty-four Basketball teapots in cobalt with gold trim. All of these teapots will be clearly marked.

Top row, left to right: Chinese Red Basketball (HSQK), $700-800; Delphinium Doughnut (H-3), $450-500; middle row: Ivory Undecorated with Gold Bird Cage (ELO Alumni), $75-100; Canary Basket (H-3), $130-160; Sandust Football (China Specialties), $60-70; front row: Green Lustre Platinum Decorated Automobile (China Specialties), $100-150.

Gold Decorated, Gold "Special," and Platinum Decorated

Twelve teapots were advertised as a Gold Decorated line in 1935. They were the Albany, Baltimore, Boston, Cleveland, French, Hollywood, Illinois, Los Angeles, Moderne, New York, Ohio, and Philadelphia. The colors available were black, blue (cobalt), brown, cadet, canary, emerald, green, green lustre, ivory, marine, maroon, rose, and yellow.

The bottom of each Hall China Gold Decorated teapot was numbered in gold. The teapots had a range of thirteen gold decorated numbers in 1935. The number identifies the color and shape of the teapot. A chart was available in the Hall catalogs to assist in ordering duplicate pots or extra covers. See the Color section later in this book for further information. The Bellevue and Newport teapots were given Gold Decorated numbers but had already been dropped from the Gold Decorated line by 1935.

Various teapots were selected from the Gold Decorated line and sold as an assortment. In the six-cup size, for instance, an assortment would consist of six shapes in six assorted colors. In open stock, to accompany the teapots, were matching six-inch round tea tiles. The Boston, Hollywood, New York, and Philadelphia shapes were the only styles with matching sugars and creamers.

In 1937 the Indiana, Kansas, and Streamline were added to the Gold Decorated line. Delphinium, orchid, and turquoise were added to the color selection. The Aladdin, Basket, Bird Cage, Melody, Nautilus, Rhythm, and Surf Side were added in 1939. The tea tiles were dropped from the advertisement at that time.

Teapots added in 1941 were the Airflow, Doughnut, Globe, Hook Cover, Parade, Saf-Handle, Sani-Grid, Star, and Windshield. Dresden was also added to the Gold Decorated line. By 1941 the Kansas, Illinois, Indiana, and Ohio had been dropped from the Gold Decorated line and in 1942 the Doughnut was dropped from the catalog.

In the 1950s several additional assortments of six teapots were advertised. These assortments were selected groups of solid colors, gold label, or gold trace. Collectors know the gold trace teapots as gold "special." They came in a variety of colors with the standard gold decoration in conjunction with bright gold decorated handles, spouts, and knobs. The "S" after the color and style code number on the bottom of the teapots stands for "solid" gold handle and spout. (Boyce, *The Glaze*, July 1986) The gold "special" teapots identified are the Airflow, Aladdin, Albany, Automobile, Baltimore, Basket, Basketball, Bird Cage, Boston, Cleveland, Doughnut, Football, French, Hollywood, Hook Cover, Kansas, Los Angeles, Melody, Nautilus, New York, Parade, Philadelphia, Saf-Handle, Star, Streamline, Surf Side, and Windshield.

Platinum was also used as a decoration rather than gold. They will have a "P" after the color and style code number. Those teapots identified with platinum decoration are the Automobile, Basket, Basketball, Kansas, Melody, and Streamline. The amount of gold or platinum decoration varied from teapot to teapot, especially on the Automobile. A Streamline has been found with platinum special-like decoration but has the bottom mark of HSQK.

An expanded "gold decorated" chart has been provided with the color section of this book. Colors added to the color chart after the 1950s were chartreuse, gray, blue turquoise, mahogany, Monterey green, camellia, and pink. Seven of the color numbers were used to represent two colors. The colors and numbers are stock brown or chartreuse (2), cobalt or gray (3), delphinium or blue turquoise (5), green lustre or Monterey green (11), camellia or butterscotch (14), pink or violet (15), and orchid or matte orchid (17). Not all teapots were available in all colors as Hall only provided those colors and styles ordered. As teapot styles have been found with a gold or platinum decorated number, the "gold decorated" chart has been expanded to include these teapots. Teapots shown in this section are gold decorated, gold "special," or platinum decorated. With each picture is the range of numbers that identify the color and shape of the teapots.

Cadet Gold Decorated Airflow, $85-100; Marine Gold Decorated Airflow, $80-95; Warm Yellow Gold "Special" Airflow, $135-165.

Decoration Numbers: #0441 - #0460. **Decoration:** Oak Leaves with and without a Rose.

Maroon Gold "Special" Aladdin, $120-150; Ivory Gold Decorated Aladdin, $80-95.

Decoration Numbers: #0661 - #0680. **Decoration:** Gold Lining.

Cobalt Gold Decorated Albany, $65-75; Warm Yellow Gold "Special" Albany, $100-120.

Decoration Numbers: #0221 - #0240. **Decoration:** Gold Medallion.

Emerald Gold Decorated Baltimore, $65-80.

Decorated Numbers: #0161 - #0180. **Decoration:** Floral and Band (also found without the floral decoration).

Canary Gold Decorated Automobile, $100-125; Black Gold "Special" Automobile, $500-575.

Decoration Numbers: #0521 - #0540. **Decoration:** Gold Lining.

Marine Gold "Special" Baltimore, $160-200.

Decoration Numbers: #0161S - #0180S. **Decoration:** Floral and Band.

Delphinium Platinum Decorated Automobile, $550-600.

Decorated Numbers: #0521 - #0540. **Decoration:** Platinum Lining.

Cadet Platinum Decorated Basket, $150-180.

Decoration Numbers: #0501 - #0520. **Decoration:** Gold and Platinum Lining.

Canary Gold "Special" Basket, $150-200.

Decoration Numbers: #0501S - #0520S. **Decoration:** Gold Lining. Gold Decorated Basket not shown.

Maroon Gold Decorated Bird Cage, $370-460.

Decoration Numbers: #0581 - #0600. **Decoration:** Gold Lining.

Delphinium Platinum Decorated Basketball, $550-600.

Decoration Numbers: #0541 - #0560. **Decoration:** Platinum Lining.

Cobalt Gold "Special" Bird Cage, $875-950.

Decoration Numbers: #0581S - #0600S. **Decoration:** Gold Lining.

Turquoise Gold "Special" Basketball, $675-750.

Decoration Numbers: #0541S - #0560S. **Decoration:** Gold Lining. Gold Decorated Basketball not shown.

Green Gold "Special" Boston, $80-100; Cobalt Gold Decorated Boston, $95-110.

Decoration Numbers: #0001 - #0020. **Decoration:** Standard Boston Gold Decoration

131

Ivory Gold "Special" Cleveland, $150-175; Emerald Gold Decorated Cleveland, $90-110.

Decoration Numbers: #0141 - #0160. **Decoration:** Butterflies.

Warm Yellow Gold "Special" French, $80-105; Cadet Gold Decorated French, $85-105.

Decoration Numbers: #0041 - #0060. **Decoration:** French Flower.

White Gold Decorated Doughnut, $150-185; Black Gold "Special" Doughnut, $200-250.

Decoration Numbers: #0461 - #0480. **Decoration:** Gold Lining.

Maroon Gold Decorated Globe, $100-125.

Decoration Numbers: #0701 - #0720. **Decoration:** Shoulder Decal.

Decoration Numbers: #0481 - #0500. **Decoration:** Gold Lining.

Turquoise Gold "Special" Football, $900-1000; Maroon Gold Decorated Football, $700-800.

Black Gold "Special" Hollywood, $130-160; Gray Gold Decorated Hollywood, $70-85.

Decoration Numbers: #0101 - #0120. **Decoration:** Shoulder Decal.

Emerald Gold Decorated Hook Cover, $70-85.

Decoration Numbers: #0741 - #0760. **Decoration:** Gold Lining. Gold "Special" Hook Cover not shown.

Marine Gold Decorated Indiana, $320-360.

Decoration Numbers: #0281 - #0300. **Decoration:** Gold Lining.

Ivory Gold Decorated Kansas, $375-425.

Decoration Numbers: #0301 - #0320. **Decoration:** Gold Lining.

Decoration Numbers: #0241 - #0260. **Decoration:** "Illinois."

Brown Gold Decorated Illinois, $135-165.

Ivory Gold "Special" Kansas, $475-525.

Decoration Numbers: #0301S - #0320S. **Decoration:** Gold Lining.

Maroon Gold "Special" Melody, $275-325.

Decoration Numbers: #0601S - #0620S. **Decoration:** Gold Lining. Platinum Decorated Melody not shown.

Emerald Gold Decorated Los Angeles, $80-100;
Cobalt Gold "Special" Los Angeles, $130-150.

Decoration Numbers: #0081 - #0100. **Decoration:** Shoulder and Foot Decal.

Canary Gold Decorated Moderne, $65-80.

Decoration Numbers: #0201 - #0220. **Decoration:** Gold Throat, Knob, and Foot.

Cobalt Gold Decorated Melody, $325-375.

Decoration Numbers: #0601 - #0620. **Decoration:** Gold Lining.

Cadet Gold Decorated Nautilus, $225-275; Canary Gold "Special" Nautilus, $325-400.

Decoration Numbers: #0641 - #0660. **Decoration:** Gold Lining.

Brown Gold Decorated Ohio, $165-195.

Decoration Numbers: #0261 - #0280. **Decoration:** Gold Emblem.

Warm Yellow Gold Decorated New York, $65-80.

Decoration Numbers: #0021 - #0040. **Decoration:** Gold "Trillium" and Band.

Emerald Gold Decorated Parade, $90-110.

Decoration Numbers: #0781 - #0800. **Decoration:** Gold Acorns and Leaves. Gold "Special" Parade not shown.

Marine Gold Decorated No-Drip, $95-110.

Decoration Numbers: #0821 - #0840. **Decoration:** Gold Floral.

Black Gold "Special" Philadelphia, $90-110; Cadet Gold Decorated Philadelphia, $65-80.

Decoration Numbers: #0061 - #0080.

Canary Gold Decorated Rhythm, $90-110.

Decoration Numbers: #0561 - #0580. **Decoration:** Dot "Swag."

Ivory Gold Decorated Star, $85-100.

Decoration Numbers: #0721 - #0740. **Decoration:** Stars and Gold Lining. Gold "Special" Star not shown.

Emerald Gold Decorated Saf-Handle, $150-185; Canary Gold "Special" Saf-Handle, $110-160.

Decoration Numbers: #0761 - #0780. **Decoration:** Stylized Flowers and Leaf Sprays.

Emerald Gold "Special" Streamline, $200-250; Cobalt Gold Decorated Streamline, $150-180.

Decoration Numbers: #0321 - #0340. **Decoration:** Gold Lining.

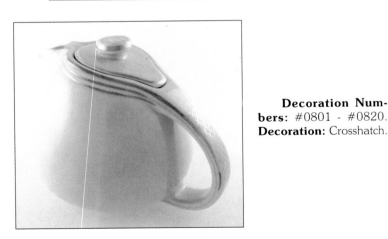

Decoration Numbers: #0801 - #0820. **Decoration:** Crosshatch.

Canary Gold Decorated Sani-Grid, $90-110.

Warm Yellow Platinum Decorated Streamline, $75-90.

Decoration: Platinum Lining.

Cobalt Gold Decorated Surf Side, $245-290.

Decoration Numbers: #0621 - #0640. **Decoration:** Gold Lines.

Cobalt Gold Decorated Windshield, $125-150.

Decoration Numbers: #0681 - #0700. **Decoration:** Gold Flowers.

Cobalt Gold "Special" Surf Side, $315-365.

Decoration Numbers: #0621S - #0640S. **Decoration:** Gold Lines.

Maroon Gold "Special" Windshield, $125-150.

Decoration Numbers: #0681S - #0700S. **Decoration:** Gold Flowers.

"Victorian" Series

Six teapots were introduced in 1946 that are referred to by collectors as the "Victorian" Series. Generally each shape is found in only one or two colors. The "Benjamin" and "Connie" are found in celadon green and yellow; the "Birch" in pastel blue; the "Murphy" in pastel blue and "steel" gray; the "Bowknot in pink, "steel" gray, and yellow, and the "Plume" in pink. They are usually found in a six-cup size; however, an eight-cup size "Bowknot" has been found.

Adding gold to solid colored teapots had been so popular, Hall China added gold to the "Victorian" Series. Hall tried a large number of gold decorations on the six teapots. The amount of gold varied from teapot to teapot. The bottom stamp found is H-3, but many of the undecorated "Victorian" teapots will not have a bottom stamp. Because of the limited production life, the "Bowknot" and any that are decorated in gold are harder to find.

Top row, left to right: Yellow "Benjamin" ("Albert"), $150-180; Blue "Birch" ("Darby"), $55-65; Celadon Green "Connie" ("Victoria"), $55-65; bottom row: "Steel" Gray "Bowknot" ("Gladstone"), $200-250; Pink "Plume" ("Disraeli"), $55-65; Pastel Blue "Murphy" ("Peel"), $55-65.

A variety of gold decorations were applied to the "Victorian" teapots; some of which are shown. Prices vary from $125-350 depending on amount of gold.

Brilliant Series

In the late 1950s, J. Palin Thorley designed the "*Brilliant Series Group 120 Hall China Decorated Teapots*" that consists of six teapots, the "Apple," "Grape," "Regal," "Royal," "Starlight," and "Windcrest." Collectors also refer to this series as the Thorley series, named after the designer. The common colors are apple green, blue turquoise, bright blue, gloss black, ivory, lemon, maroon, pink, sky blue, and white. The teapots are found with 22-carat bright gold stipple decoration and with rhinestones, usually silver, but also red or green. The rhinestones were added to the teapots later in the production cycle. The rhinestones were glued on the teapots and are frequently missing. Rhinestones added by Hall have a whitish rim around the rhinestones where the rhinestone was embedded into the glue. Rhinestones replaced by collectors usually do not have this glue rim. The "Apple" and "Grape" teapots are also found with decals. The bottom stamps found are H-3 for the solid teapots, HSQK for the decaled teapots, and H-3 with the gold decorated number on those with the gold stipple. Many of the bottom stamps will include the Hall manufacturing number. The Brilliant Series appeared in the catalogs until the late 1960s.

Top row, left to right: Apple Green "Regal" ("Dickens"), $100-125; Gloss-Black "Grape" ("Darwin"), $125-150; Sky Blue "Apple" ("Browning"), $170-215; bottom row: Pink "Starlight" ("Tennison"), $90-120; Ivory "Royal" ("Eliot"), $160-190; Lemon "Windcrest" ("Bronte"), $80-100.

Gold Label

The Gold Label Series was introduced in the mid-1950s and available through the 1960s. The bottoms of the Gold Label teapots were marked with HALL and the number in gold that identifies the color and shape of the teapot, followed with "GL." There are thirteen styles of teapots selected that came in assorted colors with bright gold decorated handles, spouts, and knobs with bright gold designs.

The thirteenth teapot that is decorated and marked on the bottom with "GL" is the T-Ball Round. Below each teapot pictured is the numbering range for color and shape identification, plus the decoration. See the Color section later in this book for more information about the Gold Label colors.

Canary Aladdin, $225-275.

Decoration Numbers: #0661 - #0680. **Decoration:** "Squiggle."

Ivory Baltimore, $100-125.

Decoration Numbers: #0161 - #0180. **Decoration:** "Nova."

Ivory Aladdin, $100-110.

Decoration Numbers: #0661 - #0680. **Decoration:** "Swag."

Ivory Boston, $60-75.

Decoration Numbers: #0001 - #0020. **Decoration:** Fleur-de-lis.

Decoration Numbers: #0221 - #0240. **Decoration:** "Reflections."

Left:
Ivory Albany, $85-110.

Ivory French, $50-65.

Decoration Numbers: #0041 - #0060. **Decoration:** Daisy.

Ivory New York, $60-75.

Decoration Numbers: #0021 - #0040. **Decoration:** Flower.

Ivory Hollywood, $80-100.

Decoration Numbers: #0101 - #0120. **Decoration:** Grid.

Ivory Parade, $45-55.

Decoration Numbers: #0781 - #0800. **Decoration:** "Squiggle."

Ivory Hook Cover, $60-75.

Decoration Numbers: #0741 - #0760. **Decoration:** Star.

Ivory Philadelphia, $55-70.

Decoration Numbers: #0061 - #0080. **Decoration:** Basket.

Decoration Numbers: #0081 - #0100. **Decoration:** "Illinois."

Ivory Los Angeles, $80-100.

Black T-Ball Round, $180-220.

Decoration Numbers: #0841 - #0860. **Decoration:** Rose.

Ivory Windshield, $85-100.

Decoration Numbers: #0681 - #0700. **Decoration:** Gold Dot.

In addition to the teapots, the Gold Label series consisted of the kitchenware pieces of French baker, "Thick Rim" three bowls set, round casserole with lid, salad bowl, Zeisel cookie jar, "Rayed" jug, and the "Terrace" eight-cup coffee pot with heavy gauge aluminum dripper with plunger-type basket for use with drip-grind coffee. Decorations on the kitchenware pieces are the Basket, Daisy, Dots, "Illinois," "Squiggle," or Star.

The colors usually found on the Gold Label kitchenware pieces and the "Terrace" coffee pots are blue turquoise, cadet, canary (maize), ivory, Monterey green, and pink. Even though the coffee pot and kitchenware pieces are generally found in a particular color and decal combination, they could be ordered in any of the six colors and decorations. The bottom mark is HSQK.

Blue Turquoise "Daisy" "Terrace," $55-65.

Sixties Decorations

The last teapot assortment produced by Hall China consisted of six of the most popular six-cup styles with new decorations. Three of the teapots, the Boston, French, and Hollywood, sported large gold decorations. The Los Angeles and Windshield featured floral bands. The Philadelphia had an unusual old-fashioned Hearth scene. This assortment of teapots was produced in the 1960s and has been dubbed the "Sixties" series. The only additional sized teapots found with any of these decals are a smaller French and Philadelphia. The bottom mark for this assortment is H-3. One other bottom mark may be found on the French, the "International Brotherhood of Pottery and Allied Workers, AFL-CLO," an organization started in 1899 of which Hall China is a member.

Top row, left to right: Hollywood (Brown body with a leafy decal in gold), $90-100; Windshield (Yellow body with a white, brown, and green floral band), $85-100; Los Angeles (Mustard body with green and yellow laurel wreath decal), $90-100; front row: Philadelphia (Blue body with a hearth scene decal in black), $70-85; French (Black body with a rose decal in gold), $70-80; Boston (Green body with a fruit decal in gold), $95-110.

Lipton Tea Company Shapes

Lipton Tea Company chose Hall's French shape teapot in 1935 for their advertising and had them made in six colors, with an incised Lipton Teas mark on the bottom. Over the years the incised bottom mark changed from almost a script Lipton to a block Lipton incising. All six teapots are solid colored inside and out. The colors are yellow, blue, warm yellow, green, black, and maroon. A story has been told that the blue and yellow were distributed on the West Coast, the warm yellow and black in the Midwest, and the maroon and green on the East Coast. A matching Boston shape creamer and sugar were made in all colors except the maroon to accompany the teapots. Teapots with strainers were produced from about 1935 to 1962 when Hall stopped making teapots with strainers. Newer Lipton teapots do not have strainers. A Lipton set that is poppy colored on the outside and warm yellow on the inside has been found. These are embossed with Lipton Tea and are also stamped with the Pearl China Company. There were only about fifty of these sets made.

In 1956 the Cozy Cover was added as a Lipton premium. With a Lipton tea box top and $2.50, one could purchase a Cozy Cover teapot. A gold-tone insulated aluminum cover with slots for the handle and spout fits over the teapot. The large handle makes it easy to hold and differs in shape from the Forman Brothers Cozy Hot Pot. The pouring spout was designed to discourage dripping, and the teapot has a built-in strainer to catch the loose tea before pouring into a cup. The bottom stamp is H-3, and it has only been seen in yellow. The large Counter Service Teapots were produced to advertise Lipton Tea.

Lipton Counter Service Teapot, $475-550.

Top row, left to right: Canary, $65-70; Maroon, $80-90; Green, $120-130; middle row: Blue, $65-75; Black, $80-90; Cozy Cover, $45-60; front row: Warm Yellow, $65-75.

Poppy and Yellow Lipton, ND.

McCormick Tea Company Shapes

The McCormick Tea Company of Baltimore, Maryland, began buying teapots from The Hall China Company in 1916 when imports from Europe were not available because of World War I. Hall provided McCormick with two-cup Boston, one-and-a-half-cup French, and two-cup New York teapots. In 1933 Hall made a white teapot with a green-band for McCormick; and when the Edwin Bennett Pottery Company closed in 1935, McCormick turned to the Hall China Company to produce all of their premium teapots. The Hall-produced teapot was a copy of the previous Bennett teapot shape. Several sizes of teapots in the Bennett shape and two new custom shapes were introduced over the years, with production ending in the middle 1990s. The teapot shapes included a two-cup teapot without infuser and with "Mc" debossed on the side, five- and six-cup teapots with infusers, a ribbed eighteen-ounce two-cup teapot, a McCormick Tea House teapot, 1.25-gallon counter service iced teapots, two-gallon counter service teapots, and a two-cup Boston teapot. The McCormick Tea Company used the teapots as premium items and sold many through the McCormick Tea House shop in Baltimore.

The first Hall-produced forty-four-ounce five-cup teapot made for McCormick was a bright-white infuser teapot with a green band and platinum trim. Alternate decorations of this teapot are a larger green band covering the lower half of the body and a band of orchid rather than green. A two-cup teapot without the infuser was added in 1938. It is found in turquoise or green with a large "Mc" on both sides of the teapot. During the late 1930s Hall produced one-and-a-quarter-gallon and two-gallon counter server teapots for McCormick, some with debossed lettering. Slogans on some of these pots included a large "Mc" with "McCormick Tea" underneath, "Keeps Hot," "McCormick Teas," and "Banquet Teas 'A *Wonderful* Flavor' Iced – Hot." The bottom mark on the Counter Service Teapots is H3.

In 1939 a thirty-six-ounce six-cup teapot was made for McCormick in solid turquoise with a white infuser. Cadet, maroon, and brown colors were added in 1946. Other known colors are blue turquoise, cascade, and pink. The six-cup McCormick infuser teapot was also produced with the Crocus decal and the "Elizabethan Bouquet" and French Flower gold decorations. These decorated McCormick teapots are hard to find. In the early 1950s Hall made a new style round ribbed-body eighteen-ounce two-cup teapot for McCormick. In the January and February 1952 Washington, D.C. newspapers, the McCormick infuser was advertised for $1.25 when you purchased McCormick teas in local grocers. The teapot was identified as a Bru-O-lator and came in maroon. (Hall McCormick Teapots, John Walker, Internet, January 9, 2000) The maroon and turquoise infuser teapots are easily found. Versailles blue, canary, Danish white, and pink infuser teapots were added to the McCormick line in 1956.

Top row, left to right: 1982 – White Souvenir Teapot, $150-180; 1946 – Gold Decorated Teapot, $100-130; middle row: 1935 – Standard McCormick Teapot, $90-110; 1933 – Green Band Teapot, $60-80; front row: 1952 – 18-ounce Ribbed Teapot, $25-35; 1938 – Two-Cup McCormick Teapot, $180-200; 1958 – Two-Cup Boston Teapot, $50-60.

In the 1980s the McCormick teapot was available in the McCormick gift shop or through their catalog in the following colors: black, canary yellow, cobalt blue, coral peach, Danish white, dark green, gourmet green, marine blue, rose, and Versailles blue. They retailed at $19.95 each. Additional colors available were blue turquoise, cascade, and pink. The metallic Golden Glo teapot retailed for $22.50. The small ten-ounce Boston shape was available in cobalt blue, dark green, marine blue, black, rose, sand dust, and ivory. They retailed for $15.95 each. The bottom stamp on the two-cup Boston is "McCormick Collection."

The McCormick Tea Company constructed a sixteenth century teahouse replica in the McCormick building in the harbor in Baltimore in 1934. For many years McCormick operated this tearoom and gift shop, referring to it as "Ye Old McCormick Teahouse." A white, thirty-six-ounce six-cup infuser teapot was made with a decal of "Ye Old McCormick Teahouse" on the side, trimmed in brown, and sold as a souvenir in 1982. A twelve-ounce collector's mug with the same decal was also available. A set of four mugs sold for $37.50 and the teapot for $23.50.

This was followed in 1984 and 1985 with the "Ann Hathaway Cottage Teapot" designed by Don Schreckengost. This teapot came undecorated and with a decal of the McCormick Tea House. The decoration shows the inside of an early English shop. On one side a waitress is standing at the door with her tray and customers are seen through the windows with their afternoon tea. Above the red door is 1984 or 1985, like a house number, indicating the year this teapot was distributed. The decal on the other side of the teapot shows workers making tea and cookies. The waitress was designed to resemble the woman who worked in the McCormick Tea House. The bottom stamp is "McCormick Tea, Baltimore, Md., Made in U.S.A."

McCormick teapots produced by Hall China were available by mail order up until 1996. McCormick teapots made after 1996 were made in China and are marked as such. Bottom stamps on the six-cup infuser teapot are "McCormick & Co., Banquet Teas, Balto" or "McCormick Tea, Baltimore, Md., Made in U.S.A." The two-cup is marked "McCormick, Balto., Md., Made in U.S.A."

1.25-Gallon Debossed Counter Service Teapot, $475-550.

1985 – "Ann Hathaway Cottage Teapot" (front and back), $130-150.

Crocus McCormick, ND.

1.25 Gallon Counter Service Teapot, $300-350.

"Elizabethan Bouquet" McCormick, ND.

Enterprise Aluminum Company Shapes and Decorations

Blaine Zuver founded the Enterprise Aluminum Company in 1914. The Enterprise Aluminum Company has been one of the world's leading manufacturers of cookware, including a broad assortment of kitchen items and utensils. Enterprise also produced a line of stainless cookware starting in 1962.

Enterprise general offices and warehouses were located in Massillon, Ohio, until 1956. A new plant was started in Oneonta, New York, in 1953, but was closed in 1963 in order to centralize operations. Enterprise sold its manufacturing plant and office buildings in Massillon, Ohio, to Republic Steel Corporation in 1956. Enterprise maintained facilities in Eatonon, Georgia, and Oneonta, New York, with an additional warehouse in Los Angeles, until 1963. The Enterprise Product Division of Republic Steel was sold to Lancaster Colony Corporation of Columbus, Ohio, in 1966. The aluminum product division of Lancaster Colony Corp. operated plants in Eatonon and Tifton, Georgia. In 1972 Enterprises Corp. offices were moved to Macon, Georgia, to be closer to its manufacturing plants in Eatonon and Tifton, Georgia. Employment at Enterprise Aluminum reached its peak in 1930.

The Drip-O-lator trademark was established in 1928 and issued to the Enterprise Aluminum Company. Two forms of the Drip-O-lator mark were in general use, but only one of these marks has been associated with the products produced by Hall China.

Enterprise ordered coffee pots from the Hall China Company starting in 1934 with large volumes of new orders and reorders continuing through the 1950s. In the early 1960s reorders slowed considerably and stopped in the late 1960s.

Enterprise added aluminum drips to china bodies it purchased from various potteries, reselling the completed units through national merchandisers like Montgomery Ward and major hardware wholesalers. During the war years, Enterprise sold all-china drip coffee pots to its distributors while the production of aluminum drips was restricted.

Very little ephemeral data has been found for the Enterprise Aluminum Company, so most of the coffee pot and teapot names for the Hall-produced pots are derived from collectors and authors. Some of the coffee pots Hall produced for Enterprise were sold to other distributors with other decorations and bottom marks, and some shapes were enlarged to fit West Bend aluminum drips. Bottom stamps will be shown at the end of this section. Only one identified coffee pot is not pictured, the #691 coffee bottom with the Drip-O-lator bottom stamp. The prices listed are for the china pieces; add $10-15 for a metal drip.

U.S. Patent 1370782 was issued on March 8, 1921, to Benjamin H. Calking for his inventive idea involving the control in the flow of hot water into contact with the roasted and ground coffee berry. Richard F. Krause of Massillon, Ohio, was issued U.S. Patent 1743925 on January 14, 1930, for the invention as it relates to coffee pots for making drip coffee by the leaching action of boiling water upon the ground coffee.

"Orange Floral Bouquet" "#2 Coffee Shape," $50-60.

Blue "Basketweave," $50-65.

Also available in solid colors of orange, white, and yellow.

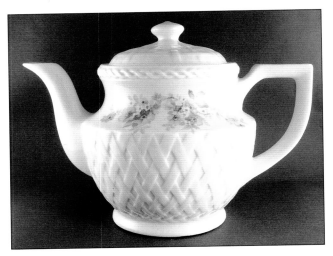

"Wild Rose Floral Garland" "Basketweave," $40-55.

"June" Flower "Bauhaus," $45-60.

Also available in "Jonquil" Flower.

"Orange Floral" Round Handle "Bricks and Ivy," $40-65.

"Ivory Beauty" Square Handle "Bricks and Ivy," ND.

Also appears with the same "Orange Floral" decal shown on the round handle "Bricks and Ivy."

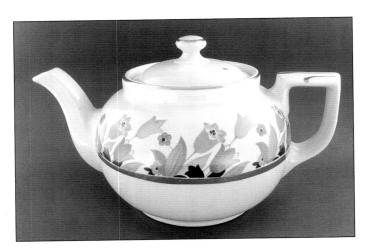

Crocus Boston Tea-O-lator, $225-275.

Daisy "Cathedral" ("Arch"), $50-65.

"Daisy Bouquet" "Cathedral" ("Arch"), $75-90.

Crocus "Colonial" ("Medallion"), $85-100.

"Shrub Rose Garland" "Colonial" ("Medallion"), $50-65.

"Green Poppy" "Colonial Tall" ("Medallion"), $180-220.

"Pink Rose" "Dart" ("Russell"), $65-80.

"Mini Floral" "Drape" ("Swathe"), $40-60.

"Yellow Tulip" "Duse," $65-80.

Red with White Accents "Jerry" ("Monarch"), $45-60.

"Floral Lattice" "Jerry" ("Monarch"), $45-60.

Homewood "Kadota" All-China Drip, $110-135.

Also available in "Parrot Tulip," Serenade, "Tulip," and Wild-flower.

"Three Poppies" "Lewis," $40-55.

"Impatiens" "Lotus," $40-55.

Red, White Accents, and Platinum Trim "Meltdown," $50-65.

Also available in black, blue, green, or yellow.

"Piggly Wiggly" "Norse" ("Everson"), ND.

"Bird of Paradise" "Orb," $45-60.

"Potted Flowers" "Panel," $40-55.

Variation shows two pots rather than three.

"Sutter's Gold" "Petal," $50-65.

Wildflower Two-Cup "Rounded Terrace" ("Step Round"), $35-45.

Also available in Floral.

"Rambling Rose" Four-Cup "Rounded Terrace" ("Step Round"), $40-55.

Also available in "Pasture Rose."

Floral Six-Cup "Rounded Terrace" ("Step Round"), $40-55.

"Floral Rose" Six-Cup "Rounded Terrace" ("Step Round"), $40-55.

Also available in "Rambling Rose" and "Pink and Gray Floral Bouquet."

Blue Band and Stars "Sash," $95-120.

Also available in red or green.

Red Band without Stars "Sash," $85-100.

Also available in blue or green.

"Brand" "Scoop," $50-65.

Also available in Wildflower.

"Modern Tulip" "Sweep," $40-55.

Also available in Wildflower.

"Dutch Couple" "Target" ("Bullseye"), $40-55.

White with Green Trim Six-Cup "Terrace" ("Step Down"), $45-60.
   Not verified as Hall.

"Windmill" "Target" ("Bullseye"), $40-55.

White with Green Flowers Six-Cup "Terrace" ("Step Down"), $45-60.
   Not verified as Hall.

"Shrub Rose Garland" Two-Cup "Terrace" ("Step Down"), $30-45.

Art Glaze Yellow "Trellis," $65-80.

Also available in art glaze colors of blue, green, orange, or red.

Cactus "Viking" ("Bell"), $60-75.

Also available in "Bird of Paradise" and "Flamingo."

"Floral Bouquet" "Trellis," $45-60.

"Minuet" "Waverlet" ("Crest"), $45-60.

"Flower Pot" "Viking" ("Bell"), $65-80.

Also available with two pots rather than three.

"Jonquil" Flower "Waverly" ("Crest"), $45-60.

Also available in "June" Flower and "Minuet."

"Tulip" "Waverly" ("Crest"), $45-60.

"Yellow Rose" "Waverly" ("Crest"), $45-60.

18-Cup Coffee Urn, $175-225.

"Shrub Rose Garland" "Wicker," $40-55.

Red Poppy "Wicker," ND.

48-Cup Coffee Urn, $175-225.

Trademarks and
Bottom Marks

The trademark for the Enterprise Aluminum Co. is "Drip-O-lator." The first usage was in 1926 and registered in March 1930 to the Automatic Drip-O-lator Corp. in Kansas City, Missouri. It was assigned to the Enterprise Aluminum Co. with first usage in November 1928 and registered in June 1930. Last renewal was in June 1970. The trademark has expired.

The bottom mark shown incorporating the Drip-O-lator trademark is the only one associated with Hall-produced coffee pots. Other pottery companies also used this bottom stamp.

This bottom mark has not been found on coffee pots known to have been made by Hall China.

A version of the bottom stamp with Tea-O-lator was also used. It is most commonly found on the eight-cup free pour Boston teapot with the Crocus decal. The bottom stamp was used in 1934.

Forman Family, Inc.
Shapes and Decorations

Forman Family, Inc., a manufacturer of chrome and silver items, purchased coffee pots and teapots between 1932 and 1982 from The Hall China Company to be combined with their products. A Beaded Electric Percolator, Urn, creamer, and sugar were introduced in August 1932 and discontinued in 1945. This set was replaced by the Basket Weave set. A picture of the Beaded set is not included. The coffee pots and teapots reflect the design and decoration styles of the period in which they were produced. Hall China products made for the Forman Family products were frequently embellished with metal covers and/or stands, some with provisions for warmers. Other products sold by Forman include casseroles, baking dishes, marmites, and serving dishes and plates employing the same decorations as the coffee pots and teapots. Bottom marks include Forman Bros. and Forman Family or Forman 4 Family as their central feature. Forman Family, Inc. was located in Brooklyn, New York.

"Pink and Gray Floral Bouquet" Basket Weave ("Straw Weave") Electric Urn, $125-150.

White Adjusto, $90-110.

Also available in Chinese red.

"Fruit" Adjusto, $200-250.

"Gold Floral" Basket Weave ("Straw Weave") Electric Urn, $125-150; Percolator, $100-125.

Pink Cozy Cover Hot Pot, $55-65.

Also available in turquoise and yellow.

Mat Black Cozy Cover Hot Pot, $50-60.

Also available in white.

Fuji "Dart" ("Russell"), $60-75.

Art Glaze Orange "Dodecagon" with China Cover, $200-250.

White and Gold Band "Dodecagon" with Metal Cover, $300-350.

"Chrysler" "Dodecagon" with Metal Cover, $300-350.

"Chrysler" "Dodecagon" with Metal Cover, $300-350.

"Apple Blossom" "Duse," $70-85.

Fuji "Duse," $65-80.

Mother of Pearl Floral Panels "Dutch" with China Cover, $100-125.

"Christopher" "Dutch" with China Cover, $125-150.

"Oriental Butterfly" "Dutch" with Metal Cover, $125-150.

"Chrysler" "Dutch" with China Cover, $150-175.

Rust and Mother of Pearl "Edwards" with Metal Cover, $125-150.

Also available in blue and green.

Blue and Mother of Pearl "Dutch" with China Cover, $100-125.

Rust and Mother of Pearl "Edwards" with China Cover, ND.

White and Greek Key Four-Matic Electric Percolator, $70-90.

Also available in black.

Black Forman Carafe, $45-55.

Also available in pink, turquoise, white, and yellow.

Also available in pink and yellow.

Left:
Turquoise Four-Matic
Electric Percolator, $65-85.

"Apple Blossom" "Gibson" Electric Percolator, $75-85.

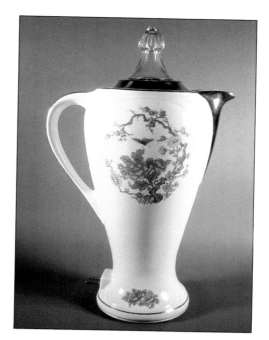

"Oriental Butterfly" "Gibson" Electric Percolator, $75-85.

"Apple Blossom" "Gibson" Electric Percolator, $75-85.

Fuji "Gibson" Electric Urn, $80-95; Percolator, $70-85.

"Tree of Life" "Gibson" Electric Percolator, $75-85.

Golden Glo "Ribbed Band" Hot Water Pot and Teapot, $125-150 each.

Black with Greek Key "Tip-Pot" and Stand, $220-260.

Also available in canary, Golden Glo, Silver Glo, and white.

Bottom Marks

Tricolator Company Shapes and Decorations

The Tricolator Company, Inc. was established in 1908 and located in New York City. On March 20, 1928, Patent No. 1,663,317 was issued to I. D. Richheimer, President and originator of Tricolation (brewing method), for the design of the spout used on the Tricolator coffee pots. Mr. Richheimer wrote in his patent application, "A common complaint incident to the use of coffee pots and the like arises from the fact that, after a pouring operation, the coffee or other contents will drip from the lip or drivel down the spout and stain the table cloth. The housewife often wipes the spout with a napkin to prevent this dripping and driveling. The dripping can be prevented to a large extent by exercising special care in pouring, and also by engaging a cup with the lip of the spout to remove the drop which generally forms thereon; but the drivel down the spout may occur without attracting attention and it makes an unsightly spot on the table cloth and presents a messy appearance. It is my object to overcome this defect in pouring spouts of coffee pots, or the like, and to provide a spout which will prevent driveling and to a large extent also prevent dripping."

The Tricolator method of making coffee is fundamentally the clarifying and refining of coffee through a Tricolator filter sheet, a fresh one used for each coffee making. The Tricolator filter is made up of different fibers that are woven strongly together yet remain very porous to permit coffee filtration. The filters were packed ten packets of 100 each and available in sizes from 2.875" to 22" diameter.

Tricolator named the different shapes of the coffee pots in their earlier brochures; but, by the early 1940s, the company began referring to the pots by number rather than by name. In a 1930s Tricolator catalog, the coffee pots are listed by name and model number. When ordering a coffee pot, an example of an Autocrat number is "1718PA." The "17" refers to the shape (Autocrat); the "1" to the color of the pot; the "8" to the coffee pot capacity; and the "PA" to the drip top style which was shown in the catalog. An illustration of the different drip styles is shown in this section. Also shown in this section is a Tricolator flame pad. The flame pad was used for protection over an open flame and carried an insurance policy. Tricolator would replace any Tricolator coffee pot without cost that would break while using the flame pad. All an individual had to do was send in a copy of the Insurance Certificate and a piece of the broken Tricolator coffee pot and receive a replacement.

Colors advertised for some of the Tricolator coffee pots were cardinal, coral, emerald, jade, orchid, sky, yale, and yellow. These colors are matte art glazes with decoration numbers Dec.-T-141 through Dec-T-149. The number of the color was stamped on the bottom of many of the Tricolator pots. These colors and color numbering system were also used on the Cube, Tea for Four Sets, Tea for Two Sets, and the Twin-Tee sets. The matte art glazes are soft and easily damaged. Some of the other colors found on the Tricolator pots are coral, delft, egg blue, henna, jade, lavender, lettuce, marine, Ming red, navy blue, Nile green, old rose, olive green, peacock green, seal brown, tan, white, and yellow.

Some styles of the Tricolator coffee pots were given two names depending upon whether they came in solid colors or were decorated. Some styles had different names depending upon whether they had a regular or a screw-top lid. Some styles were given different names because they had both long and short spouts. When known, we have tried to use the names that were given to the coffee pots when they were first sold. We know that this may cause confusion, but we wanted to call the Tricolator coffee pots by their proper name.

From the late twenties to the sixties, Hall China made coffee pots for the Tricolator Company with most of the production in the thirties and forties. Tricolator provided the metal drips and heaters that could be ordered to go with the coffee pot. One of the drips was called the Crown and was made to fit any style coffee server. The drip had a metal cover that could serve as a drip tray when turned over. All of the china coffee pots were sold with china covers. The latest coffee pots made for the Tricolator Company were the Coffee Princess, Coffee Queen, and the Coffee Empress.

The bottom stamp is Tricolator Pour Right U. S. Patent 1663317, with and without HALL incised. Some of the Tricolator shapes will not have the Tricolator bottom stamp. There are some coffee pots marked Tricolator that were not made by Hall China.

In this section are shown the various shapes and decorations of the Tricolator coffee pots. More decorations than are shown will be found on the Autocrat, Bride, and Regent. Also shown is a Flame Tamer that was used on open flames to protect the pot. A sample of an Autocrat serving station is illustrated.

Marine Ambassador ("Blossom"), $65-85.

Decorated Ambassador ("Blossom"),
$250-300.

Autocrat ("Buchanan") Counter Service. (Reprint from a 1927
Tricolator brochure.)

Warm Yellow "Amory," $70-85.

Also available in black with colored covers.

Decorated Eight-Cup Autocrat ("Buchanan"), ND.

Maroon Eight-Cup Autocrat ("Buchanan"),
$55-65.

Decorated Eight-Cup
Autocrat ("Buchanan"),
$150-175.

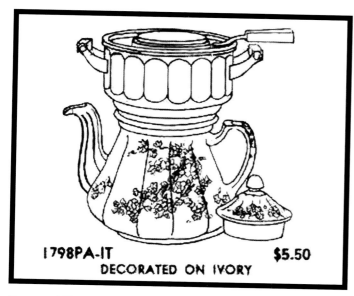

Decorated Eight-Cup Autocrat ("Buchanan"). (Reprint from a 1930s Tricolator brochure.)

Yellow Solid Color Beacon ("Diver"), $60-75.

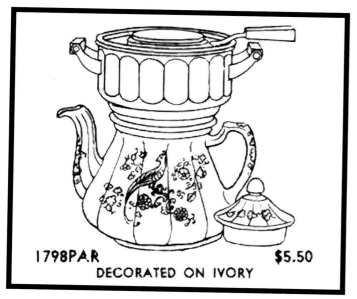

Decorated Eight-Cup Autocrat ("Buchanan"). (Reprint from a 1930s Tricolator brochure.)

Black Lustre with Red Cover Bride ("Diver"), $95-110.

Chinese Red Autocrat, Jr. ("Buchanan" with Screw Locking Cover), $70-85.

Decorated Bride ("Diver"), $125-150.

Decorated Bride ("Diver"), $125-150.

Decorated Bride ("Diver"), $125-150.

Decorated Bride ("Diver"), $125-150.

Decorated Bride ("Diver"), $125-150.

Decorated Bride ("Diver"), $125-150.

Decorated Bride ("Diver"), $150-175.

Decorated Bride ("Diver"), $100-125.

3795CA-3 $4.50

Decorated Bride ("Diver"). (Reprint from a 1930s Tricolator brochure.)

Decorated Bride ("Diver"), ND.

Decorated Bride ("Diver"), $100-125.

Decorated Bride ("Diver"), $100-125.

3795CA-73 $4.50

Decorated Bride ("Diver"). (Reprint from
a 1930s Tricolator brochure.)

Decorated Bride ("Diver"), $125-150.

Nile Green Clipper (Long-Spout "Carraway"), $60-75.

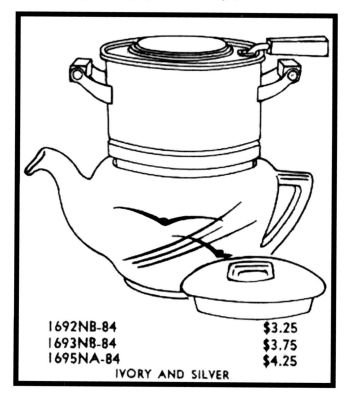

1692NB-84	$3.25
1693NB-84	$3.75
1695NA-84	$4.25

IVORY AND SILVER

Decorated Clipper (Long-Spout "Carraway").
(Reprint from a 1930s Tricolator brochure.)

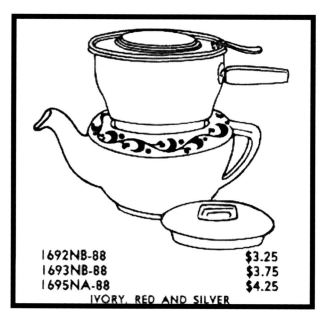

1692NB-88	$3.25
1693NB-88	$3.75
1695NA-88	$4.25

IVORY, RED AND SILVER

Decorated Clipper (Long-Spout "Carraway"). (Reprint from a 1930s Tricolator brochure.)

1692NB-102	$3.25
1693NB-102	$3.75
1695NA-102	$4.25

DECORATED ON IVORY

Decorated Clipper (Long-Spout "Carraway"). (Reprint from a 1930s Tricolator brochure.)

Lune Blue Eight-Cup Coffee Empress, $35-50.

Four-Cup Coffee Princess, Six-Cup Coffee Queen

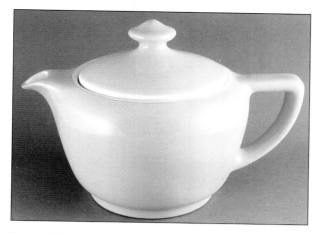

Emerald Screw Locking Cover "Dave," $80-95.

French Flower Erie ("Wilson"), ND.

Brown with White Knob One-Gallon Encore ("Crown"), $45-60.

Eight-Cup Solid Color Encore ("Wilson").

Marine "Imperial" ("Clover"), $40-60.

Black with White Cover "Imperial" ("Clover"), $50-65.

1898AFA-100 $5.50
DECORATED ON IVORY

8 CUP CAPACITY POTS

Decorated Erie ("Wilson"). (Reprint from a 1930s Tricolator brochure.)

Decorated "Imperial" ("Clover"), $125-150.

Decorated "Imperial" ("Clover"), $125-150.

Matte Art Glaze Yellow Norfolk ("Hoyt"), $65-80.

Nile Green New Yorker (Short-Spout "Carraway"), $60-75.

Decorated New Yorker (Short-Spout "Carraway"), $250-300.

Decorated Norfolk ("Hoyt"), $125-150.

Decorated New Yorker (Short-Spout "Carraway"), ND.

Decorated Norfolk ("Hoyt"), $150-175.

Decorated Norfolk ("Hoyt"). (Reprint from a 1930s Tricolator brochure.)

Decorated Panther ("Ritz"), $100-125.

Yellow Solid Color Panther ("Ritz"), $60-75.

Decorated Panther ("Ritz"), $125-150.

Also available with other color covers.

Left:
Black Lustre with Orange Cover Panther ("Ritz"), $100-125.

3098AFA-83 $6.00
RED AND SILVER ON IVORY

Decorated Panther ("Ritz"). (Reprint from a 1930s Tricolator brochure.)

Matte Art Glaze Lavender Plaza ("Susannah"/"Ansel"), $100-125.

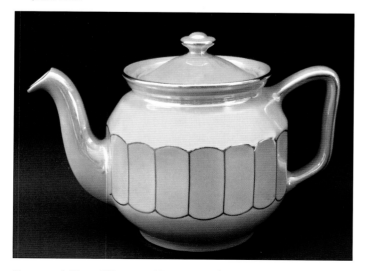

Decorated Plaza ("Susannah"/"Ansel"), $125-150.

Decorated Six-Cup Regent ("Buchanan"), $125-150.

3296MA-101 $4.50
DECORATED ON IVORY

Decorated Six-Cup Regent ("Buchanan"). (Reprint from a 1930s Tricolator brochure.)

Decorated Six-Cup Regent ("Buchanan"), $125-150.

3256MB $3.75
JET BLACK LUSTER WITH COLORED
COVERS — YELLOW, GREEN, RED

Black Lustre with Colored Cover Six-Cup Regent ("Buchanan"). (Reprint from a 1930s Tricolator brochure.)

Marine "Steve," $65-80.

Lettuce Roosevelt ("Blaine"), $70-85.

Decorated "Steve," $150-175.

Green Lustre Royal Park ("Lincoln"), $70-85.

Yellow "Wellman," $60-75.

Coral Pink Solid Color Six-Cup Windsor ("Buchanan"), $60-75.

Tricolator Flame Tamer, $35-45.

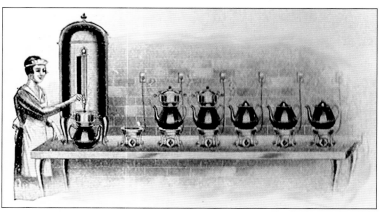

Reprinted from a 1927 Tricolator Company, Inc. catalog.

Tricolator Bottom Marks

Tricolator's trademark is the word "TRICOLATOR" in block letters, first used in May 1922, which has expired. The trademark was acquired from the Filtrator Coffee Apparatus Company, Inc. of New Jersey.

Types of Tricolator Aluminum Drips

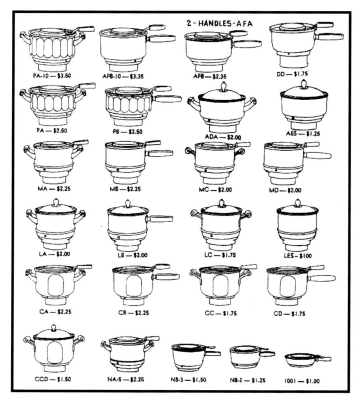

(Reprint from a 1930s Tricolator brochure.)

Decorations

What to include in this section? We wanted to show all the decorations used on Hall teapots and coffee pots. That seems too large an undertaking if you consider color as a decoration. So, we decided not to include solid colors, but to note them in the shape sections of this book. We also decided not to include hand-painted designs; commercial, club, or organization decals or decorations; or silver overlays. We are also not including decals added to Hall undecorated china bodies that are not bottom stamped. These teapots and coffee pots are interesting to collect, but we feel that the quantity of these decorated items makes them too many to include.

Next, we decided to exclude from this section those decorations or decals that only appear on one shape of teapot or coffee pot. Instead, we would include these decorations or decals in the shape sections of the book. This, however, causes a problem with some Enterprise Aluminum, Forman, and Tricolator pots, since several decals are used on these pots that were not used on another shape. These decaled items are included as decorations in the Enterprise Aluminum, Forman, or Tricolator sections of the book.

Finally, we had to try to name the remaining decorations or decals that we did include. China decorators seem to use a lot of decals where the primary flower is some type of rose. So many of the decals are rose sprays, rose bouquets, or rose swags. We have used other author's names for these rose-floral mixes where known, but we have added some of our own names. Names such as Rose Decal 1, Rose Decal 2, etc., while appealing, just did not seem to fill the bill. Without a doubt, some will argue that we are not botanist and cannot tell a rose from a tulip, but we tried and are open to other interpretations.

Below are the decorations in alphabetical order with a listing of the pots that they have been found on thus far. We have tried to be inclusive, but we are sure that others exist.

Shapes with same decorations: Older Teapots – Baltimore, New York, "Radiance," "Rutherford;" Older Coffee Pots – #691 All-China Drip, "Meltdown," "Radiance" All-China Drip, "Terrace" (8 cup).

Acacia "Radiance," $185-210.

Shapes with same decoration: Older Teapots – "Radiance," "Rutherford;" Older Coffee Pots – #691 All-China Drip, "Baron," Bride, "Radiance" All-China Drip, Tea for Four Set, "Terrace" (8 cup).

"Antique Rose" Philadelphia, $65-80.

Shapes with same decoration: Newer Teapots – Airflow, Boston (3 cup), Philadelphia (3, 6, and 8 cup).

#488 "Radiance," $275-300.

"Apple Blossom" "Gibson" Electric
Percolator, $75-85.

Shapes with same decoration: Older Teapot – "Radiance;"
Older Coffee Pots – "Duse" (Forman), "Gibson" Electric Percolator
and Urn.

"Autumn Harvest" Airflow, $90-125.

Shapes with same decoration: Newer Teapots – Airflow,
Boston (8 cup), Philadelphia.

Autumn Leaf (Jewel Tea) Aladdin, $65-85.

Shapes with same decoration: Older Teapots – Aladdin (7-
cup round with infuser), Boston (2 cup), "Demi" Teapot (only 2
made), Newport, "Rayed;" Older Coffee Pots – "Jordan" All-China
Drip, "MJ" Electric Percolator, "Rayed," "Rayed" Teapot/Coffee Pot;
Newer Teapots – Airflow, Automobile, Basketball, Bellevue, Bird
Cage, Boston, Centennial (only 2 made), Counter Server, Cube,
Doughnut, Football, French (2 cup), Hook Cover, Musical, Nautilus,
New York, Philadelphia (4 cup), Saf-Spout, Solo, St. Louis Choco-
late Pot, Streamline, T-Ball Square, Tea for Two Set, Windshield;
Newer Coffee Pots – Bellevue (3 cup), Washington (12 Cup).

Autumn Leaf Flare-Ware, $60-75.

Shapes with same decoration: Older Teapot – Flare-Ware;
Older Coffee Pots – Flare-Ware Coffee Server and Urn.

"Black Beauty" "Rutherford," $290-330.

Shapes with same decoration: Older Teapots – "Radiance,"
"Rutherford;" Older Coffee Pot – #691 All-China Drip.

Black Gold Aladdin, $125-155.

Shapes with same decoration: Older Teapots – Aladdin (Round), French (2 cup); Older Coffee Pot – Washington (15 cup).

Blue Belle with Blue Flowers "Demi" Teapot, $90-110.

Shapes with same decoration: Older Teapot – "Demi" Teapot; Older Coffee Pot – Demi Coffee Pot.

Blue Blossom Saf-Handle, $375-450.

Shapes with same decoration: Older Teapots – Airflow, Baltimore, "Demi" Teapot, Hook Cover, New York (6, 10, and 12 cup), Saf-Handle (6 cup) Streamline; Older Coffee Pots – #691 All-

China Drip, French Coffee Biggin (2 cup), Saf-Handle Coffee Server; Newer Teapots – Automobile, Counter Server, Cube, Football, Musical, Saf-Spout.

Blue Bouquet Aladdin, $190-230.

Shapes with same decoration: Older Teapots – Aladdin (oval and round with Infuser), Boston; Older Coffee Pots – "Carrie" All-China Drip with electric heater, "Carrie" with glass dripper with electric heater, "Five Band 'D'-Handle," "Kadota" All-China Drip, "Terrace" (8 cup); Newer Teapots – Automobile, Cube, Football, Hook Cover, Musical, St. Louis Chocolate Pot, Streamline, Windshield.

"Blue Dresden" (Newer) Two-Cup Boston, $50-65.

Blue Garden "Demi" Teapot, $325-375.

Shapes with same decoration: Older Teapots – Airflow, Aladdin (oval with colored infuser), "Demi" Teapot, Doughnut, New York (6, 10, and 12 cup), Saf-Handle (6 cup), Streamline; Older Coffee Pots – French Coffee Biggin (4 cup), Saf-Handle Coffee Server, "Terrace" (8 cup), "Terrace" All-China Drip, Washington.

Blue Willow Philadelphia, $475-525.

Blue Willow Boston, $300-350.

Blue Willow Boston, $300-350.

Shapes with same decoration: Older Teapots – Boston (2, 4, and 6 cup), New York (8 cup), Philadelphia (5 cup), Twin-Tee Hot Water Pot; Older Coffee Pot – Washington (2 cup).

Bouquet Hallcraft Tomorrow's Classic Coffee Pot, $75-125.

Shapes with same decoration: Older Teapots – "Grape," Hallcraft Tomorrow's Classic; Older Coffee Pots – "Flared" Coffee Server (Sohn), Hallcraft Tomorrow's Classic, "MJ" Electric Percolator, Samovar (Sohn).

"Bronze Rose" "MJ" Electric Percolator, $85-100.

Brown-Eyed Susan (Older) Aladdin, $250-300.

Buttercup with Yellow Flowers Demi Coffee Pot, $90-110.

Shapes with same decoration: Older Teapot – "Demi" Teapot; Older Coffee Pot – Demi Coffee Pot.

Cactus "Viking," $60-75.

Shapes with same decoration: Older Teapots – French (6 and 8 cup), Manhattan, "Radiance," "Rutherford," Streamline; Older Coffee Pots – "Five Band 'D' Handle," "Viking".

"California Poppy" French, ND.

Shapes with same decoration: Older Teapots – French (2 cup); St. Louis Chocolate Pot; Older Coffee Pot – Bride.

Cameo Rose E- Style, $100-125.

Shapes with same decoration: Older Teapot – E-Style; Newer Teapots – Automobile, Counter Server, Cube, Football, Hook Cover, Musical.

Carrot "Radiance," ND.

Shapes with same decoration: Older Teapots – "Radiance," Windshield.

Cat-Tail "Betty" Electric Urn, $160-175.

Shapes with same decoration: Older Coffee Pots – "Betty" Electric Percolator and Urn; Newer Teapots – Automobile, Cube, Football, Hook Cover, St. Louis Chocolate Pot, Streamline, Windshield.

Chestnut Flare-Ware Teapot, $40-50.

Chinese Red Aladdin, $250-300.

Shapes with same decoration: (Chinese red pots with HSQK bottom marks are sometimes referred to as Red Kitchenware) Teapots – Airflow, Aladdin (round, oval with and without colored in-

fuser), Albany, Alma, Automobile, Baltimore, Basket, Basketball, Bellevue, Bird Cage, Boston, Chicago, Cleveland, Cube, "Demi" Teapot, Doughnut, Football, French (2 and 6 cup), Globe, Hollywood (4 and 6 cup), Hook Cover, Iconic, Illinois, Irvine, Kansas, Los Angeles, "Medallion," Melody, Moderne, Nautilus, New York (2 and 6 cup), Newport, Ohio, Parade, Philadelphia (3 and 6 cup), "Radiance," Rhythm, "Ribbed" Globe, "Ribbed Rutherford," "Rutherford," Saf-Handle (1.5, 2, and 6 cup), Solo Tea Set, Star, Streamline, Surf Side, T-Ball Round, Tea for Four Set, Tea for Two Set, Tea Taster, Twin-Tee Set, Twinspout, Windshield; Coffee Pots – #691 All-China Drip, Autocrat Jr., Bellevue, Coffelator, "Five Band" Coffee Server, French Coffee Biggin, "Medallion" All-China Drip, Million Dollar Coffee Pot, "Radiance" All-China Drip, Saf-Handle Coffee Server, "Terrace" (8 cup), "Terrace" All-China Drip, Washington.

Christmas (Older) Heirloom, $110-135.

Christmas Tree Demi Coffee Pot, $150-175.

Shapes with same decoration: Older Coffee Pot – Demi Coffee Pot; Newer Teapots – Automobile, Boston Sunken Cover (2 cup), Cube, Football, Hook Cover, Musical.

"Color Band" (Older) "Rutherford," $250-275.

Decorations have the color band or color band and a black line below. Color band variations include green, red, red and black, and yellow and black.

Copper Lustre (Older) Airflow, $175-200.

"Country Cottage" (Newer) Two-Cup Boston, $50-65.

Crocus Aladdin, ND.

Shapes with same decoration: Older Teapots – Aladdin (hi-white or ivory oval with infuser, ivory round with infuser), Boston (8 cup), Doughnut, McCormick, Melody, New York, (2, 4, 6, 8, and 12 cup), "Rayed," Streamline; Older Coffee Pots – "Arthur," "Colonial," "Deco," "Five Band" (Partial Tab Cover), "Jordan" All-China Drip, "Kadota" All-China Drip, "Meltdown," "Terrace" (8 cup), "Terrace" All-China Drip; Newer Teapots – Automobile, Bellevue (Green - 2 cup), Counter Server, Cube, Football, Hook Cover, Musical, Saf-Spout, St. Louis Chocolate Pot, Windshield; Newer Coffee Pot – Bellevue (Green - 1 cup).

"Duberry" (Newer) Two-Cup Boston, $50-65.

Eggshell Lines New York, $150-175.

Shapes with same decoration: Older Teapots – Aladdin (with infuser), New York (white – 6 cup), "Rutherford" (ivory).

Eggshell Swag "Rutherford," $450-500.

Shapes with same decoration: Older Teapot – "Rutherford;" Older Coffee Pot – #691 All-China Drip.

Eggshell Plaid #691 All-China Drip, ND.

Shapes with same decoration: Older Teapot – "Rutherford;" Older Coffee Pot – #691 All-China Drip.

Fantasy Streamline, $475-550.

Shapes with same decoration: Older Teapots – "Demi" Teapot, Saf-Handle (6 cup), Streamline; Older Coffee Pot – Saf-Handle Coffee Server.

Eggshell Polka Dot "Rutherford," $325-375.

Shapes with same decoration of either black, blue, green, red, or yellow dots: Older Teapots – French (2 cup), "Rutherford;" Older Coffee Pot – #691 All-China Drip.

"Fantasy Dragon" (Newer) London, $45-60.

Flamingo Streamline, $530-600.

Shapes with same decoration: Older Teapots – French, Streamline; Older Coffee Pots – #691 All-China Drip, "Viking."

Shapes with same decoration: Older Teapots – Manhattan, New York (2, 6, and 12 cup); Older Coffee Pots – "Jerry," French Coffee Biggin (2, 6, and 10 cup), "Kadota" All-China Drip, Washington (6, 12, and 15 cup).

"Floral Sprig" Boston, $75-100.

Shapes with same decoration: Older Teapots – Aladdin (round), Boston (2 cup).

"Floral" (Newer) Doughnut, $125-175.

"Flower Garden" Boston, ND.

Shape with same decoration: Newer Teapots – Boston (3 and 8 cup).

"Floral Lattice" ("Flower Pot") Six-Cup New York, $250-300.

French Flower French, $85-105.

Shapes with same decoration: Older Teapots – Airflow, Aladdin (round with infuser), Boston, Buffet Teapot, Cube, Detroit, French, French Light Weight, Infuser, Los Angeles, McCormick, New York, Parade, "Philbe," Star, Windshield; Older Coffee Pots – Erie (8 cup and 1 gallon), French Coffee Biggin, Washington (15 cup).

"Fruit" Adjusto, $200-250.

Shapes with same decoration: Older Teapots – Adjusto, "Ribbed Band" Teapot, "Ribbed Band" Hot Water Server.

Fuji "Duse," $65-80.

Shapes with same decoration that could come in other flower colors (Duke, *Superior Quality China*, page 92)**:** Older Coffee Pots – "Andrew" Electric Percolator and Urn, "Dart" (Forman), "Duse" (Forman), "Gibson" Electric Percolator and Urn.

"Gaillardia" Boston, $200-250.

Shapes with same decoration: Older Teapot – Boston; Older Coffee Pot – "Terrace" (8 cup).

Game Bird (Ring Neck Pheasants) "Apple," $175-200.

Game Bird (Bob White Quail) "MJ" Electric Percolator, $125-150.

Game Bird (Canada Geese) "MJ" Electric Percolator, $125-150.

Coffee Server (Sohn), "MJ" Electric Percolator (Hall and Sohn); Newer Teapots – Cube, Football, French, Hook Cover, Musical, Saf-Spout, St. Louis Chocolate Pot, Streamline.

Gold Band Philadelphia, $50-75.

Shapes with same decoration (width of band can be of varying size): Older Teapots – Boston, "Grape," New York, Philadelphia; Older Coffee Pot – "Terrace" (8 cup).

Game Bird (Mallard Ducks) "MJ" Electric Percolator, $125-150.

Shapes with Game Bird decorations: Older Teapots – "Apple," "Grape," New York (2 and 6 cup), Windshield; Older Coffee Pots – Flame Ware Coffee Biggin Bottom (Sohn), Flame Ware

Gold Deer "MJ" Electric Percolator, $85-100.

Shapes with same decoration: Older Teapot – Windshield; Older Coffee Pot – "MJ" Electric Percolator.

185

Gold Dot Windshield, $85-100.

Shapes with same decoration: Older Teapots – Boston (2, 4, and 6 cup), French (2 cup), New York (2 and 6 cup), Ohio, Windshield; Older Coffee Pots – Coffee Carafe, "Terrace" (8 cup).

Golden Clover Windshield, $225-275.

Shapes with same decoration: Older Teapots – "Radiance," Windshield; Older Coffee Pot – "Radiance" All-China Drip.

Gold Lace Flare-Ware Teapot, $60-75.

Shapes with same decoration: Older Teapots – Flare-Ware (black or gold bottom), Flare-Ware with Heather Rose; Older Coffee Pots – Flare-Ware Coffee Server and Urn.

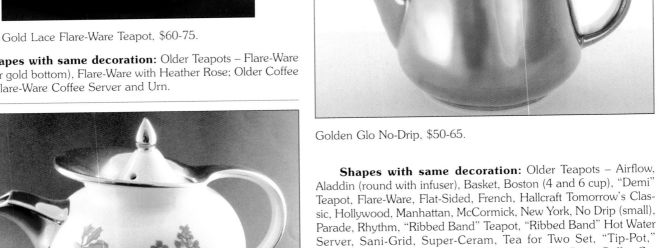

Golden Glo No-Drip, $50-65.

Shapes with same decoration: Older Teapots – Airflow, Aladdin (round with infuser), Basket, Boston (4 and 6 cup), "Demi" Teapot, Flare-Ware, Flat-Sided, French, Hallcraft Tomorrow's Classic, Hollywood, Manhattan, McCormick, New York, No Drip (small), Parade, Rhythm, "Ribbed Band" Teapot, "Ribbed Band" Hot Water Server, Sani-Grid, Super-Ceram, Tea for Two Set, "Tip-Pot," Twinspout; Older Coffee Pots – Demi Coffee Pot, Doric Coffee Carafe (Sohn), French Coffee Biggin (all sizes), Hallcraft Tomorrow's Classic, Super-Ceram, Washington.

Golden Carrot Windshield, $325-350.

Shapes with same decoration: Older Teapots – "Radiance," Windshield.

Golden Oak French, $175-200.

Shapes with same decoration: Older Teapots – E-Style, French, New York; Older Coffee Pot – "Kadota" Large Coffee Base.

"Green Poppy" "Rutherford," ND.

Shapes with same decoration: Older Teapots – Boston, "Rutherford;" Older Coffee Pot – "Colonial Tall."

Harlequin Hallcraft Tomorrow's Classic Coffee Pot, $175-225.

Shapes with same decoration: Older Teapots – "Grape," Hallcraft Tomorrow's Classic; Older Coffee Pot – Hallcraft Tomorrow's Classic.

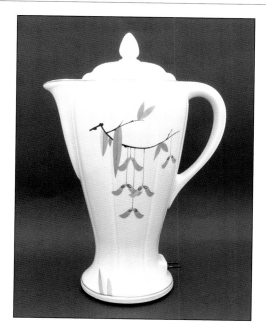

Shapes with same decoration: Older Coffee Pots – "Andrew" Electric Percolator and Urn, "Gibson" Electric Percolator and Urn.

"Hanging Vine" "Andrew" Electric Percolator, $150-175.

"Heather Rose" London, $40-60.

Shapes with same decoration with flowers available in pink or yellow: Older Teapots – Flare-Ware, London, New York; Older Coffee Pots – Flare-Ware Coffee Server, "Terrace" (8 cup), Washington Knob Cover (2 and 6 cup); Washington Sunken Cover (2 cup); Newer Teapots – Cube, Football, French, Hook Cover, Streamline.

Homewood "Terrace," $60-75.

Shapes with same decoration: Older Teapot – New York; Older Coffee Pots – "Kadota" All-China Drip, "Terrace" (8 cup).

"Holly" (Older) Demi Coffee Pot, $195-225.

"Hunt Scene" (Newer) Three-Cup Boston, $50-65.

Left:
"Holly" (Newer)
Longaberger, $135-160.

"Hunting Dog" (Brittany) "MJ" Electric Percolator, $125-150.

"Hunting Dog" (Golden Retriever) "MJ" Electric Percolator, $125-150.

"Hunting Dog" (Pointer) "MJ" Electric Percolator, $125-150.

"Hunting Dog" (Pointer) "MJ" Electric Percolator, $125-150.

"Ivory Beauty" "Bricks and Ivy," ND.

Shapes with same decoration: Older Teapot – "Radiance;" Older Coffee Pot – "Bricks and Ivy."

"Ivy Trellis" Airflow, $90-125.

Shapes with same decoration: Newer Teapots – Airflow, London, Philadelphia.

"Leaf and Vine" Hollywood, $165-200.

Shapes with same decoration (can be found in other colors – see Early Decals Section): Older Teapots – Baltimore, French, Hollywood, Philadelphia.

"Lilac Mist" Boston, $50-65.

Shapes with same decoration: Newer Teapots – Airflow, Boston (3 cup).

Little Red Riding Hood Hook Cover, $80-100.

Shapes with same decoration: Newer Teapots – Automobile, Hook Cover.

Meadow Flower (Older) Streamline, $850-950.

Mexicana Windshield, $90-120.

Shapes with same decoration: Newer Teapots – Automobile, Football, Streamline, Windshield.

"Mini-Fleurette" Parade, $275-325.

Shapes with same decoration: Older Teapots – Aladdin, Benjamin, Birch, French, Hook Cover, Los Angeles, Parade, Streamline; Older Coffee Pot – "Waverly."

"Minuet" French, $150-175.

Shapes with same decoration: Older Teapots – Baltimore, French (4 and 7 cup), Philadelphia; Older Coffee Pots – "Waverlet," "Waverly."

Morning Glory Aladdin, $175-200.

Shapes with same decoration: Older Teapot – Aladdin (7 cup with infuser); Older Coffee Pot – "Jordan" All-China Drip.

Mother of Pearl Hollywood, $175-200.

Shapes with same decoration of canary or ivory: Older Teapots – Airflow, Hollywood, New York, Philadelphia, Sani-Grid.

"Mums" ("Pink Mums") "Colonial," $125-150.

Shapes with same decoration: Older Teapots – Boston (8 cup), "Colonial," New York, "Rutherford;" Older Coffee Pots – "Colonial Tall," "Daniel," "Meltdown," "Terrace" (8 cup).

"New Rose" (Newer) Three-Cup Boston, $50-65.

"No Blue" French, $125-150.

Shapes with same decoration: Older Teapots – Aladdin (6 cup), French, Hook Cover, Parade, Sani-Grid (white lid); Newer Teapot – Boston (8 cup).

"Old Garden Rose" "MJ" Electric Percolator, $85-100.

"Old Garden Rose" "MJ" Electric Percolator, $85-100.

"Orange Poppy" ("Poppy") Melody, $325-375.

Shapes with same decoration: Older Teapots – Bellevue (2 cup), Boston, Doughnut, Melody, Streamline, Windshield; Older Coffee Pots – Bellevue (2 cup), Great American, S-Handle; Newer Teapots – Automobile, Counter Service Teapot, Cube, Football, Hook Cover, Musical, Saf-Spout, St. Louis Chocolate Pot.

"Parrot Tulip" ("Shaggy Tulip") "Radiance," $275-325.

Shapes with same decoration: Older Teapot – "Radiance;" Older Coffee Pots – "Kadota" All-China Drip, "Perk," "Radiance" All-China Drip.

Oyster White and Red Cooking China Washington, $95-115.

Shapes with same decoration: Older Teapot – Aladdin (round with infuser); Older Coffee Pot – Washington (15 cup).

"Pastel Morning Glory" ("Pink Morning Glory") "Rutherford," $275-325.

Shapes with same decoration: Older Teapots – Aladdin (round with infuser), Boston, "Colonial," New York, "Radiance," "Rutherford;" Older Coffee Pots – "Perk," "Radiance" All-China Drip, "Terrace" (8 cup), Washington (15 cup).

Pewter Portland, $40-55.

Shapes with same decoration: Older Teapots – Detroit, Portland, Tea Taster.

"Piggly Wiggly" "Norse," ND.

Shapes with same decoration: Older Teapot – "Radiance;" Older Coffee Pots – "Norse".

Poinsettia and Holly (Newer) Musical, $90-120.

Radial Flare-Ware Teapot, $60-75.

Shapes with same decoration: Older Teapot – Flare-Ware; Older Coffee Pots – Flare-Ware Coffee Server and Urn.

Shapes with same decoration: Older Coffee Pots – Basket Weave Electric Percolator and Urn, "Kadota" Large Coffee Base, "MJ" Electric Percolator, "Rounded Terrace."

"Pink and Gray Floral Bouquet" "Kadota" Large Coffee Base, $45-60.

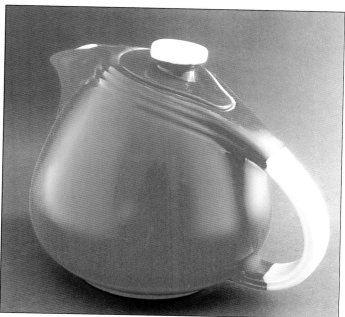

"Red and White" Sani-Grid, $65-85.

Shapes with same decoration: Older Teapots – Sani-Grid (3 and 6 cup).

Red, White Accent, and Platinum "Deca-Flip," $65-80.

Shapes with same decoration (may come in black, blue, green, or yellow): Older Teapot – Boston; Older Coffee Pots – "Arthur," "Baron," "Bingham," Deca Flip, "Meltdown," "Perk," "Terrace" (8 cup), "Terrace" All-China Drip.

Red Poppy Aladdin, $175-200.

Shapes with same decoration: Older Teapots – Aladdin (oval with infuser), New York; Older Coffee Pots – "Daniel," "Wicker;" Newer Teapots – Airflow, Automobile, Counter Server, Cube, Football, Hook Cover, Musical, Saf-Spout, St. Louis Chocolate Pot, Streamline, Windshield.

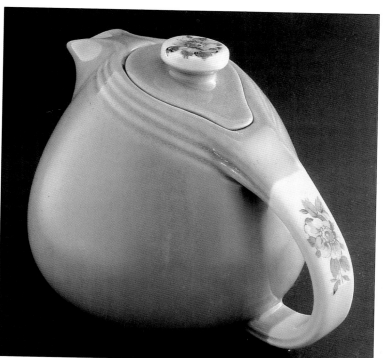

Rose Parade Sani-Grid, $100-125.

Shapes with same decoration: Older Teapots – Sani-Grid (3 and 6 cup); Older Coffee Pot – "Jordan" All-China Drip.

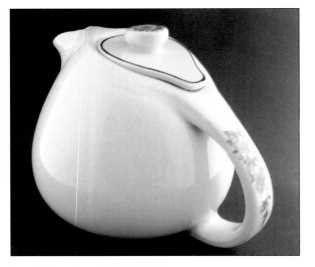

Rose White Sani-Grid, $75-95.

Shapes with same decoration: Older Teapots – Sani-Grid (3 and 6 cup).

RX New York, $90-100.

Shapes with same decoration: Older Teapot – New York; Older Coffee Pot – "MJ" Electric Percolator (Hall and Sohn).

Royal Rose Aladdin, ND.

Shapes with same decoration: Older Teapots – Aladdin (round with infuser), French.

Serenade New York, $130-160.

Shapes with same decoration: Older Teapots – Aladdin (round with infuser), New York; Older Coffee Pots – "Jordan" All-China Drip, "Kadota" All-China Drip, "Terrace" (8 cup).

Shapes with same decoration: Older Teapot – Boston (2 cup), Buffet Teapot, French (2 and 6 cup), "Ribbed" Globe, "Ribbed Rutherford," "Rutherford;" Older Coffee Pots – #691 All-China Drip, California, French Coffee Biggin.

Left:
Russet "Rutherford,"
$225-275.

"Shaggy Floral" (Older) "Radiance," ND.

Silhouette ("Taverne") New York, $250-300.

Shapes with same decoration: Older Teapots – "Colonial," New York, Streamline; Older Coffee Pots – "Colonial" All-China Drip, "Colonial Tall," "Five Band" (Partial Tab Cover), "Five Band 'D' Handle," "Kadota" All-China Drip, "Terrace" (8 cup); Newer Teapots – Airflow, Automobile, Counter Server, Cube, Football, Hook Cover, Musical, Saf-Spout, St. Louis Chocolate Pot, Windshield.

Silver Glo Aladdin, $140-160.

Shapes with same decoration: Older Teapots – Airflow, Aladdin (round with infuser), Baltimore, Boston (2, 4, and 6 cup), Hollywood, Hook Cover, Parade, Philadelphia, T-Ball Round, "Tip-Pot," Windshield; Older Coffee Pots – Demi Coffee Pot, Four-Matic (4-Matic) Electric Percolator.

"Spring Blossoms" (Older) Streamline, ND.

Springtime French, $85-110.

Shapes with same decoration: Older Teapot – French; Older Coffee Pots – "Kadota" Large Coffee Base, Washington.

"Stonewall" ("Banner N' Basket") "Radiance," $375-425.

Shapes with same decoration: Older Teapot – "Radiance" (Eggshell or Ivory); Older Coffee Pots – "Kadota" All-China Drip (Eggshell or Ivory), "Radiance" All-China Drip (Eggshell).

Sunnyvale (Older) Flare-Ware Teapot, $75-100.

"Summer Song" Boston, $60-75.

Shapes with same decoration: Newer Teapots – Airflow, Boston (3 and 8 cup), Philadelphia.

"Tulip" "Kadota" All-China Drip, $135-160.

Shapes with same decoration: Older Teapot – Aladdin (Round with infuser); Older Coffee Pots – "Daniel," "Kadota" All-China Drip with and without gold trim, "Perk," "Rayed."

Sun Porch (Newer) Automobile, $125-150.

Two-Tone Boston, $70-85.

Shapes with same decoration of either forest green and citron, mahogany and canary, or mahogany and blue mist: Older Teapot – Boston; Older Coffee Pot – French Coffee Biggin (4, 6, and 10 cup).

Watusi (Older) Up-Beat Stoneware, $65-80.

White Bake Ware Boston, $45-60.

Shapes with same decoration: Older Teapots – Aladdin (round with infuser), Boston, "Demi" Teapot; Older Coffee Pots – Demi Coffee Pot, French Coffee Biggin (all sizes), Washington (15 cup).

Brown "White Rim Band" Boston, ND (Reprint from 1920s Hall China catalog)

Shapes with same decoration in either brown or green: Older Teapots – Boston Knob Cover (1, 1.5, and 2 cup), Chicago (1 and 1.5 cup); Older Coffee Pot – Washington (2 cup).

"Wild Poppy" ("Poppy and Wheat") "Radiance," $300-350.

Shapes with same decoration: Older Teapots – Baltimore, "Demi" Teapot, French, Infuser, New York (all sizes), "Radiance," Tea for Four Set, Tea for Two Set; Older Coffee Pots – #691 All-China Drip, French Coffee Biggin (3, 4, and 6 cup), "Jordan" All-China Drip, "Radiance" All-China Drip, "Terrace" All-China Drip, Washington (2 and 12 cup).

Wildfire Aladdin, $150-175.

Shapes with same decoration: Older Teapots – Aladdin (oval and round with infuser), Boston, Sani-Grid (6 cup), Streamline; Older Coffee Pot – S-Handle (with and without glass drip).

Wildflower "Scoop," $45-60.

Shapes with same decoration: Older Coffee Pots – "Kadota" All-China Drip, "Rounded Terrace" (small), "Scoop," "Sweep."

"Winter Berry" London, $50-65.

Shapes with same decoration: Older Teapot – Hollywood; Newer Teapots – Airflow, London.

"Winter Rose" (Newer) Three-Cup Boston, $50-65.

Woven Traditions Longaberger, $125-160.

Came in red, blue, green, or holly.

"Yellow Rose" ("Pastel Rose") New York, $150-165.

Shapes with same decoration: Older Teapot – New York (4 and 6 cup); Older Coffee Pots – "Kadota" Coffee Bottom with "Jordan" China Drip, "Kadota" Large Coffee Base, "Norse," "Waverly."

Eva Zeisel Designs

Eva Zeisel, in her nineties at the time of this writing, was still very active in industrial design projects and teaching. As a freelance designer, she has designed for A. H. Heisey and Company; Bryce Brothers; Federal Glass Company; Castleton China Company; Charm House; Clover Box and Manufacturing Company; General Mills; The Hall China Company; Hyalyn Porcelain; Red Wing Pottery; Riverside Ceramics Company; Salisbury Artisans; Sears, Roebuck and Company; United China and Glass; Western Stoneware Company; and others. She is known for designing the first all-white modernist dinnerware in the United States. Her design projects also included plexiglass, metal craft, glass, and pottery.

Eva Zeisel came to the United States in 1938 and taught ceramic design for mass production at the Pratt Institute in Brooklyn, New York, from 1939 to 1953. In 1942 she designed her first important dinnerware line, called Stratoware, for Sears, Roebuck and Company.

Between 1942 and 1943, she collaborated with Castleton China Company and the Museum of Modern Art to produce her famous Museum Shape dinnerware line. Museum Shape dinnerware was produced by Shenango Pottery, a division of Castleton, and marketed by Castleton. Because of the war, Museum Shape dinnerware was not exhibited until 1946 and not actively marketed until 1949 with some of the shapes having been changed from their original design. The Museum design gained her a reputation as a first-class designer.

Eva Zeisel's next major design was the free-spirited Town and Country Earthenware dinnerware for Red Wing Pottery, Minnesota, in 1946. Eva designed next for the Riverside Ceramic Company. In 1949-1950, the Hallcraft Tomorrow's Classic line was designed for the Midhurst China Company. Hall China produced the Hallcraft Tomorrow's Classic line from 1951 to 1958.

The year 1954 saw a new design of classical, simple shapes in the Zeisel "Monmouth" line designed for Western Stoneware and part of the Orchard Ware series for the Watt Pottery Company. Also Eva Zeisel designed for Hall the Zeisel Kitchenware line that year. In 1957, she created the Hallcraft Century dinnerware design that was also produced by The Hall China Company. Her last dinnerware design, "Z" dinnerware, was for Hyalyn. Eva Zeisel retired from designing in 1964 but returned to industrial design and teaching in 1983.

In 1998 The Hall China Company gave Eva Zeisel the production molds for the Tomorrow's Classic and Hallcraft Century dinnerware lines. The company is releasing the production rights for the Eva Zeisel designs produced by Hall China. An article in a 2004 *Modernism* magazine says you can expect in the near future to find reproduced Tomorrow's Classic pieces made by Royal Stafford of Burslem and sold at Crate & Barrel.

Hallcraft Century

Hallcraft Century dinnerware was designed in 1957 and produced in 1957 and 1958 by the Hall China Company. While considered equal in design to the earlier Tomorrow's Classic design, it did not achieve nearly the same commercial success. The Century din-

nerware line was more limited than Tomorrow's Classic with only twenty-three pieces and five patterns – Century White, Fern, Flight, Garden of Eden, and Sunglow. The delicate shapes of the Century design did not ship well and breakage was common. Charles Seliger designed the Garden of Eden decoration. A teapot may be found in the Flight decoration that is shown. A Hallcraft Tomorrow's Classic Coffee Pot with a Century style lid is shown. This pot has not been proven to have been part of the Hallcraft Century line.

Fern, $175-195.

Garden of Eden Pattern, ND.

Sunglow, $175-195.

White, $200-225.

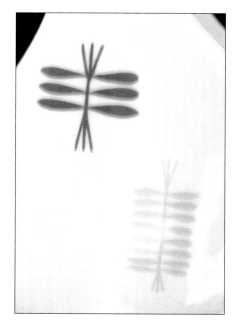

"Flight" Pattern.

Hallcraft Century Coffee Pot (not proven as Hall), ND.

Hallcraft
Tomorrow's Classic

Tomorrow's Classic was designed in 1949-1950 and produced between 1951 and 1958 by the Hall China Company. The dinnerware was distributed by Midhurst China Company and has been called the best selling dinner set in the United States. The Midhurst China Company was the result of a Hall China and Johnathan Higgins partnership for the distribution of Hall's Hallcraft dinnerware to department stores. This dinnerware line has forty pieces, including teapot, coffee pot, creamer, and sugar, and was produced in many patterns.

The book, *Eva Zeisel*, states that this line almost did not reach production. "The manufacturer, Hall China, was on the point of shelving it when the president of Commercial Decal stepped in saying he thought the pieces were ideal for decorating. Consequently, Eva was required to present nine patterns the first year and three each subsequent years."

Most of the design patterns were not created by Eva but by her associates and design studios, including Irene Haas, her assistant, who designed Flair, Frost Flower, and Lyric; Eric Blegvard, a student, designed Buckingham; Ross Littell designed Fantasy and Harlequin; John Carlos designed Studio 10; Alfred Durhrssen adapted Bouquet from a Stig Lunberg design; Charles Seliger of the decal company designed Arizona, Dawn, Palo Duro, Prairie Grass, Rain Tree, and Spring; and Sascha Brastoff designed "Surf Ballet." Eva Zeisel designed the Hi-White, Satin Gray, and Satin Black patterns.

Not shown are the Hallcraft Tomorrow's Classic teapot and coffee pot in Golden Glo. A creamer has been found with the Gold Deer decal. It is not known whether teapots and coffee pots were made in the Hallcraft Tomorrow's Classic patterns shown at the end of this section. Some Tomorrow's Classic patterns were shown in advertising, but never produced.

Arizona Coffee Pot, $175-225; Arizona Teapot, $375-425.

Caprice Coffee Pot, $75-125; Caprice Teapot, $100-150.

Bouquet Coffee Pot, $75-125; Bouquet Teapot, $125-175.

Dawn Coffee Pot, $225-275; Dawn Teapot, $375-425 (not shown).

Buckingham Coffee Pot, $175-225;
Buckingham Teapot, $225-275.

Fantasy Coffee Pot, $75-125; Fantasy Teapot, $75-125 (not shown).

Frost Flowers Coffee Pot, $125-175; Frost Flowers Teapot, $275-325.

Harlequin Coffee Pot, $175-225; Harlequin Teapot, $175-225.

Flair Coffee Pot, $175-225; Flair Teapot, $275-325 (not shown).

Hi-White Coffee Pot, $125-175; Hi-White Teapot, $175-225.

Holiday Coffee Pot, $175-225; Holiday Teapot, $275-325.

Lyric Coffee Pot, $175-225; Lyric Teapot, $275-325.

Peach Blossom Coffee Pot, $175-225; Peach Blossom Teapot, $275-325 (not shown).

Mulberry Coffee Pot, $175-225; Mulberry Teapot, $275-325.

Pinecone Coffee Pot, $125-175; Pinecone Teapot, $225-275.

Satin Black Coffee Pot, $125-175; Satin Black Teapot, $175-225.

Spring Coffee Pot, $175-225; Spring Teapot, $225-275.

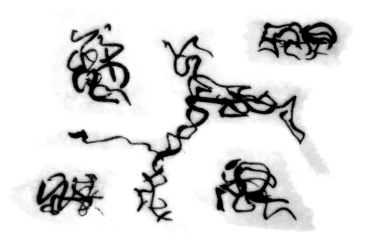

Studio Ten Pattern. Studio Ten Coffee Pot, $275-325 (not shown); Studio Ten Teapot, $375-425 (not shown).

"Surf Ballet" ("Platinum Splatter") Coffee Pot, $175-225; Teapot, $325-375 (not shown).

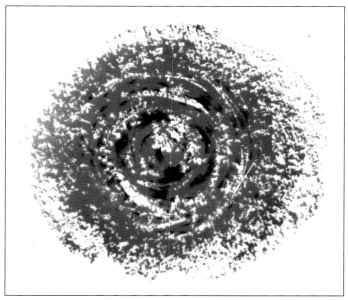

"Palo Duro" Pattern.

"Prairie Grass" Pattern.

Zeisel Kitchenware

In 1954, Eva Zeisel designed the Zeisel Kitchenware that consists of a twenty-piece cooking ware and kitchen accessories line. The Zeisel Kitchenware was produced in three patterns, Casual Living, Tri-Tone and Elena. The Elena pattern is marked Hostess Ware.

Casual Living Zeisel Kitchenware, $85-110.

"Raintree" Pattern.

Tri-Tone Zeisel Kitchenware, Side-Handled, $350-400.

"Romance" Pattern.

"Elena" ("Bodine") Zeisel Kitchenware, $450-500.

Red-Cliff Ironstone

The Red-Cliff Company of Chicago, Illinois, was a decorating and distributing company. The company distributed beautiful ironstone pieces that were reproductions of old English patterns and shapes. The Red-Cliff Company operated from about 1950 to 1980.

A 1965 Red-Cliff Retail Price Brochure states, "Red-Cliff reproductions are as faithful as research and skillful crafting can produce. The original color has been as closely maintained as possible. The original formula, however, has been altered to create a ware of great thermal properties and strength together with a fully vitrified body in fine Ironstone china. Red-Cliff Ironstone is true ovenware doing double duty as a casserole in the oven and a beautiful service piece on the table. It will retain heat and keep the foods warm well beyond the normal serving period. Dishes and beverages may be kept warm on top of the stove over medium heat if an asbestos pad is used. Red-Cliff Early American Pattern Glass is reproduced with the same meticulous care, detail and quality as our famous Ironstone Fine China."

Mr. Fred Clifford, president of Red-Cliff, purchased original pieces of English Ironstone and sent them to the Hall China Company to copy for reproductions. Red-Cliff's intent was never to deceive, only to present a modernized version of English Ironstone ware. Each piece is plainly marked. Hall China made the hollow ware and molded pieces, and Walker China Company of Bedford Heights, Ohio, made the flatware pieces.

Red-Cliff Ironstone was made in two styles – undecorated Barium White ware and Tea Leaf patterned. The Tea Leaf patterned ware was not considered successful because Hall was unable to develop a bronze tea leaf that would withstand dishwashers. The English method of years ago was to decorate the item with a brown tea leaf underglaze. After the piece had been fired, they would apply a luster and fire again. This worked reasonably well for hand washing. In the case of the British product, as the luster wears off, the brown tea leaf remains. Hall's production processes did not allow the application of the leaf underglaze; consequently, they applied the tea leaf by decal only. This made the ware microwave safe but did not result in the bright luster of the English items. Tea Leaf ware was only made from the late 1950s to the early 1960s.

Red-Cliff made ten undecorated ironstone teapots, undecorated coffee pot and coffee urn, and two Tea Leaf teapots. The teapots not shown are Hall Nos. #4165 Wheat, #4204 (not named), and #4276 Wheat (Ceres). Most of the pots have matching creamer, sugar, and tray.

Red-Cliff Ironstone Teapots

Early American Wheat, $95-110.

12 cup, 72 ounces, 8" high without cover, 11" high with cover, 10.125" wide, Hall No. 4140

Grape Cluster, $95-110.

8 cup, 56 ounces, 7" high without cover, 9" high with cover, 8.5" wide, Hall No. 4169

Grape Leaf, $80-90.

    8 cup, 48 ounces, 7.75" high without cover, 10" high with cover, 8.625" wide, Hall No. 412

Grape Melon Rib, $95-110.

    8 cup, 56 ounces, 8.125" high without cover, 9.875" high with cover, 9.75" wide, Hall No. 4256

Grape Leaf, $75-85.

    8 cup, 48 ounces, 7.75" high without cover, 10" high with cover, 8.5" wide, Hall No. 4141

Heirloom, $80-90.

    8 cup, 52 ounces, 7.375" high without cover, 9.875" high with cover, 8.875" wide, Hall No. 4198

Sydeham, $75-85.

8 cup, 52 ounces, 6.5" high without cover, 9.75" high with cover, 9.375" wide, Hall No. 4127

Red-Cliff Ironstone
Coffee Pots

Grape Leaf, $90-110.

8 cup, 52 ounces, 7.25" high without cover, 9.5" high with cover, 8.25" wide, Hall No. 4145

Grape Coffee Urn and Stand, $150-175.

Coffee Urn – 25 cup, 4.5 quarts brimful, 12" high without cover, 15" high with cover, 9.75" wide, Hall No. 4301; Stand – 3.875" high, 7.25" wide, Hall No. 4302.

Red-Cliff Ironstone Teapots and Coffee Pots Bottom Stamps

Royal-Cliff, $195-225 - (Enoch) Wedgwood shape.

8 cup, 60 ounces, 6.875" high without cover, 9.5" high with cover, 9.25" wide, strainer, Hall No. 4214 (Square)

Red-Cliff Ironstone Tea Leaf Teapots

Chinese Shape, $375-425.

8 cup, 56 ounces, 7.25" high without cover, 8.625" high with cover, 8.375" wide, Hall No. 4211 (Octagonal)

Red-Cliff Ironstone Tea Leaf Bottom Stamp

Ernest Sohn Creations

Ernest Sohn's designs are quite different from other Hall-produced pottery. The pieces are generally quite large and have wood or stainless steel, copper, or brass components. Sales literature or distributor's data has been hard to find. Even though catalogs were produced twice a year, not much is known about Sohn's product names. Ernest Sohn had products produced by Red Wing Potteries as well as other foreign and domestic potteries. Hall China Company produced a large number of Sohn's pieces between the mid-1950s and 1960s.

Ernest Sohn was born in Antwerp, Belgium, in 1913 and moved to the United States in 1938 with an education in engineering and industrial design. His first pottery job was with Glidden Pottery in New York. Shortly after starting at Glidden, Mr. Sohn, Louis Dreyfuss, and Raymond Loewy started the Industrial Design Institute. The group donated items to the Museum of Modern Art and promoted the design profession. The Industrial Design Institute later evolved into the Industrial Designers Society of America. Mr. Sohn worked for Rubel and Company between 1945 and 1951. He continued to design for Glidden while working for Rubel and created Glidden's Menagerie and Circus lines.

Ernest Sohn exhibited at the New York's Museum of Modern Art and was a winner of the Good Design Award. He started the Ernest Sohn Associates in New York City in 1951 as a one-man company. Jack Orenstein Associates became exclusive sales agents for Ernest Sohn Creations that year. Mr. Orenstein had been sales manager for Everlast Metal Products. By the mid-1950s, Ernest Sohn Associates had changed to Ernest Sohn Creations. In the late 1950s, Sohn expanded by hiring two additional designers. In 1960 Sohn worked with Red Wing personnel to produce molded ceramic cooking and serving pieces with Pennsylvania Dutch butter mold designs. Next, Mr. Sohn designed modern ceramic dinnerware and accessories pieces produced by The Hall China Company.

Mr. Sohn also owned ETCO Industries in LaCross and Ettrick, Wisconsin. The ETCO plants were small and produced stainless steel and copper cooking utensils. His Houseware and Giftware Division used combinations of Hall's ceramic cooking china and coffee pots with copper and brass components for buffet service, serving trays, and coffee servers, many with warmers for the Ambiance line.

At its peak, Ernest Sohn Creations grew to twelve salesmen with showrooms in Cleveland, Los Angeles, Dallas, and Chicago. Ernest Sohn Creations was sold in 1978.

While many of Sohn's ceramic pieces were produced by Hall China, many of the earlier and later pieces were not. The pieces shown may have been produced by the Hall China Company, but they have not been confirmed.

Ambiance, $45-65.

6 cup, 30 ounces brimful, 6" high without cover, 7.5" high with cover, 6.5" wide; Stand 5.375"

"Beaded" Coffee Server, $75-95.

8 cup, 64 ounces brimful, 10.25" high without cover, 12.75" high with cover, 10" wide, Hall No. 5355

Coffee Server, ND.

5.5" high to the top of the cover, 9.25" high to top of handle (Confirmed as made by Hall China but not confirmed as a production item.)

Coffee Server, $90-110.

10 cup, 92 ounces brimful, 10.125" high without cover, 11.275" high with cover, 8.25" wide, Hall No. 5404

Doric Coffee Carafe, $45-60.

10 cup, 84 ounces brimful, 10.5" high without cover, 11" high with cover, 9.5" wide, Hall No. 5370

Doric Coffee Server and Electric Percolator, $75-95 each.

Coffee Server: 10 cup, 96 ounces brimful, 11.75" high without cover, 13.25" high with cover, 11" wide, Hall No. 5386

Percolator: 8 cup, 80 ounces brimful, 13" high without cover, 14.25" high with cover, 10.625" wide, Hall No. 5384

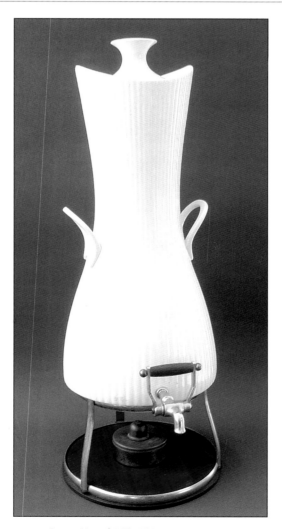

Doric Urn, $150-175.

Flame Ware Coffee Biggin, $85-100.

6 cup, 42 ounces brimful, 6.125" high without cover or biggin, 11.5" high with cover, 8.75" wide, Hall No. 5489

Flame Ware Coffee Biggin Pieces.

5.75 quarts brimful, 16" high without cover, 18" high with cover, 23.25" high with stand, 10.625" wide, Hall No. 5388

Flame Ware Coffee Biggin Bottom, $75-95.

6 cup, 42 ounces brimful, 6.125" high without cover, 8.875" high with cover, 8.75" wide, Hall No. 5489

Flame Ware Coffee Server, $90-110.

8 cup, 80 ounces brimful, 12" high without cover, 13.5" high with cover, 11" wide, Hall No. 5440 (locking tab cover)

Flame Ware Coffee Server, $80-100.

8 cup, 80 ounces brimful, 12" high without cover, 13.5" high with cover, 11" wide, Hall No. 5440 (locking tab cover)

"Flared" Coffee Server, $125-160.

6 cup, 52 ounces brimful, 10.5" high, 8.5" wide

"Formal" ("Gold Band") Coffee Server, $80-100.

8 cup, 68 ounces brimful, 8.625" high without cover, 10" high with cover, 10.25" wide, Hall No. 5456 (goes with formal dinnerware)

"Octagon" "Tip-Pot," $125-150.

6 cup, 37 ounces brimful, 4.125" high without cover, 5.875" high with cover, 10.25" high with stand, 13.125" wide, Hall No. 5243; Without lugs – Hall No. 5250

"MJ" Electric Percolator, $100-125.

8 cup, 74 ounces brimful, 10.625" high without cover, 11.5" high with cover, 8.5" wide, Hall No. 5200

"Octagon" Coffee Server and Electric Percolator, $75-95 each.

Coffee Server: 8 cup, 76 ounces brimful, 10.25" high without cover, 12" high with cover, 9.5" wide, Hall No. 5249
Percolator: 6 cup, 67 ounces brimful, 10.5" high without cover, 12.75" high with cover, 9.75" wide, Hall No. 5234

"Petal" Coffee Server, $80-100.

10 cup, 105 ounces brimful, 9" high without cover, 11.75" high with cover, 11.75" wide, Hall No. 5430

"Rivera" Coffee Server, $150-180.

8 cup, 66 ounces brimful, 9" high with cover, 11.25" wide, Hall No. 5393

"Round" Coffee Server, $80-100.

4 cup, 30 ounces brimful, 10.125" high without cover, 11.375" high with cover, 8.25" wide, Hall No. 5233

"Round" Electric Percolator, ND.

Hall No. 5439

"Royal" Electric Percolator without decal, $75-95.

8 cup, 68 ounces brimful, 10.5" high without cover, 15" high with cover, 12.25" wide, Hall No. 5405

Samovar, $200-225.

5.5 quarts, 9" high without cover, 11" high with cover, 10" wide, Hall No. 5468

"Royal" Electric Percolator with decal, $80-100.

8 cup, 68 ounces brimful, 10.5" high without cover, 15" high with cover, 12.25" wide, Hall No. 5405

Bottom Stamp

Colors

The Hall China Company probably formulated more color formulas than any other American pottery company. In addition, Hall offers to match any colors to a customer's request through their custom shop.

Colors vary because (1) of the variation in manufacturing techniques, kiln temperatures, and raw materials used; (2) the color glazes were produced in batches; and (3) changes in the time between the stirring of the glazes and the length of time an item was in the glaze. This is truer of older products, as the newer manufacturing processes use automated spraying of the glaze and more precise kiln temperature controls. The variation in colors resulting from manufacturing and the large number of Hall's colors, some just a shade different, make color identification difficult. The hardest colors to match between product runs are reds and yellows.

Most of Hall's colors are under-glaze colors fired with the greenware, but some over-glaze colors were used. Most notable among these are the Chinese red and DuPont "screaming" colors used in the late 1930s. Other early over-glaze colors were the matte art glazes used on the Tricolator coffee pots, Twin-Tee Sets, and Cube teapots and coffee pots. The over-glaze colors are more eas-

ily damaged because the glaze was applied after the initial firing. They were applied more like decals and gold lining and fired the second time at a lower temperature allowing them to be more susceptible to wear. New over-glaze colors are Copper Lustre, Golden Glo, Mother of Pearl, and Silver Glo.

Hall started with three colors, white, "stock" green, and "stock" brown, and they now offer eighteen colors on the Super Express Lines and over 150 standard additional colors for the General Product line. Super-Ceram colors are shown on the Sample General Line Colors table.

Table 1 - General Line Colors Offered Over Time
Table 2 - Sample General Line Colors
Table 3 - Decorated Teapot Colors Offered Over Time
Table 4 - Gold Decorated Teapot Available Colors
Table 5 - Gold Decorated Teapot Most Common Colors
Table 6 - Gold Label Teapot Available Colors
Table 7 - Gold Label Teapot Most Common Colors
Table 8 - Gold "Special" and Platinum Decorated Available Colors
Table 9 - Group Number for Decorated Teapot Styles
Table 10- Decorated Teapot Color Numbers

Table 1 – General Line
Colors Offered Over Time

Hall Number	Color	1935	1937	1940	1956–1964	1973	1982	1984–1989	1992
1	Brown	X	X	X	X	X	X	X	X
2	Green	X	X	X	X	X	X	X	X
3	Green Lustre	X	X	X	X	X	X	X	X
4	Gray	X	X	X	X	X	X	X	
5	Ivory	X	X	X	X	X	X	X	X
6	Black	X	X	X	X	X	X	X	X
7	White				X	X	X	X	X
8	Sandust				X	X	X	X	X
9	Dark Cobalt Blue	X	X	X	X	X	X	X	X
10	Lettuce	X	X	X	X	X	X	X	X
11	Cadet	X	X	X	X	X	X	X	
12	Flesh		X	X	X	X	X	X	X
13	Lune Blue		X	X	X	X	X	X	
14	Canary	X	X	X	X	X	X	X	X
15	Pink	X	X	X	X	X	X	X	
16	Marine	X	X	X	X	X	X	X	X
17	Emerald	X	X	X	X	X	X	X	
18	Dresden		X	X	X	X	X	X	X
19	Yellow	X	X	X	X	X	X	X	
20	Delphinium				X	X	X	X	
21	Tan	X	X	X	X	X	X	X	
22	Sea Spray			X	X	X	X	X	X
23	Turquoise		X	X	X	X	X	X	
24	Maroon	X	X	X	X	X	X	X	X
25	Monterey Green				X	X	X	X	
26	Rose	X	X	X	X	X	X	X	
27	Mat Black					X	X	X	X
28	Addison Gray					X	X	X	
29	Mahogany					X	X	X	X
30	Antique Mahogany						X	X	
31	Antique Lenox Brown						X	X	X
32	Walnut					X	X	X	X
33	Lenox Brown					X	X	X	X
34	Pewter					X	X	X	
35	Weathered Oak					X	X	X	X
36	Bone White						X	X	X
37	Brianwood						X	X	
38	Mustard					X	X	X	X
39	Golden Olive					X	X	X	
40	Leaf Green						X	X	
41	Daffodil					X	X	X	
42	Oakwood						X	X	X
43	Stone Tan						X	X	
44	Taupe Brown						X	X	
45	Beechwood							X	

Hall Number	Color	1935	1937	1940	1956–1964	1973	1982	1984–1989	1992
46	Beige					X	X	X	
47	Camellia					X	X	X	X
48	Avocado					X	X	X	
49	Chamois							X	
50	Ivory Spice							X	
51	Honey							X	
52	Lemon Yellow							X	
53	Provincial Two Tone							X	
54	Amber Spice					X	X	X	
55	Blue Spice					X	X	X	
56	Burnt Orange					X	X	X	
57	Almond						X	X	X
58	Terra Cotta						X	X	X
59	Butterscotch							X	
60	Wheat							X	
61	Pecan Brown							X	
62	Arctic Blue							X	
63	Laurel Green							X	
64	Dove Gray							X	
65	Coral Peach							X	X
66	Oxford Gray							X	
67	Chocolate							X	X
68	Chestnut						X		
69	Copen Blue							X	
70	Myrtle Green							X	
71	Teal							X	
72	Caramel Spice							X	X
73	Mint Green							X	
74	Alabaster							X	
75	Cork Tan							X	
76	Aqua Blue							X	
77	Caramel							X	
78	Forest Green							X	X
79	Oatmeal							X	
80	Peco Brown (Mat)							X	
81	Sky Blue							X	
82	Spring Green							X	
83	Sunlight Yellow							X	X
84	Spruce Green							X	
85	Vanilla							X	
86	Apple Green							X	
87	Stone Gray							X	
88	Colonial Blue							X	
89	Horizon Blue							X	
90	Versailles Blue							X	X
91	Blue Turquoise							X	
92	Platinum Blue							X	X
93	Powder Blue							X	

Hall Number	Color	1935	1937	1940	1956–1964	1973	1982	1984–1989	1992
94	Wedgewood Blue							X	
95	Blue Mist							X	
96	Coral Red							X	
97	Poppy							X	
98	Mandarine Red							X	
99	Chinese Red							X	
100	Indian Red							X	
101	Golden Glo							X	
102	Silver Glo							X	
103	Copper Lustre							X	
106	Coral Pink								X
108	Concord Blue								X
110	Orchid Pink								X
114	Powder Rose								X
117	Cascade								
129	Sterling White								
	Clay		X	X					
	Devon Cream								X
	Dusty Pink								
	Lavender								
	New Ivory								
	Orchid	X	X	X					
	Teal Blue								
	Violet	X	X	X					

Table 2 – Same General Line Colors

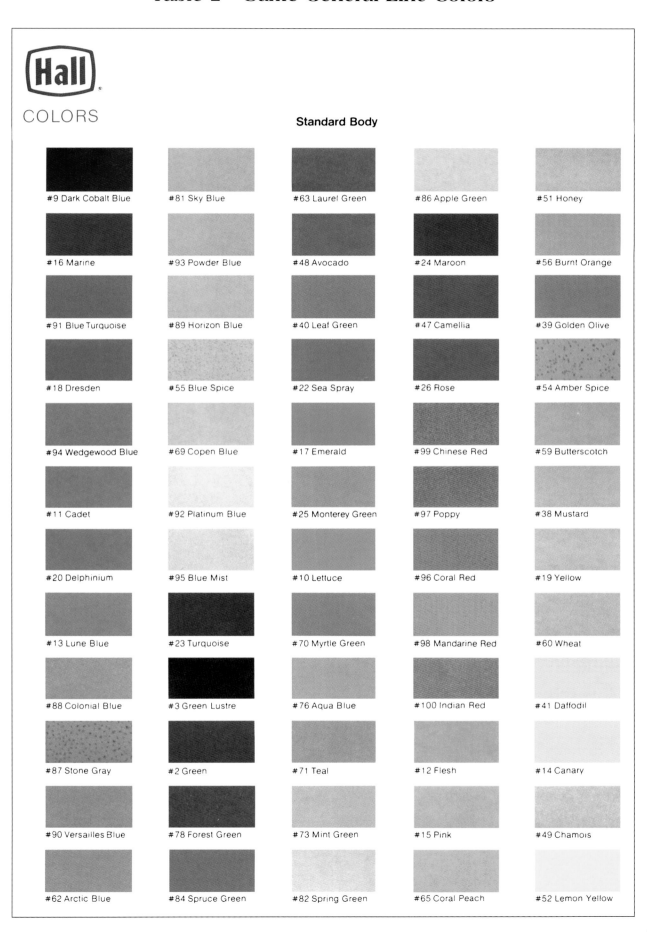

COLORS

Standard Body

#9 Dark Cobalt Blue	#81 Sky Blue	#63 Laurel Green	#86 Apple Green	#51 Honey
#16 Marine	#93 Powder Blue	#48 Avocado	#24 Maroon	#56 Burnt Orange
#91 Blue Turquoise	#89 Horizon Blue	#40 Leaf Green	#47 Camellia	#39 Golden Olive
#18 Dresden	#55 Blue Spice	#22 Sea Spray	#26 Rose	#54 Amber Spice
#94 Wedgewood Blue	#69 Copen Blue	#17 Emerald	#99 Chinese Red	#59 Butterscotch
#11 Cadet	#92 Platinum Blue	#25 Monterey Green	#97 Poppy	#38 Mustard
#20 Delphinium	#95 Blue Mist	#10 Lettuce	#96 Coral Red	#19 Yellow
#13 Lune Blue	#23 Turquoise	#70 Myrtle Green	#98 Mandarine Red	#60 Wheat
#88 Colonial Blue	#3 Green Lustre	#76 Aqua Blue	#100 Indian Red	#41 Daffodil
#87 Stone Gray	#2 Green	#71 Teal	#12 Flesh	#14 Canary
#90 Versailles Blue	#78 Forest Green	#73 Mint Green	#15 Pink	#49 Chamois
#62 Arctic Blue	#84 Spruce Green	#82 Spring Green	#65 Coral Peach	#52 Lemon Yellow

Standard Body

#83 Sunlight Yellow   #61 Pecan Brown   #75 Cork Tan   #85 Vanilla   #28 Addison Gray

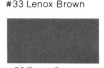

#30 Antique Mahogany   #1 Brown   #46 Beige   #74 Alabaster   #64 Dove Gray

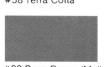

#67 Chocolate   #33 Lenox Brown   #8 Sandust   #50 Ivory Spice   #5 Ivory

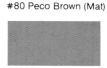

#32 Walnut   #58 Terra Cotta   #53 Provincial Two Tone   #36 Bone White   #7 White

#44 Taupe Brown   #80 Peco Brown (Mat)   #42 Oakwood   #6 Black

#37 Briarwood   #77 Caramel   #45 Beechwood   #27 Mat Black

#29 Mahogany   #72 Caramel Spice   #43 Stone Tan   #34 Pewter

#68 Chestnut   #35 Weathered Oak   #79 Oatmeal   #4 Gray

#31 Antique Lenox Brown   #21 Tan   #57 Almond   #66 Oxford Gray

Metallic Colors
#101 Golden Glo
#102 Silver Glo
#103 Copper Lustre

Colors illustrated are not true reproductions. Please contact your Hall China representative for either the actual colors or additional colors.

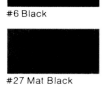

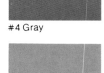

Super-Ceram® Body

Dresden Blue   Old Wine   Flesh   Ivory   Pearl Gray

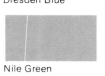

Nile Green   Pink   Shell   Black   White

Table 3 – Decorated
Teapot Color Availability Over Time

This table shows when colors were introduced that were used on Hall products. The data is from available catalogs and does not indicate the exact year a color was first available on Hall's products.

		1935	1937	1941	After 1950s
0001	Stock Green	X	X	X	X
0002	Chartreuse				X
0002	Stock Brown	X	X	X	X
0003	Cobalt	X	X	X	X
0003	Gray				X
0004	Rose	X	X	X	X
0005	Blue Turquoise				X
0005	Delphinium		X	X	X
0006	Dresden			X	X
0007	Mahogany				X
0008	Yellow (Warm)	X	X	X	X
0009	Cadet	X	X	X	X
0010	Black	X	X	X	X
0011	Green Lustre	X	X	X	X
0011	Monterey Green				X
0012	Emerald	X	X	X	X
0013	Maroon	X	X	X	X
0014	Camellia				X
0014	Butterscotch				X
0015	Pink				X
0015	Violet				X
0016	Marine	X	X	X	X
0017	Orchid		X	X	X
0017	Matte Orchid				X
0018	Ivory	X	X	X	X
0019	Canary	X	X	X	X
0020	Turquoise		X	X	X

Table 4 – Gold Decorated
Teapot Colors

The table shows the colors found on the Hall Gold Decorated Teapot line by a review of major collectors. Any colors not in the table would be considered unusual.

AIRFLOW	ALADDIN	ALBANY	AUTOMOBILE	BALTIMORE	BASKET
Black	Black	Black	Cobalt	Black	Cadet
Cadet	Blue Turquoise	Blue Turquoise	Dresden	Cadet	Canary
Canary	Cadet	Cadet	Emerald	Canary	Maroon
Cobalt	Camellia	Canary	Ivory	Cobalt	
Dresden	Canary	Cobalt	Marine	Emerald	
Emerald	Chartreuse	Dresden	Maroon	Ivory	
Ivory	Cobalt	Emerald	Turquoise	Mahogany	
Marine	Dresden	Ivory		Marine	
Maroon	Emerald	Mahogany		Maroon	
Rose	Gray	Marine		Stock Brown	
Stock Brown	Green Lustre	Maroon		Warm Yellow	
Turquoise	Ivory	Pink			
Warm Yellow	Marine	Stock Green			
	Maroon	Turquoise			
	Orchid	Violet			
	Pink	Warm Yellow			
	Rose				
	Turquoise				
	Warm Yellow				
	White				

BASKETBALL	BELLEVUE	BIRD CAGE	BOSTON	CLEVELAND	DOUGHNUT
Cadet	Cadet	Cadet	Black	Black	Black
Canary	Cobalt	Canary	Blue Turquoise	Cadet	Cadet
Cobalt	Green Lustre	Cobalt	Cadet	Canary	Canary
Emerald	Ivory	Emerald	Camellia	Cobalt	Cobalt
Ivory	Stock Brown	Marine	Canary	Emerald	Delphinium
Marine		Maroon	Chartreuse	Ivory	Emerald
Maroon		Turquoise	Cobalt	Marine	Ivory
Turquoise			Dresden	Maroon	Marine
Warm Yellow			Emerald	Orchid	Maroon
			Gray	Pink	Turquoise
			Ivory	Turquoise	
			Marine	Warm Yellow	
			Maroon		
			Monterey Green		
			Pink		
			Rose		
			Stock Brown		
			Stock Green		
			Turquoise		
			Warm Yellow		

FOOTBALL	FRENCH	GLOBE	HOLLYWOOD	HOOK COVER	ILLINOIS
Black	Black	Cadet	Black	Black	Black
Cadet	Blue Turquoise	Camellia	Cadet	Cadet	Cadet
Canary	Cadet	Canary	Canary	Canary	Canary
Cobalt	Camellia	Chartreuse	Chartreuse	Cobalt	Cobalt
Delphinium	Canary	Emerald	Cobalt	Delphinium	Emerald
Dresden	Chartreuse	Ivory	Delphinium	Emerald	Marine
Emerald	Cobalt	Marine	Dresden	Marine	Maroon
Ivory	Dresden	Maroon	Emerald	Maroon	Stock Brown
Marine	Emerald	Rose	Ivory	Turquoise	Stock Green
Maroon	Gray	Turquoise	Marine		
Turquoise	Green Lustre	Warm Yellow	Maroon		
Violet	Ivory		Old Rose		
Warm Yellow	Marine		Pink		
	Maroon		Stock Brown		
	Monterey Green		Stock Green		
	Pink		Turquoise		
	Rose		Warm Yellow		
	Stock Brown				
	Stock Green				
	Turquoise				
	Warm Yellow				

INDIANA	KANSAS	LOS ANGELES	MELODY	MODERNE	NAUTILUS
Cobalt	Emerald	Black	Black	Black	Cadet
Ivory	Ivory	Cadet	Cadet	Cadet	Canary
Marine	Maroon	Canary	Canary	Canary	Cobalt
Maroon		Cobalt	Cobalt	Cobalt	Delphinium
Orchid		Dresden	Emerald	Delphinium	Dresden
Warm Yellow		Emerald	Marine	Dresden	Emerald
		Ivory	Maroon	Emerald	Marine
		Marine	Turquoise	Ivory	Maroon
		Maroon	Warm Yellow	Marine	Turquoise
		Old Rose		Maroon	Warm Yellow
		Pink		Old Rose	
		Stock Brown		Orchid	
		Stock Green		Pink	
		Turquoise		Turquoise	
		Warm Yellow		Warm Yellow	

NEW YORK
Black
Blue Turquoise
Cadet
Camellia
Canary
Chartreuse
Cobalt
Dresden
Emerald
Gray
Green Lustre
Ivory
Marine
Maroon
Monterey Green
Pink
Rose
Stock Brown
Stock Green
Turquoise
Warm Yellow

NEWPORT
Pink
Warm Yellow

NO-DRIP
Cadet
Camellia
Canary
Chartreuse
Gray
Marine
Rose
Turquoise

OHIO
Black
Cadet
Canary
Cobalt
Emerald
Maroon
Stock Brown
Stock Green

PARADE
Black
Cadet
Canary
Cobalt
Delphinium
Emerald
Ivory
Marine
Maroon
Stock Brown
Turquoise
Warm Yellow

PHILADELPHIA
Black
Blue Turquoise
Cadet
Canary
Cobalt
Delphinium
Dresden
Emerald
Gray
Ivory
Marine
Maroon
Pink
Rose
Stock Brown
Stock Green
Turquoise
Warm Yellow

RHYTHM
Black
Cadet
Canary
Cobalt
Emerald
Ivory
Maroon
Turquoise

SAF-HANDLE
Black
Cadet
Canary
Cobalt
Dresden
Emerald
Ivory
Marine
Maroon
Pink
Turquoise
Warm Yellow

SANI-GRID
Cadet
Canary
Cobalt
Emerald
Ivory
Maroon
Turquoise
Warm Yellow

STAR
Cadet
Canary
Cobalt
Delphinium
Emerald
Ivory
Marine
Maroon
Pink
Turquoise
Warm Yellow

STREAMLINE
Black
Cadet
Canary
Cobalt
Delphinium
Dresden
Emerald
Ivory
Marine
Maroon
Pink
Turquoise
Warm Yellow

SURF SIDE
Black
Cadet
Canary
Cobalt
Delphinium
Dresden
Emerald
Ivory
Maroon
Old Rose
Turquoise
Warm Yellow

WINDSHIELD
Black
Cadet
Camellia
Canary
Cobalt
Delphinium
Dresden
Emerald
Green Lustre
Ivory
Maroon
Turquoise
Warm Yellow

Table 5 – Gold Decorated Teapots – Most Common Colors

This table shows the most common colors as identified by a review of major collectors.

AIRFLOW
Canary
Cobalt
Warm Yellow

ALADDIN
Black
Canary
Cobalt
Marine
Maroon

ALBANY
Cobalt
Mahogany
Turquoise

AUTOMOBILE
Canary
Maroon

BALTIMORE
Canary
Emerald
Marine
Maroon

BASKET
Canary

BASKETBALL
Turquoise

BELLEVUE
Green Lustre

BIRD CAGE
Maroon

BOSTON
Canary
Cadet
Cobalt
Dresden
Gray
Maroon

CLEVELAND
Canary
Emerald
Turquoise
Warm Yellow

DOUGHNUT
Black
Canary
Cobalt
Maroon

FOOTBALL
Maroon
Turquoise

FRENCH
Black
Cadet
Canary
Cobalt

GLOBE
Canary
Emerald
Maroon

HOLLYWOOD
Canary
Cobalt
Chartreuse
Ivory
Maroon

HOOK COVER
Cadet
Canary
Emerald
Ivory

ILLINOIS
Brown
Cobalt
Maroon

INDIANA
Marine
Warm Yellow

KANSAS
Emerald
Ivory

LOS ANGELES
Black
Brown
Canary
Cobalt
Emerald

MELODY
Cobalt
Maroon
Turquoise

MODERNE
Cadet
Canary
Ivory

NAUTILUS
Canary
Maroon
Turquoise

NEW YORK
Cadet
Canary
Cobalt
Emerald
Maroon
Warm Yellow

NEWPORT
Pink

NO-DRIP
Cadet
Camellia
Chartreuse
Gray

OHIO
Brown

PARADE
Cadet
Canary
Cobalt
Emerald
Maroon

PHILADELPHIA
Cadet
Canary
Ivory
Turquoise

RHYTHM
Canary

SAF-HANDLE
Canary
Cobalt

SANI-GRID
Cadet
Cobalt

STAR
Cadet
Canary
Cobalt
Emerald
Ivory
Turquoise

STREAMLINE
Canary
Cobalt
Dresden

SURF SIDE
Canary
Emerald
Turquoise

WINDSHIELD
Cadet
Camellia
Cobalt
Maroon

Table 6 – Gold Label
Available Colors

The Gold Label teapots were available in a limited number of colors. This table shows those colors identified by collectors. Any colors not in the table would be considered unusual.

ALADDIN – SWAG
Black
Blue Turquoise
Cadet
Chartreuse

Cobalt
Dresden
Gray
Ivory
Marine
Maroon
Matte Orchid

ALADDIN – SQUIGGLE
Canary
Ivory

ALBANY
Blue Turquoise
Ivory
Mahogany
Maroon

Matte Orchid
Pink

BALTIMORE
Black
Cadet
Ivory
Maroon

Matte Orchid
Pink

BOSTON
Canary
Chartreuse
Cobalt
Dresden

Ivory
Matte Orchid
Monterey Green
Pink
Turquoise

FRENCH
Black
Blue Turquoise
Cadet
Camellia

Canary
Chartreuse
Cobalt
Dresden
Emerald
Gray
Ivory
Marine

Matte Orchid
Monterey Green
Pink

INFUSER
Ivory

HOLLYWOOD
Black
Blue Turquoise
Chartreuse
Ivory

Marine
Maroon
Matte Orchid
Monterey Green
Pink

HOOK COVER
Cadet
Ivory

LOS ANGELES
Black
Blue Turquoise
Cobalt
Dresden
Emerald
Ivory
Monterey Green
Pink

NEW YORK
Black
Blue Turquoise
Cadet
Canary
Chartreuse
Cobalt
Emerald
Gray
Ivory
Marine
Matte Orchid
Monterey Green
Pink
Warm Yellow

PARADE
Black
Canary
Ivory

PHILADELPHIA
Blue Turquoise
Camellia
Chartreuse
Gray
Ivory
Maroon
Monterey Green
Pink
Turquoise

WINDSHIELD
Camellia
Canary
Dresden
Ivory
Pink

Table 7 – Gold Label
Most Common Colors

This table shows the most common colors found on the Gold Label teapots as identified by a review of major collectors.

ALADDIN – SWAG	ALBANY	BALTIMORE	BOSTON	FRENCH	HOLLYWOOD
Ivory	Blue Turquoise	Ivory	Cobalt	Black	Chartreuse
Marine	Ivory	Maroon	Dresden	Blue Turquoise	Ivory
Maroon	Mahogany		Ivory	Cadet	Maroon
Pink	Pink			Canary	
				Ivory	
ALADDIN – SQUIGGLE					
Canary					

HOOK COVER	LOS ANGELES	NEW YORK	PARADE	PHILADELPHIA	WINDSHIELD
Cadet	Cobalt	Blue Turquoise	Canary	Ivory	Camellia
Ivory	Ivory	Canary	Ivory	Pink	Ivory
	Monterey Green	Ivory		Turquoise	

Table 8 – Gold "Special" and
Platinum Decorated Available Colors

This table shows the colors found on the Gold "Special" and Platinum Decorated teapots by a review of major collectors. Any colors not in the table would be considered unusual.

AIRFLOW	ALADDIN	ALBANY	AUTOMOBILE	BALTIMORE	BASKET
Black	Canary	Cobalt	Black	Cobalt	Canary
Canary	Cobalt	Maroon		Ivory	
Cobalt	Maroon	Monterry	*PLATINUM*	Marine	*PLATINUM*
Emerald	Turquoise	Turquoise	Black	Maroon	Black
Ivory		Warm Yellow	Cadet		Cadet
Maroon			Canary		Canary
Turquoise			Cobalt		Cobalt
Warm Yellow			Delphinium		Delphinum
			Emerald		Emerald
			Marine		Marine
			Maroon		Maroon
			Warm Yellow		Turquoise
					Warm Yellow

BASKETBALL	BASKETBALL	BIRD CAGE	BOSTON	CLEVELAND	DOUGHNUT
Cadet	*PLATINUM*	Cadet	Canary	Canary	Black
Canary	Black	Canary	Cobalt	Cobalt	
Turquoise	Cadet	Cobalt	Emerald	Emerald	
Warm Yellow	Cobalt	Maroon	Maroon	Ivory	
	Delphinium		Stock Green	Marine	
			Warm Yellow	Turquoise	
				Warm Yellow	

FOOTBALL	FRENCH	HOLLYWOOD	HOOK COVER	KANSAS	LOS ANGELES
Turquoise	Maroon	Black	Canary	Ivory	Canary
	Warm Yellow	Canary			Cobalt
		Cobalt		*PLATINUM*	Ivory
	INFUSER	Maroon		Emerald	Maroon
	Cobalt	Stock Green			Warm Yellow
		Warm Yellow			

MELODY	NAUTILUS	NEW YORK	PARADE	PHILADELPHIA	SAF-HANDLE
Maroon	Cadet	Cobalt	Cobalt	Black	Canary
	Canary	Ivory		Cadet	Cobalt
PLATINUM	Cobalt	Marine		Cobalt	Emerald
Ivory		Maroon		Maroon	
		Stock Green			

STAR	STREAMLINE	STREAMLINE	SURF SIDE	WINDSHIELD	
Cobalt	Cadet	*PLATINUM*	Canary	Maroon	
	Canary	Canary	Cobalt		
	Cobalt		Emerald		
	Delphinium				
	Emerald				
	Turquoise				
	Warm Yellow				

Hall Decorated Teapots have a gold number on the bottom to identify the shape and color. This number can be decoded as follows:

(1) Locate the number from the bottom of the teapot and find the number in the Group Number in Table 9. For example, if the number is 0.6.5.S, find 0065 in Table 9. The number falls between 0061 and 0080. The teapot style is Philadelphia. A suffix of "S" indicates the pot is a Gold "Special" and "P" indicates the pot is a Platinum "Special." "X" indicates a modified decoration or shape. Periods between the number digits are not important.

(2) To identify the teapot color, take the number you found on the teapot and subtract the first number from the Group Number found in Table 9. For example, 0065 (from teapot) minus 0061 (from Table 9), equals 0004. Next add 1 to 0004 and find the color in Table 10. The 0065 Philadelphia is Delphinium. There is only one complication. Some numbers are associated with two different colors. However, it is usually easy to tell which color applies to your teapot.

Table 9 – Group Number
for Decorated Teapot Styles

This table shows the range of numbers (group numbers) that identifies the shape of a Gold Decorated teapot.

Group Number	Teapot	Group Number	Teapot	Group Number	Teapot
0001 - 0020	Boston	0261 - 0280	Ohio	0601 - 0620	Melody
0021 - 0040	New York	0281 - 0300	Indiana	0621 - 0640	Surf Side
0041 - 0060	French	0301 - 0320	Kansas	0641 - 0660	Nautilus
0061 - 0080	Philadelphia	0321 - 0340	Streamline	0661 - 0680	Aladdin
0081 - 0100	Los Angeles			0681 - 0700	Windshield
0101 - 0120	Hollywood	0441 - 0460	Airflow	0701 - 0720	Globe
0121 - 0140	Newport	0461 - 0480	Doughnut	0721 - 0740	Star
0141 - 0160	Cleveland	0481 - 0500	Football	0741 - 0760	Hook Cover
0161 - 0180	Baltimore	0501 - 0520	Basket	0761 - 0780	Saf-Handle
0181 - 0200	Bellevue	0521 - 0540	Automobile	0781 - 0800	Parade
0201 - 0220	Moderne	0541 - 0560	Basketball	0801 - 0820	Sani-Grid
0221 - 0240	Albany	0561 - 0580	Rhythm	0821 – 0840	No Drip
0241 - 0260	Illinois	0581 - 0600	Bird Cage	0841 – 0860	T-Ball Round

Table 10 – Decorated
Teapot Color Numbers

This table shows the color number used to identify the color of a Gold Decorated teapot.

0001	Stock Green	0007	Mahogany	0014	Butterscotch
0002	Chartreuse	0008	Warm Yellow	0015	Pink
0002	Stock Brown	0009	Cadet	0015	Violet
0003	Cobalt	0010	Black	0016	Marine
0003	Gray	0011	Green Lustre	0017	Orchid
0004	Rose	0011	Monterey Green	0017	Matte Orchid
0005	Blue Turquoise	0012	Emerald	0018	Ivory
0005	Delphinium	0013	Maroon	0019	Canary
0006	Dresden	0014	Camellia	0020	Turquoise

Bibliography

Books

Atterbury, Paul (consultant). *Miller's Antique Checklist: 20th Century Ceramics*. Docklands, London: Octopus Publishing Group Ltd., 2003.

Conroy, Barbara J. *Restaurant China, Volume 1, Identification and Value Guide for Restaurant, Airline, Ship and Railroad Dinnerware*. Paducah, Kentucky: Collector Books, A Division of Schroeder Publishing Co., Inc., 1998.

_____. *Restaurant China, Volume 2, Identification and Value Guide for Restaurant, Airline, Ship and Railroad Dinnerware*. Paducah, Kentucky: Collector Books, A Division of Schroeder Publishing Co., Inc., 1999.

Cunningham, Jo. *The Best of Collectible Dinnerware*, 1st Edition. Atglen, Pennsylvania: Schiffer Publishing, 1995.

_____. *The Collector's Encyclopedia of American Dinnerware*, 1st Edition. Paducah, Kentucky: Collector Books, A Division of Schroeder Publishing Co., Inc., 1982.

_____. *Hall China Price Update, Including Jewel Tea's Famous Autumn Leaf Pattern*. Copyright 1982 by Jo Cunningham (Typesetting and layout by The Glaze Art Service).

_____. *The Best of Collectible Dinnerware*, 2nd Edition. Atglen, Pennsylvania: Schiffer Publishing, 1999.

Duke, Harvey. *HALL 2*. ELO Books, First Printing,1985.

_____. *Official Price Guide to Pottery and Porcelain*, 8th Edition. New York, New York: House of Collectibles, 1995.

_____. *Superior Quality Hall China. A Guide for Collectors*. ELO Books, 1977.

Gates, William C. *The East Liverpool, Ohio, Pottery District (Identification of Manufacturers Marks)*. Pennsylvania: The Society for Historical Archaeology, 1982.

_____. *The City of Hills and Kilns – Life and Work in East Liverpool, Ohio*. East Liverpool, Ohio: The East Liverpool Historical Society, 1984.

Knous, Bill and Sue. *Railroadiana, The Official Price Guide for the Year 2000 and Beyond*, 1st Edition. Denver, Colorado: RRM Publishing, 2000.

Lehner, Lois. *Lehner's Encyclopedia of U.S. Marks on Pottery, Porcelain & Clay*. Paducah, Kentucky: Collector Books, A Division of Schroeder Publishing Co., Inc., 1988.

Luckin, Richard W. *Dining on Rails (An Encyclopedia of Railroad China)*. Denver, Colorado: RK Publishing, 1983.

Marsh, Madeleine. *Miller's Collecting the 1950s*. Wappingers' Falls, New York: Antique Collectors Club Ltd., 1997.

Miller, C. L. *The Jewel Tea Company, Its History and Products*. Atglen, Pennsylvania: Schiffer Publishing, 1994.

_____. *Jewel Tea Sales and Household Collectibles*. Atglen, Pennsylvania: Schiffer Publishing, 1995.

Pratt, Michael. *Mid-Century Modern Dinnerware*, Atglen, Pennsylvania: Schiffer Publishing, 2003.

Snyder, Jeffrey B. *Depression Pottery*, 2nd Edition. Atglen, Pennsylvania: Schiffer Publishing, 2002.

_____. *Hall China*. Atglen, Pennsylvania: Schiffer Publishing, 2002.

Vodrey, Catherine. *A Centennial History of the Hall China Company*. Cleveland, Ohio: Stevens Daron Communications, Inc., 2003.

Whitmyer, Margaret & Kenn. *Collector's Encyclopedia of Hall China*. Paducah, Kentucky Collector Books, A Division of Schroeder Publishing Co., Inc., 2001.

Young. Lucie. *Eva Zeisel*. San Francisco: Chronicle Books, 2003.

Advertisements, Brochures, Catalogs, Magazines, Newspapers, Periodicals, and Videos

Better Tea in a Hall Teapot. East Liverpool, Ohio: The Hall China Company, 1930.

China and Glass, 1944-1946.

China, Glass, and Decorative Accessories, 1946-1954.

China, Glass and Lamps, 1927-1941.

China and Glass Tableware, 1964-1965.

"Directors for Using London Teabob." Milwaukee, Wisconsin: Teabob, Inc., undated.

East Liverpool – Our Potteries and Their Leaders. Ohio: East Liverpool Area Chamber of Commerce, 2003.

"Electrical Household Appliances" Catalog. Mansfield, Ohio: Westinghouse Electric Company, 1934.

"First Modern China," *China, Glass and Decorative Accessories*, 1946.

From Fire and Clay: East Liverpool, Ohio. East Liverpool, Ohio: Phoenix Studios, 2003.

Good Housekeeping. September 1916, 163.

Hall China Company Catalogs. East Liverpool, Ohio, 1920s to 2003.

"Hall China Company Catalogs and Data." Seattle, Washington: Hall Mania, 2003.

Hall China – A Centennial Celebration. East Liverpool, Ohio: Phoenix Studios, 2003.

Hallcraft by Eva Zeisel – Tomorrow's Classic. New York: Midhurst China Co., undated.

Hellick Coffee Company's Home Service News. Easton, Pennsylvania: George F. Hellick Company, undated.

Hotel and Restaurant Suppliers. Kansas City, Missouri: Racket Merchandise Company, 1950.

Hotel Monthly, 1937.

"How to Make Delicious Drip Coffee With Your Drip-O-lator." Massillon, Ohio: The Enterprise Aluminum Company, undated.

"How to Use Your Electromatic Coffeemaker." Electromatic Coffee Company, undated.

"Introducing Modernistic Colors with the Tricolators." New York City: Tricolator Company, Inc., undated.

Jewel Tea Price Guide. National Autumn Leaf Collectors Club, February 1997.

"Learn How to Tricolate Coffee." New York City: Tricolator Company, Inc., undated.

Literary Digest, 1930.

"Massillon Firm Was Leader in Aluminum Field." Massillon, Ohio: *The Evening Independent*, November 21, 1988.

Montgomery Ward Catalogs. Chicago, Illinois, Fall and Winter 1931-1932, 1937, 1940-41.

Pottery, Glass, and Brass Salesman, 1914 – 1938.

"Red-Cliff Retail Price Brochure." Chicago, Illinois: Red-Cliff Company, 1965.

"Red-Cliff Retail Price Brochure." Chicago, Illinois: Red-Cliff Company, 1976.

Restaurant Management. 1930-1931.

Sears, Roebuck, and Company Catalogs, 1927, 1928, 1941-1942, 1956, 1957.

Shapleigh Catalog. St. Louis, Missouri: Shapleigh Hardware Company, 1951.

Sherlock Holmes-Master Sleuth Teapot and Beverage Mugs, Flushing, Michigan, Holmes by Hall, 1992.

"Special Offer to Gold Star Dairy Customers." East Liverpool, Ohio: The Wilcox Electric Appliance Company, Inc., undated.

Springtime I Crestware Gift Offer. Toledo, Ohio, Owens-Illinois Company, 1963-1964.

Teapot Tidings. East Liverpool, Ohio: The Hall China Company. October 1957 – January 1958.

"The Enterprise Story." Massillon, Ohio. Massillon, Ohio, Historical Society, undated.

The Geo. Worthington Co. Catalog. Cleveland, Ohio.

The Glaze. Springfield, Missouri, April 1977 - June 1984.

The New Glaze. Birmingham, Alabama, September 1985 - May 1992.

"The Secret of Perfect Coffee Making in Your Drip-O-lator." Massillon, Ohio: The Enterprise Aluminum Company, undated.

"The Tricolator Makes Savoury Coffee." New York City: Tricolator Company, Inc., 1927.

Thorley, Paul. "Pottery Fundamentals." China, Glass, and Lamps. 1938-1939.

"Tricolator – Points of Advantage in Modern Coffee Making." New York City: Tricolator Company, Inc., undated.

Walkerstein, Ed. "Hotshot Teapots." *Collectibles Illustrated*, July-August 1984, 35-37.

Wilson, Joel. "Ernest Sohn Designs in Hall China." *The Quarterly Newsletter of the Hall China Collectors Club and Jewel Tea and Other Tea Company China Collectors Club*, Winter 2003-2004.

Internet

"Century Dinnerware by Hall China." www.ohioriverpotteries.com.

Edward Don and Company Food Service. "Equipment and Supplies." www.don.com.

"Golden Tea Tips. Archives: The History of Tea." http://www.dilmahtea.com/press/Golden/golden_ tea_tips.html

Great Britain Patent Office Web Site. www.gb.espace net.com/

"Hall China – Casual Living by Eva Zeisel." 2003, www.ohioriverpotteries.com.

Jiamachello, Tom. "The Manning Bowman Co., 1900-1950." Art Metal – Part Four, www.imakernews.com, 2004.

Labaco, Ronalt T. "Serving Modern to America." www.modernismmagazine.com, Spring 2004.

Longaberger Home, The Longaberger Company, 2002. www.longaberger.com

"Lost Molds and Found Dinnerware: Rediscovered Eva Zeisel's Hallcraft." 2004, www.collecting channel.com.

"Modern Objects." 2003. http://cgi.ebay.com.

Nelson, Linda. "Eva Zeisel: Woman of Design." Suite University Internet Site, 2003.

Pratt, Michael. "Spotlight on Sohn Creations."

Service Ideas Product Catalog. Service Ideas, Inc., 2003. www.serviceideas.com.

Sterling China Product Catalog. Wellsville, Ohio: Sterling China Company, 2003. www.sterlingchina.com.

Thompson, Lynne. "Weaving Success." Great Lakes Publishing Company, February 2001. www.infotrack.galegroup.com.

"Tomorrow's Classics Dinnerware by Hall China." 2003, www.ohioriverpotteries.com.

"Unbreakable Porcelain." 2003, www.washington post.com.

United States Patents Web Site. www.uspto.gov.

Walker, John. "McCormick Teapots." Lunenburg, Maine, July 2000. http://public.surfree.com/walker/mccormick.htm

Woodard, Kathy L. *American Ceramics Society Bulletin*, 2001. www.ceramicbulletin.org

Appendix
Name Cross Reference

This is a cross reference of names used in this book with those used by prominent authors on Hall China.

BOOK NAME	WHITMYER	DUKE	BOOK NAME	WHITMYER	DUKE
Ambassador	"Blossom"	"Blossom"	"Imperial"	"Imperial"	"Clover"
"Apple"	"Apple"	"Browning"	Infuser	French with infuser	French with infuser
Autocrat	"Buchanan"	"Buchanan"	"Jerry"	"Jerry"	"Monarch"
Autocrat Jr.	"Buchanan"	"Buchanan"	Lipton Cozy Pot	"Coverlet"	"Cozy Cover"
"Baron"	"Baron"	"Rochester"	"Medallion"	"Medallion"	"Colonial"
Basket Weave	"Straw Weave"	"Straw Weave"	"Murphy"	"Murphy"	"Peel"
Beacon	"Diver"	"Diver"	New Yorker	"Carraway"	"Carraway"
"Benjamin"	"Benjamin"	"Albert"	No Drip	"Globe No Drip"	No Drip
"Birch"	"Birch"	"Darby"	Norfolk	Hoyt	Hoyt
Bird Cage	Birdcage	Bird Cage	"Norse"	"Norse"	"Everson"
"Bowknot"	"Bowknot"	"Gladstone"	Panther	"Ritz"	"Ritz"
"Bowling Ball"	"Bowling Ball"	"Pepper"	"Perk"	"Perk"	"Deca Plain"
Bride	"Diver"	"Diver"	Plaza	"Ansel"	"Susannah"
"Carrie"	"Carrie"	"Connie"	"Plume"	"Plume"	"Disraeli"
"Cathedral"	"Cathedral"	"Arch"	"Radiance"	"Radiance"	"Sunshine"
Clipper	"Carraway"	"Carraway"	"Rayed"	"Rayed"	"Eliot"
"Colonial"	"Medallion"	"Colonial"	"Regal"	"Regal"	"Dickens"
"Colonial Tall"	"Medallion"	"Colonial"	Regent	"Buchanan"	"Buchanan"
"Connie"	"Connie"	"Victoria"	"Ribbed"	"Ribbed"	"Flute"
"Daniel"	"Daniel"	"Rickson"	Roosevelt	"Blaine"	"Blaine"
"Dart"	"Dart"	"Russell"	"Rounded Terrace"	"Rounded Terrace"	"Step Round"
Demi Coffee	"No. 2 Coffee"	"No. 2 Coffee"	"Royal"	"Royal"	"Eliot"
"Demi" Teapot	Morning Teapot	Morning Teapot	Royal Park	"Lincoln"	"Lincoln"
"Dohrco"	"Dohrco"	"Irene"	"Rutherford"	"Rutherford"	"Alton"
Doughnut	Donut	Doughnut	S-Handle	"S-Lid"	"S-Lid"
"Drape"	"Drape"	"Swathe"	Saf-Handle	"Sundial"	Saf-Handle
Electromatic Coffee Maker	"Big Boy"	"Big Boy"	Saf-Spout	"Baby Melody"	Saf-Spout
Encore	"Crown" / "Wilson"	"Wilson"	"Starlight"	"Starlight"	"Tennison"
Erie	"Crown" / "Wilson"	"Wilson"	Surf Side	Surfside	Surf Side
"Five Band"	"Five Band"	"Banded"	"Target"	"Target"	"Bullseye"
French Light Weight	French	French	"Terrace"	"Terrace"	"Step Down"
Gardiner	Gardiner	"Corydon"	"Viking"	"Viking"	"Bell"
"Grape"	"Grape"	"Darwin"	"Waverlet"	"Waverlet"	"Crest"
Great American	Great American	"Golden Key"	"Waverly"	"Waverly"	"Crest"
Hallcraft Century	Century	Century	"Windcrest"	"Windcrest"	"Bronte"
Hallcraft Tomorrow's Classic	Tomorrow's Classic	Tomorrow's Classic	Windsor	"Buchanan"	"Buchanan"
"Hoyt R"	"Hoyt"	"Hoyt"	Windsor	"Buchanan"	"Buchanan"

Index

The book index is broken into three parts. The first part is an index of the shapes; the second index is of the decorations; and the third index is for company names, designers, distributors, etc. The primary references are bolded.

Shapes

"#1 Teapot", 14
"#2 Coffee Shape", **67**, 84, 147
#691 All-China Drip, **67-68**, 175, 176, 177, 180, 182, 183, 196, 199
"Adele", **14**, 127
Adjusto, **14-15**, 54, 157, 184
Airflow, 5, **15**, 31, 34, 51, 128, 129, 175, 176, 177, 178, 180, 181, 183, 186, 190, 191, 195, 197, 198, 200, 226, 229, 232, 233
Aladdin, Oval, **16**, 20, 45, 177, 178, 180, 181, 195, 200
Aladdin, Round (Six Cup), **16-17**, 50, 129, 140, 177, 179, 180, 181, 183, 186, 191, 192, 193, 196, 197, 198, 199, 200, 226, 229, 230, 231, 232, 233
Aladdin, Round (Seven Cup), **17**, 176, 191, 192
Albany, 8, **17**, 25, 27, 129, 130, 140, 180, 226, 229, 230, 231, 232, 233
"Albert" - see "Benjamin"
"Alcony", 68
Alma, **17**, 40, 61, 64, 180
"Alton" - see "Rutherford"
Amano Beverage Pot, 68
Ambassador, **68-69**, 163, 164
"Amory", **69**, 164
"Andrew" Electric Percolator and Urn, **69**, 184, 187
"Ansel" - see Plaza
Apple, 18
"Apple", **18**, 139, 184, 185
"Arch" - see "Cathedral"
"Arthur", **69**, 181, 195
Autocrat, **70**, 106, 116, 163, 164, 165
Autocrat Jr., **70**, 165, 180
Automobile, **18**, 19, 128, 130, 176, 177, 179, 180, 181, 190, 191, 193, 195, 197, 198, 226, 229, 232, 233
Baltimore, 8, **18-19**, 124, 125, 129, 130, 140, 175, 177, 180, 190, 191, 197, 199, 226, 229, 230, 231, 232, 233
"Banded" Coffee Carafe - see "Five Band" Carafe
"Banded" Coffee Pot - see "Five Band - Partial Tab Cover" and "Five Band 'D' Handle"
"Baron", **70**, 175, 195
"Bartow" - see Bellevue Teapot
Basket, 18, **19**, 128, 129, 130, 180, 186, 226, 229, 232, 233
Basket Weave Electric Percolator and Urn, **70-71**, 157, 194
Basketball, 18, **19**, 128, 129, 131, 176, 180, 226, 229, 232, 233
"Basketweave", 12, **71**, 147, 148
"Bauhaus", **71**, 148
Beacon, **71**, 74, 165
"Beaded" Coffee Server, 213
"Beaver Falls", **71-72**, 82
"Bell" - see "Viking"
Bellevue Coffee Pot, **72**, 121, 176, 180, 181, 193
Bellevue Teapot, **19-20**, 40, 72, 117, 119, 120, 129, 176, 180, 181, 193, 226, 229, 233
"Benjamin", **20**, 138, 191
"Betty" Electric Percolator and Urn, **72-73**, 180
Beverage Pot, **73**, 78
Big Boy - see Electromatic Coffeemaker
"Bingham", **73**, 195
"Birch", **20**, 51, 138, 191
Bird Cage, 16, **20-21**, 45, 128, 129, 131, 176, 180, 226, 229, 232, 233
"Blaine" - see Roosevelt
"Blossom" - see Ambassador
Boston, 6, 8, **21-22**, 35, 48, 55, 117, 118, 119, 123, 129, 131, 140, 143, 145, 148, 175, 176, 177, 178, 180, 181, 183, 184, 185, 186, 187, 188, 190, 192, 193, 195, 196, 197, 198, 199, 200, 226, 229, 230, 231, 232, 233
Boston with Infuser, 16, **22**
Boston Long Metal Tip Spout, 22
Boston Short Metal Tip Spout, 23
"Bowknot", **23**, 138
"Bowling Ball", 23
"Bricks and Ivy", **74**, 148, 190
Bride, **74**, 86, 163, 165-168, 175, 179
"Bronte" - see "Windcrest"
"Browning" - see "Apple"
"Buchanan" - see Autocrat, Autocrat Jr., Regent, Windsor
Buffet Hot Water Pot and Teapot, **24**, 183, 196
"Bullseye" - see "Target"
California, **74-75**, 196
"Canoy", 75
Carafe (No Cover), 75-76
"Carraway" Long Spout - see Clipper

"Carraway" Short Spout - see New Yorker
"Carrie" with and without All-China Drip, **76**, 177
"Cathedral", **76**, 148, 149
Centennial, **24-25**, 176
Ceylonator, 16, 17, **25**
Chicago, **25**, 180, 199
Chinese Shape Teapot, 211
Chrome Cozy, 26
Classic Series Beverage Pot Metal Tip Spout, 77
"Clayman", 77
Cleveland, 8, **26**, 118, 129, 132, 180, 226, 229, 232, 233
Clipper, **77**, 101, 168
"Clover" - see "Imperial"
Club, 78
Coffee Carafe, **78**, 186
Coffee Pot Metal Tip Spout, 73, **78**
Coffee Princess, Coffee Queen, Coffee Empress, **79**, 163, 168
Coffee Server, 213
Coffee Urn - Drip-O-lator, **79-80**, 155
Coffelator, **80**, 180
"Colonial" All-China Drip, **80-81**, 197
"Colonial" Coffee Pot, 81, 149, **181**
"Colonial" Teapot, **26**, 192, 193, 197
"Colonial Tall", **81**, 149, 187, 192, 197
"Columbia", 8, 17, **27**, 117, 121
"Connie", **27**, 138
"Connie" with and without All-China Drip - see "Carrie" All-China Drip
"Corrie", 81
"Corydon" - see Gardiner
Counter Service, **27**, 144, 176, 177, 179, 181, 193, 195, 197
Cozy Cover - see Lipton Cozy Teapot
Cozy Hot Pot, **28**, 158
"Crest" - see "Waverlet" and "Waverly"
"Crown" - see Encore and Erie
Cube Coffee Pot, 12, **81-82**, 163, 219
Cube Teapot, 12, **28**, 82, 119, 163, 176, 177, 179, 180, 181, 183, 185, 188, 193, 195, 197, 219
"Damascus", 14, **28**, 127
"Daniel", 72, **82**, 192, 195, 198
"Danielle", 14, **29**, 127
"Darby" - see "Birch"
"Dart", **82-83**, 149, 158, 184
"Darwin" - see "Grape"
"Dave", **83**, 169

"Deca-Flip", **83**, 195
"Deca-Plain" - see "Perk"
"Deco", **84**, 181
Demi Coffee Pot, **84**, 177, 179, 180, 186, 188, 197, 199
"Demi" Teapot, **29**, 176, 177, 178, 179, 180, 182, 186, 199
Denver, 29
Detroit, **29-30**, 119, 183, 194
"Devon", 84
"Dickens" - see "Regal"
"Disraeli" - see "Plume"
"Diver" - see Beacon and Bride
Dodecagon, **30**, 158
"Donut" - see Doughnut
Dorhco, 30
Doric Coffee Carafe, 186, **213**
Doric Coffee Server, 214
Doric Electric Percolator, 214
Doric Urn, 214
Doughnut, 13, 15, **31**, 34, 128, 129, 132, 176, 178, 180, 181, 183, 193, 226, 229, 232, 233
"Drape", **84-85**, 149
"Duse", **85**, 149, 158, 159, 176, 184
"Dutch", **85-86**, 159
E-Style, **31**, 179, 187
E-Style All-China Drip, 86
Early American Wheat Teapot, 208
Eastern, 86
Edward Don Beverage Pot, 87
Edward Don Open Teapot, 31-32
Edward Don StakUps Teapot, 32
Edward Don Stakups Metal Tip Spout, 87
Edwards, **32**, 159, 160
Electrodrip All-China Drip, **87**, 97
Electromatic Coffeemaker, 88
"Eliot" - see "Royal"
Encore, **88**, 116, 169
Erie, **88-89**, 169, 183
Ever Fresh Coffee, 89
"Everson" Coffee Pot - see "Norse"
"Everson" Ribbed Teapot, **32**, 44
Facetation, 33
"Five Band - Partial Tab Cover", **89**, 90, 181, 197
"Five Band Carafe", **90**, 180
"Five Band 'D' Handle", 89, **90**, 177, 179, 197
Flame Ware Coffee Biggin, 185, **214-215**
Flame Ware Coffee Server, 185, **215**
"Flared" Coffee Server, 178, **215**
Flare-Ware Teapot, **33**, 176, 180, 186, 188, 194, 198
Flare-Ware Coffee Server, **90**, 176, 186, 188, 194
Flare-Ware Coffee Urn, **90-91**, 176, 186, 194

Flared Tabletop Beverage Pot, 91
Flat-Sides Teapot, **33**, 186
"Fluted Alton" - see "Ribbed Rutherford"
"Fluted" Coffee Carafe - see Doric Coffee Carafe
"Fluted" Coffee Server and Electric Percolator - see Doric Coffee Server and Electric Percolator
"Fluted Globe" - see "Ribbed Globe"
Football, 5, 15, 31, **33-34**, 128, 129, 132, 176, 177, 179, 180, 181, 185, 188, 191, 193, 195, 197, 227, 229, 232, 233
"Formal" Coffee Server, 216
Forman Carafe, **91-92**, 160
Four-Matic (4-Matic) Electric Percolator, **92**, 160, 197
French, 6, **34-35**, 39, 117, 118, 119, 120, 121, 123, 124, 125, 129, 132, 141, 143, 144, 145, 176, 177, 179, 180, 182, 183, 185, 186, 187, 188, 190, 191, 192, 196, 197, 199, 227, 229, 230, 231, 232, 233
French Coffee Biggin, **92-93**, 177, 178, 180, 183, 186, 196, 199
French Drip Coffee Maker - see French Coffee Biggin
French Light Weight, 8, 34, **35**, 48, 119, 121, 122, 123, 183
"Gardiner", 93
"Gibson" Electric Percolator and Urn, **93-94**, 161, 176, 184, 187
"Gladstone" - see "Bowknot"
Globe, **35-36**, 49, 54, 129, 132, 180, 227, 229, 233
"Globe No-Drip" - see No Drip
"Gold Band" Coffee Server - see "Formal" Coffee Server
"Golden Key" - see Great American
"Grape", **36**, 139, 178, 185, 187
Grape Cluster Teapot, 208
Grape Coffee Urn, 210
Grape Leaf Coffee Pot, 210
Grape Leaf Teapot, 209
Grape Melon Rib Teapot, 209
Great American, **94**, 107, 193
Hallcraft Century, 36, **201-202**
Hallcraft Tomorrow's Classic Coffee Pot, 94, 178, 186, 187, **202-207**
Hallcraft Tomorrow's Classic Teapot, 36-37, 178, 186, 187, **202-207**
Heirloom, **94-95**, 180
Heirloom Teapot, 209
Hi-Tech Metal Tip Spout Beverage Pot, 95
Hollywood, 8, **37**, 120, 129, 133, 141, 143, 180, 186, 190, 191, 197, 200, 227, 229, 230, 231, 232, 233
Hook Cover, 10, **37**, 129, 133, 141, 176, 177, 179, 180, 181, 185, 188, 190, 191, 192, 193, 195, 197, 227, 229, 230, 231, 232, 233
Hospital Set - see Solo Tea Set
Hot Beverage Pot - Tray Service, 95
Hot Pot, **37-38**, 62
"Hoyt" - see Norfolk
"Hoyt R", **95**, 102
Iconic Coffee Pot, 96

Iconic Hot Water Pot and Teapot, **38**, 180
Illinois, 8, **38**, 42, 47, 120, 121, 129, 133, 180, 227, 229, 233
"Imperial" with and without All-China Drip, **96**, 97, 169, 170
Indiana, 8, **38**, 129, 133, 227, 229, 233
Infuser Teapot, 16, 34, 35, **39**, 118, 119, 120, 122, 183, 199, 230, 232
International Teapot, **39**, 97
International Coffee Pot, 39, **96-97**
"Irene" - see Dohrco
Irvine, 17, **40**, 61, 64, 180
"J-Sunshine" Coffee Pot - see "Rayed" Coffee Pot
"J-Sunshine" Teapot or Coffee Pot - see "Rayed" Teapot and Coffee Pot
"Jerry", **97**, 150, 183
"Johnson", 8, 20, **40**, 117, 119
"Jordan" All-China Drip, 87, 96, **97**, 176, 181, 191, 195, 196, 199, 200
"Kadota" All-China Drip, 67, **97-98**, 150, 177, 181, 183, 188, 193, 196, 197, 198, 200
"Kadota" Large Coffee Base, **98**, 187, 194, 197, 200
Kansas, 8, 11, **40**, 129, 133, 134, 180, 227, 229, 232, 233
"Lassitter", **98**, 104
"Lewis", **98-99**, 150
"Lincoln" - see Royal Park
Lipton, 144
Lipton Cozy Teapot, **40-41**, 144
London, **41**, 182, 188, 190, 200
London Teabob, 41
Longaberger, **42**, 188, 200
Los Angeles, 8, 38, **42**, 47, 117, 121, 123, 124, 125, 129, 134, 141, 143, 180, 183, 191, 227, 229, 230, 231, 232, 233
"Lotus", **99**, 150
"Madeline" - see "Bingham"
Manhattan, **42-43**, 179, 183, 186
Manhattan Pot (Side-Handled), **43**, 120, 121
Manning Bowman - see Chrome Cozy
McCormick, **43**, 119, 145, 146, 181, 183, 186
McCormick Counter Service Teapot, **44**, 145, 146
McCormick Ribbed Teapot, 32, **44**, 145
McCormick Tea House, **44**, 145, 146
McCormick – Two Cup, **44**, 145
"Medallion" All-China Drip, **99**, 180
"Medallion" Teapot, **45**, 180
"Medallion" Coffee Pot - see "Colonial" Coffee Pot
"Medallion" Teapot - see "Colonial" Teapot
Melody, 16, 20, **45**, 56, 129, 134, 180, 181, 193, 227, 229, 232, 233
"Meltdown", **99**, 150, 175, 181, 192, 195
Million Dollar Coffee Pot, **100**, 180
"MJ" Electric Percolator, **100**, 176, 178, 184, 185, 189, 192, 194, 196, 216

Moderne, 8, **45**, 129, 134, 180, 227, 229, 233
"Monarch" - see "Jerry"
"Morning Teapot" - see "Demi" Teapot
"Murphy", **45-46**, 138
Musical, **46**, 176, 177, 179, 180, 181, 185, 193, 194, 195, 197
Musical - Rose Petal, 46
"Naomi", 8, 38, 42, **46-47**, 117, 120
National Coffee Pot, 47, **100-101**
National Teapot, **47**, 100-101
Nautilus, **47**, 129, 135, 176, 180, 227, 229, 232, 233
New York, 6, 8, 21, 35, **47-48**, 117, 118, 119, 120, 121, 122, 123, 129, 135, 141, 145, 175, 176, 177, 178, 180, 181, 183, 185, 186, 187, 188, 191, 192, 193, 195, 196, 197, 199, 200, 228, 229, 230, 231, 232, 233
New Yorker, 77, **101**, 170
Newport, 6, 8, 10, **48-49**, 53, 117, 118, 120, 122, 124, 125, 129, 176, 180, 228, 229, 233
No Drip, **49**, 186
No Drip (Six-Cup), 36, **49**, 135, 228, 229, 233
"Nolte", 101
Norfolk, 95, **101-102**, 170, 171
"Norse", **102**, 151, 194, 200
"Octagon" Coffee Server, 216
"Octagon" Electric Percolator, 216
"Octagon" Tip-Pot, 216
Ohio, 8, **49**, 129, 135, 180, 186, 228, 229, 233
"Orb", **102**, 109, 151
"Panel", **102**, 151
Panther, **102-103**, 171, 172
Parade, **50**, 84, 129, 135, 141, 180, 183, 186, 191, 192, 197, 228, 229, 230, 231, 232, 233
Pear, 50
"Peel" - see "Murphy"
"Pepper" - see "Bowling Ball"
Percolator Teapot - see Infuser Teapot
"Perk", 83, **103**, 193, 195, 198
"Petal", **103**, 151
"Petal" Coffee Server, 217
Philadelphia, 6, **50-51**, 118, 119, 121, 122, 124, 125, 129, 135, 141, 143, 175, 176, 178, 180, 185, 190, 191, 197, 198, 228, 229, 230, 231, 232, 233
"Philbe", **51**, 183
"Pineapple", 51
Pittsburg, 51
Plaza, **103-104**, 172
"Plume", **51-52**, 138
Plymouth, 52
Portland, **52**, 194
"Radiance" All-China Drip, **104**, 175, 180, 186, 193, 198, 199
"Radiance" Teapot, **52**, 175, 176, 179, 180, 186, 190, 193, 194, 197, 198, 199
"Ralston", 104
"Rayed" Coffee Pot, **104-105**, 176, 198
"Rayed" Teapot and Coffee Pot, 48, **52-53**, **105**, 176, 181
Reagan, 53
"Red Coach" - see Teapot Liners

"Regal", **53**, 139
Regent, 70, **105-106**, 116, 163, 172, 173
Rhythm, 5, 13, **53**, 129, 136, 180, 186, 228, 229, 233
"Ribbed Band" Electric Percolator, 54, **106**
"Ribbed Band" Hot Water Server and Teapot, 54, 106, 161, 184, 186
"Ribbed Globe", **54**, 180, 196
"Ribbed Rutherford", **54**, 55, 180, 196
"Rickson" - see "Daniel"
"Ritz" - see Panther
"Rivera" Coffee Server, 217
"Rochester" - see "Baron"
Roosevelt, **106**, 173
"Round" Coffee Server, 217
"Round" Electric Percolator, 217
"Rounded Terrace", **106-107**, 151, 152, 194, 200
"Royal", **54-55**, 139
"Royal" Electric Percolator, 218
Royal Park, **107**, 173
Royal-Cliff Teapot, 211
"Russell" - see Dart
"Rutherford", 54, **55**, 175, 176, 179, 180, 181, 182, 187, 192, 193, 196
S-Handle, 94, **107**, 193, 200
"S-Lid" - see S-Handle
"Saben", 55
Saf-Handle Coffee Pot, 55, **108**
Saf-Handle Coffee Server, **108**, 177, 178, 180, 182
Saf-Handle Teapot, **55-56**, 108, 129, 136, 177, 178, 180, 182, 228, 229, 232, 233
Saf-Spout Coffee Pot, 56, **108**, 177
Saf-Spout Teapot, **56**, 108, 176, 181, 185, 193, 195, 197
Samovar, 178, **218**
Sani-Grid, **56**, 129, 136, 186, 191, 192, 195, 196, 200, 228, 229, 233
Sanka and Sanka Embossed Coffee, 109
"Sash", 102, **109**, 152
"Scoop", **109**, 152, 200
Seawinds Beverage Pot, 110
Service Ideas Carafe, 110
Sherlock Holmes, 56-57
Short Spout Hot Water Pot, 57
"Side-Handled Chocolate Pot", 57
Sixties Decorations, 21, 34, 37, 42, 50, 65, 143
Solo Tea Set, **57**, 176, 180
St. Louis Chocolate Pot, **58**, 118, 121, 123, 176, 177, 179, 180, 181, 185, 193, 195, 197
Star, **58**, 66, 129, 136, 180, 183, 228, 229, 232, 233
"Starlight", **58**, 139
"Step Down" - see "Terrace"
"Step Down" All-China Drip - see "Terrace" All-China Drip
"Step Round" - see "Rounded Terrace"
Sterling Coffee Pot, 59, **110**
Sterling Teapot, 58-59
"Steve", **110-111**, 173
"Straw-Weave" Electric Percolator and Urn - see Basket Weave

Electric Percolator and Urn Streamline, 8, **59**, 129, 136, 176, 177, 178, 179, 180, 181, 182, 183, 185, 188, 191, 193, 195, 197, 200, 228, 229, 232, 233

"Sundial" Coffee Pot - see Saf-Handle Coffee Pot

"Sundial" Coffee Server - see Saf-Handle Coffee Server

"Sundial" Teapot - see Saf-Handle Teapot

"Sunshine" All-China Drip - see "Radiance" All-China Drip

"Sunshine" Teapot - see "Radiance" Teapot

Super-Ceram Coffee Pot, **111**, 186

Super-Ceram Teapot, **59**, 186

Surf Side, 47, 51, **59**, 129, 137, 180, 228, 229, 232, 233

"Suzannah" - see Plaza

"Swathe" - see "Drape"

"Sweep", **111**, 152, 200

Sydeham Teapot, 210

"Target", **111**, 153

T-Ball Round, **60**, 140, 142, 180, 197

T-Ball Square, **60**, 176

Tea for Four Set, 6, 12, 38, 42, 47, **60-61**, 117, 120, 124, 125, 126, 163, 175, 180, 199

Tea for Two Set, 6, 8, 12, 38, 42, 47, 57, **61**, 117, 120, 124, 125, 126, 163, 176, 180, 186, 199

Tea Taster, 12, 15, 17, 40, **61**, 64, 180, 194

Teabagger, 62

Teapot, 38, **62**

Teapot Liners, 62

Teapot Metal Tip Spout, 63

"Tennison" - see "Starlight"

"Terrace", **112**, 142, 153, 175, 177, 178, 180, 181, 184, 185, 186, 188, 192, 193, 195, 196, 197

"Terrace" All-China Drip, **112-113**, 178, 180, 181, 195, 199

"Tip-Pot", **63**, 162, 186, 197

"Trellis", 12, **113**, 154

Trieste Beverage Pot, 113

Twin-Tee Set, 6, 38, 42, 47, **64**, 117, 119, 120, 122, 123, 124, 125, 126, 163, 178, 180, 219

Twinspout, 17, 40, 61, **64**, 180, 186

Up-Beat Beverage Pot, **113**, 199

"Victoria" - see "Connie"

"Viking", **114**, 154, 179, 183

Washington, 73, 78, **114-115**, 118, 119, 176, 177, 178, 180, 183, 186, 188, 193, 197, 199, 212

"Waverlet", **115**, 124, 154, 191

"Waverly", **115**, 124, 154, 155, 191, 200

"Wellman", **115**, 173

"Wicker", **116**, 155, 195

Wilshire Coffee Pot, 65, **116**

Wilshire Teapot and Hot Water Pot, **64-65**, 116

"Wilson" - see Encore and Erie

"Wilson", 88, **116**

"Windcrest", **65**, 139

Windshield, **65**, 129, 137, 142, 143, 176, 177, 179, 180, 181, 183, 185, 186, 191, 193, 195, 197, 228, 229, 230, 231, 232, 233

Windsor, 70, 106, **116**, 174

World's Fair, 58, **65-66**

Zeisel Kitchenware, **66**, 207

Zeisel Kitchenware Side-Handled, **66**, 207

Decorations

#488, 18, 48, 52, 55, 67, 99, 104, 112, **175**

Acacia, 52, 55, 60, 67, 70, 74, 104, 112, **175**

"Alexander", 124

"All Over Daisy", 117

"Antique Rose", 15, 21, 22, 50, 51, **175**

"Apple Blossom", 52, 85, 94, 158, 161, **176**

Arizona, 37, 94, 202, **203**

"Art Nouveau", 117

"Autumn Harvest", 15, 50, 51, **176**

"Autumn Leaf" (Jewel Tea), 13, 15, 17, 18, 19, 20, 21, 24, 27, 28, 29, 31, 34, 37, 46, 47, 48, 50, 51, 52, 53, 56, 57, 58, 59, 60, 61, 65, 72, 97, 100, 104, 105, 114, 128, **176**

Autumn Leaf (Flare-Ware), 33, 90, 91, **176**

"Band and Lace", 117

"Band and Lines", 118

"Band and Lines with Gold Handle", 118

"Banner n' Basket" - see "Stonewall"

Basket, **141**, 142

"Bird of Paradise", 102, 114, **151**, 154

"Black Beauty", 52, 55, 67, **176**

"Black Garden", 124

Black Gold, 17, 34, 114, **177**

Blue Bell with Blue or Pink Flowers, 29, 84, **177**

Blue Blossom, 15, 18, 27, 28, 29, 34, 37, 46, 48, 55, 56, 59, 67, 92, 108, **177**

Blue Bouquet, 16, 18, 21, 28, 34, 37, 46, 58, 59, 65, 76, 90, 98, 112, **177**

"Blue Dresden", 21, 22, **177**

Blue Garden, 15, 16, 29, 31, 48, 55, 59, 92, 108, 112, 113, 114, **177**

Blue Willow, 21, 48, 50, 64, 114, **178**

"Bodine" - see "Elena"

Boston Standard Gold Decoration, 118, 131

Bouquet, 36, 37, 94, 100, **178**, 202, **203**, 215, 218

"Brand", 109, **152**

"Bronze Rose", 100, **178**, 216

Brown-Eyed Susan, 16, 31, **179**

Bubble, 118

Buckingham, 37, 94, 202, **203**

Burbick, 118

Buttercup with Blue or Yellow Flowers, 29, 84, **179**

Butterflies, 132

Cactus, 34, 42, 52, 55, 59, 90, 114, 154, **179**

"California Poppy", 34, 58, **179**

Cameo Rose, 18, 27, 28, 31, 34, 37, 46, **179**

Caprice, 37, 94, **203**

Carrot, 52, 65, **179**

Casual Living, 66, **207**

Cat-Tail, 18, 28, 34, 37, 58, 59, 65, 72, 73, **180**

Chestnut, 33, **180**

Chinese Red, 11, 15, 16, 17, 18, 19, 20, 21, 23, 25, 26, 28, 29, 31, 34, 36, 37, 38, 40, 42, 45, 47, 48, 49, 50, 52, 53, 54, 55, 57, 58, 59, 60, 61, 64, 65, 67, 70, 72, 80, 90, 92, 99, 100, 104, 108, 112, 113, 114, 128, 165, **180**, 219, 222

"Chintz", 124

Christmas, 95, **180**

Christmas Tree, 18, 21, 22, 28, 34, 37, 46, 84, **180**

"Christopher", **85**, **86**, 159

"Chrysler", 30, 86, **158, 159**

Color Band, 55, **181**

Color Bands, 67, 68

Copper Lustre, 5, 12, 15, **181**, 219, 222

"Country Cottage", 21, 22, **181**

Crocus, 16, 18, 20, 21, 22, 26, 27, 28, 31, 34, 37, 43, 45, 46, 48, 53, 56, 58, 59, 65, 69, 72, 81, 84, 89, 97, 98, 99, 112, 113, 145, 146, 148, 149, **181**

Crosshatch, 136

Daisy, 141, 142

"Daisy" and "Daisy Bouquet", 76, **148, 149**

"Daisy and Poppy", 125

Dawn, 37, 94, 202, **203**

Dot "Swag", 136

"Duberry", 21, 22, **181**

"Dutch Couple", 111, **153**

"Eden Bird", 86

Eggshell Lines, 48, 55, **181**

Eggshell Plaid, 55, 67, 68, **182**

Eggshell Polka Dot, 34, 55, 67, **182**

Eggshell Swag, 55, 67, **182**

"Elena", 66, **207**

"Elizabethan Bouquet", 119, 145, 146

"Emblem", 119

Fantasy, 29, 55, 59, 108, **182**

Fantasy (Zeisel), 37, 94, 202, **204**

"Fantasy Dragon", 41, **182**

Fern, 36, **201**

Flair, 37, 94, 202, **204**

Flamingo, 34, 59, 67, 114, 154, **183**

Fleur-de-lis, 140

Flight, 36, 201, **202**

"Floral", 31, **183**

"Floral Band", 125

"Floral Basket", 125

"Floral Bouquet", 113, **154**

"Floral Fan", 125

"Floral Garland", 87

"Floral Lattice", 42, 48, 92, 97, 98, 114, 150, **183**

"Floral Pot", 106, **152**

"Floral Sprig", 17, 21, **183**

"Floral Vine", 119

Flower (Gold), 141

"Flower Garden", 21, 22, **183**

"Flower Pot" - see "Floral Lattice"

"Flower Pot", 114, **154**

Folk Song, 113

French Flower, 15, 16, 21, 24, 28, 29, 34, 35, 39, 42, 43, 48, 50, 51, 58, 65, 88, 89, 92, 114, 117, 119, 132, 145, 169, **183**

Frost Flowers, 37, 94, 202, **204**

"Fruit", 15, 54, 157, **184**

Fuji, 69, 82, 83, 85, 86, 93, 94, 158, 159, 161, **184**

"Gaillardia", 21, 112, **184**

Game Bird, 18, 28, 34, 36, 37, 46, 48, 56, 58, 59, 65, 100, **184-185**, 215

Garden of Eden, 36, **201**

Gold Acorns and Leaves, 135

Gold Band, 21, 36, 48, 50, 112, **185**

"Gold Blossom", 119

Gold Deer, 65, 100, **185**, 202

Gold Dot, 21, 34, 48, 49, 78, 142, **186**

Gold Floral, 71, **157**

"Gold Frize", 119

"Gold Fruit", 22

Gold Label, 6, 16, 17, 18, 21, 22, 34, 37, 42, 48, 50, 51, 60, 65, 112, **140-142**, 219

Gold Lace, 33, 90, **186**

"Gold Lined" (Gold Lining), 14, 120, 129-137

Gold Medallion, 130

"Gold Mini-Floral with Matte Gold Band", 120

"Gold Rosettes", 120

"Gold Trim", 120

Golden Carrot, 52, 65, **186**

Golden Clover, 52, 65, 104, **186**

Golden Glo, 5, 11, 12, 15, 16, 19, 21, 29, 33, 34, 37, 42, 43, 48, 49, 50, 53, 54, 56, 59, 61, 63, 64, 84, 92, 94, 111, 114, 161, 162, **186**, 202, 219, 222

Golden Oak, 31, 34, 48, 98, **187**

"Golden Renaissance", 120

Greek Key, 63, 91, 92, **160**, 162

"Green Poppy", 21, 55, 81, 149, **187**

Grid, 141

"Hanging Vine", 69, 73, **187**

Harlequin, 36, 37, 94, 187, 202, **204**

"Hearth Scene", 50, **143**

"Heather Rose", 28, 33, 34, 37, 41, 48, 59, 90, 112, 114, **188**

Hi-White (White), 36, 37, 94, 202, **204**

Holiday, 37, 94, **205**

"Holly", 42, 84, **188**

"Hollywood Standard Gold Decoration", 120

Homewood, 48, 97, 98, 112, 150, **188**

"Hunt Scene", 21, 22, **188**

Hunting Dog, 100, **189**

"Illinois", 38, 42, 47, **120**, 141, 142

"Impatiens", 99, **150**

Impressions, 113

"Ivory Beauty", 52, 74, 148, **190**

"Ivy Trellis", 15, 41, 50, 51, **190**

"Japoneske", 120

"Jonquil" Flower, 71, 115, 148, **154**

"June" Flower, 71, 115, **148**, 154

"Lavaliere", 27, **121**

"Leaf and Vine", 18, 34, 37, 50, 124, 125, **190**

"Lilac Mist", 15, 21, 22, **190**

Little Red Riding Hood, 10, 18, 37, **190**

Loops, 121

Lyric, 37, 94, 202, **205**

"Matte Gold Trim", 121

"Mayflower", 125

Meadow Flower, 59, **191**

Mexicana, 18, 34, 59, 65, **191**
"Mini-Floral", 85, **149**
"Mini-Freurette", 17, 20, 34, 37, 42, 50, 59, 115, 121, **191**
"Minuet", 18, 35, 115, 124, 125, 154, **191**
"Modern Tulip", 111, **152**
Morning Glory, 17, 97, **191**
Mother of Pearl, 15, 30, 32, 37, 48, 50, 56, 159, 160, **191**, 219
Mount Vernon, 86
Mulberry, 37, 94, **205**
"Mums", 21, 26, 48, 55, 81, 82, 99, 112, **192**
"Nebula", 38, **121**
"New Rose", 21, 22, **192**
"No Blue", 17, 21, 34, 37, 50, 56, **192**
"Nocturne", 113
"Nouveau", 121
"Nova", 19, **140**
"Old Garden Rose", 100, **192**
"Orange Floral", 74, **148**
"Orange Floral Bouquet", 66, 67, **147**
"Orange Poppy", 18, 20, 21, 27, 28, 31, 34, 37, 45, 46, 56, 58, 59, 65, 72, 94, 107, **193**
Oriental Butterfly, 86, 94, 159, **161**
Oyster White and Red Cooking China, 16, 114, **193**
"Palm", 122
"Palm Tree", 122
Palo Duro, 37, 94, 202, **206**
"Pansy", 126
"Parrot Tulip", 52, 98, 103, 104, 150, **193**
"Pastel Morning Glory", 16, 21, 26, 48, 52, 55, 103, 104, 112, 114, **193**
"Pastel Rose" - see "Yellow Rose"
"Pasture Rose", 106, 151
Peach Blossom, 37, 94, **205**
"Perzel", 126
Pewter, 12, 29, 52, 61, **194**
"Piggly Wiggly", 52, 102, 151, **194**
Pinecone, 37, 94, **205**
"Pink and Gray Floral Bouquet", 71, 98, 100, 106, 157, **194**
"Pink Morning Glory" - see "Pastel Morning Glory"
"Pink Mums" - see "Mums"
"Pink Rose", 31, 82, **149**
"Platinum Garden", 122
"Platinum Splatter" - see "Surf Ballet"
Poinsettia and Holly, 46, **194**
"Poppy" - see "Orange Poppy"
"Poppy and Wheat" - see "Wild Poppy"
"Posey", 122
"Potted Flowers", 102, **151**
Prairie Grass, 37, 94, 202, **207**
Radial, 33, 90, **194**
Raintree, 37, 94, 202, **207**
"Rambling Rose", 106, 107, **151**
"Reflections", 17, **140**
"Red and White", 56, **195**

Red Poppy, 15, 16, 18, 27, 28, 34, 37, 46, 48, 56, 58, 59, 65, 82, 116, 155, **195**
Red, Ivory or White Accent, and Platinum, 21, 69, 70, 73, 83, 99, 103, 112, 113, 150, **195**
Romance, 37, 94, **207**
Rose (Gold), 129, **142**
Rose Parade, 56, 97, **195**
Rose White, 56, **196**
Royal Rose, 17, 34, **196**
Russet, 21, 24, 34, 54, 55, 67, 74, 92, **196**
RX, 48, 100, **196**
"Sanford", 126
Satin Black, 37, 94, 202, **206**
Satin Gray, 37, 94, 202
Serenade, 16, 48, 97, 98, 112, 150, **196**
"Shaggy Floral", 52, **197**
"Shaggy Tulip" - see "Parrot Tulip"
"Shrub Rose Garland", 26, 81, 112, 116, 149, 153, **155**
"Silhouette", 15, 18, 26, 27, 28, 34, 37, 46, 48, 56, 58, 59, 65, 80, 81, 89, 90, 98, 112, **197**
Silver Glo, 12, 15, 16, 18, 21, 37, 50, 60, 63, 65, 84, 92, 162, **197**, 219, 222
"Snow Flake", 122
"Spider Web", 122
"Sponge Gold", 123
Spring, 37, 94, 202, **206**
"Spring Blossom", 59, **197**
Springtime, 34, 98, 114, **197**
"Squiggle", 17, 50, **140**, 141, 142
Star, **141**, 142
Stars and Gold Lining, 136
"Stonewall", 52, 98, 104, **198**
Studio Ten, 37, 94, 202, **206**
"Summer Song", 15, 21, 22, 50, 51, **198**
Sun Porch, 18, **198**
Sunglow, 36, 201, **202**
Sunnyvale, 33, **198**
Surf Ballet, 37, 94, 202, **206**
"Sutter's Gold", 103, **151**
"Swag", 17, **140**
"Sycamore", 123
"Taverne" - see Silhouette
Tea Leaf, 208, **211**
"Texas Rose", 103
"The Chase", 15
"Three Poppies", 98, 99, **150**
"Tiled Band and Flowers", 123
"Toccata", 113
"Trailing Aster", 123
Tree of Life, 94, **161**
"Trillium", 48, 123, **135**
Tri-Tone, 66, **207**
"Tulip", 16, 82, 98, 103, 105, 150, **198**
"Tulip" (Drip-O-lator), 115, **155**
"Tulip and Carnation", 126
Two-Tone, 21, 92, **199**
"Victorian Swag", 123
"Walsh" - see "Tulip and Carnation"
Watusi, 113, **199**

White Bake Ware, 16, 21, 29, 84, 92, 114, **199**
"White Rim Band", 21, 25, 114, **199**
"Wild Poppy", 18, 29, 34, 39, 48, 52, 60, 61, 67, 92, 97, 104, 113, 114, **199**
"Wild Rose Floral Garland", 71, **148**
Wildfire, 16, 21, 56, 59, 107, **200**
Wildflower, 98, 106, 107, 109, 150, 151, 152, **200**
"Windmill", 111, **153**
"Winter Berry", 15, 37, 41, **200**
"Winter Rose", 21, 22, **200**
Woven Traditions, 42, **200**
"Wreath", 123
"Yellow Rose", 48, 97, 98, 102, 115, 155, **200**
"Yellow Tulip", 85, **149**

Miscellaneous
Amtrak, 47, 101
"Art Deco" Series, 6, 12, 14, 28, 29, 127
Bacharach, Inc., 60
Block China Co., 95, 113
Brilliant Series, 8, 11, 18, 36, 53, 55, 58, 65, 139
Carbone, 18, 50, 65
China Specialties, 10, 13, 14, 15, 18, 20, 21, 22, 27, 28, 30, 34, 37, 46, 58, 59, 65, 128
Coffelator Co., 80
Cook Coffee Co., 8, 26, 83, 103, 104
Dohrmann Hotel Supply Co., 30, 51, 75
Drip-A-Drop, 86, 162
Drip-O-lator, 11, 26, 67, 68, 71, 73, 74, 76, 79, 80, 81, 83, 84, 85, 97, 98, 99, 102, 103, 107, 109, 111, 112, 113, 114, 115, 116, 147, 155, 156
East Liverpool Alumni Association, 6, 10, 19, 21, 24, 31, 47, 59, 60, 65, 128
East Liverpool Potteries Co., 7, 11, 14
Edward Don and Co., 31, 32, 87
Enterprise Aluminum Co., 6, 8, 9, 11, 12, 22, 26, 67, 68, 71, 74, 76, 79, 81, 82, 83, 84, 85, 97, 98, 99, 102, 103, 109, 111, 112, 113, 114, 115, 116, 124, **147-156**, 175
Epicurio, 16, 17
F. S. Martin and Co., 100
Forman Family, 6, 9, 11, 12, 15, 26, 28, 30, 32, 54, 63, 67, 71, 82, 83, 85, 86, 92, 94, 144, **157-162**, 175
Grand Union, 82
Great American Tea Co., 94, 107
Hall American Line, 13, 15, 34, 48, 53, 57, 60, 61, 115
Hall Closet, 13, 15, 18, 20, 22, 31, 50, 53, 128
Hall Convention, 13
Hall Haul, 13, 34
Hellick Coffee Co., 80

Jewel Tea Co., 8, 10, 17, 20, 21, 29, 31, 32, 48, 51, 53, 87, 90, 97, 105, 114
Koenig Coffee Co., 89
Liberty Hall Ironstone, 95
Lipton (Thomas J.) Co., 8, 12, 34, 41, 144
Longaberger Basket Co., 8, 13, 42
Manning Bowman Co., 5, 26
Mannings Coffee Co., 75, 108
McCormick Tea Co., 8, 21, 22, 35, 43, 44, 48, **145-146**
Metal Clad, 12, 14, 18, 20, 21, 24, 25, 34, 37, 48, 57, 61, 64, 67, 84, 114
Metal Tip Spout, 22, 23, 25, 39, 41, 47, 63, 73, 77, 78, 87, 95, 96, 97, 100, 101
Midhurst China Co., 36, 37, 94, 95, 201, 202
Modern Antique Concepts, 10, 15, 21, 22, 41, 51
Montgomery Ward Catalog, 29, 42, 46, 80, 82, 147
Naomi's Antiques of San Francisco, 15, 31, 35, 48, 53, 57, 60, 61, 115, 128
National Autumn Leaf Collectors Club, 6, 10, 13, 14, 19, 20, 21, 22, 24, 31, 35, 47, 48, 51, 57, 60, 61, 67, 115, 128
"Novelty" Series, 18, 19, 20, 31, 34, 128
Red-Cliff Ironstone, 6, 8, 11, **208-211**
Royal Family Series, 79
Sanka Brand Decaffeinated Coffee, 109
Schreckengost, Don, 57
Sears, Roebuck and Co., 31, 34, 50, 86, 113, 201
Service Ideas, 33, 110
Sohn, Ernest, 6, 8, 11, 12, 78, 100, **212-218**
Standard Brands, Inc., 23
Standard Coffee Co., 76
Sterling China, 59, 110, 113
Super-Ceram, 4, 10, 12, 14, 21, 24, 34, 38, 39, 47, 48, 54, 58, 59, 61, 67, 106, 111, 114, 219
Teamaster, 17, 40, 61, 64
Tea-O-lator, 11, 21, 72, 156
Thorley, J. Palin, 4, 8, 16, 31, 36, 45, 53, 55, 56, 65, 86, 108, 139
Thornberry, 10, 15, 21, 22, 31, 51
Tricolator, Inc., 6, 9, 11, 12, 67, 69, 70, 71, 74, 77, 79, 83, 88, 95, 96, 101, 102, 103, 104, 106, 107, 111, 115, 116, **163-174**, 175, 219
Twinspout Pottery Co., 17, 40, 61, 64
"Victorian" Series, 8, 11, 20, 23, 27, 46, 51, 52, 55, 138
Westinghouse, 69, 73
Zeisel, Eva, 4, 6, 8, 13, 36, 37, 66, 67, 94, 142, **201-207**